The Color of Jazz

The Color of Jazz

Race and Representation in Postwar American Culture

Jon Panish

University Press of Mississippi
Jackson

Manufactured in the United States of America

00 99 98 97   4   3   2   1

The paper in this book meets the guidelines for permanence and
durability of the Committee on Production Guidelines for Book
Longevity of the Council on Library Resources.

Library of Congress Cataloging-in-Publication Data

Panish, Jon.
    The color of jazz : race and representation in postwar American culture / Jon Panish.
        p.   cm.
    Includes bibliographical references (p.   ) and index.
    ISBN 1-57806-035-4 (cloth : alk. paper) — ISBN 1-57806-033-8 (pbk. : alk. paper)
    1. Jazz in literature.   2. Jazz—Social aspects—United States.   3. Race in literature.
    4. Music and society—United States.   5. United States—Race relations.
    ML3849.P27   1997
    306.4'84—dc21
                                                                    97-11364
                                                                        CIP
                                                                        MN

British Library Cataloging-in-Publication Data available

Contents

Acknowledgments

I gratefully acknowledge the many heavy debts I incurred while completing this project. Since this work began its life as a dissertation, the members of my UC Irvine committee—Professors Dickran Tashjian, Dave Bruce, and John Liu—deserve my first thanks for their encouragement, criticism, and insight. Professor Raul Fernandez also helped me greatly in my extended graduate career by providing intellectual, moral, and financial support. Thanks also to Professor Lorenzo Thomas, who supported my work at crucial times.

Several friends inside and outside the academic world were essential to the creation and completion of this book. Jennifer Reed and Charles Krinsky were most influential during the planning, writing, and revising of this work. More important, each has greatly affected who I am and how I live my life. I am also grateful to the following individuals who, at various times throughout my academic career, have powerfully affected my perceptions, ideas, and knowledge: Robin Reynolds, Anthony Bernier, Curtiss Rooks, and Gary Cale.

My extended family has always supported my work, although they haven't always known just what I was up to. Barbara Seebart and David Elliott have been especially generous with their advice, encouragement, and criticism. For everything they've done, I also thank Lee Schullinger; Greta, Jay, Debbie, and Adam Panish; and Joyce and Don Seebart.

I thank everyone at the University Press of Mississippi for their help—especially Seetha A-Srinivasan for her early and continued support, Anne Stascavage for paying attention to the details, Evan Young for his excellent copyediting, and the anonymous reader whose insightful comments increased the clarity, logic, and persuasiveness of my argument.

My apologies to Emma and Lily for all the time I spent "at the computer" during the seemingly endless writing and rewriting of this book; in the competition between parenting and scholarship for my time and energy, this book almost (and maybe should have) lost out. Finally, without Virginia none of this would have been possible.

Introduction

> After twenty years in the marginal wilderness, jazz is gearing up to slip out of its ghetto again. While it's still true that only 3–4 percent of recording consumers pick up the CDs in jazz bins, jazz is showing up in mainstream forums that only a few years ago would have shrugged the stuff off as elitist. . . .
>
> This upsets some folks in the jazz world. They don't like the less informed grazing randomly on hallowed turf. Many jazzbos, after all, really are cultist and elitist. Like ham-radio operators, baseball card or pog collectors, audiophiles and wine connoisseurs, they're not looking to share passion, information or even space with the great unwashed. (Santoro 1996: 36)

At the risk of seeming like one of the "elitist jazzbos" gently satirized above by music journalist Gene Santoro, I take a look in this book at the representation of jazz music in the U.S. cultural mainstream. Comparing representations of jazz and jazz musicians during the 1950s and early 1960s, I argue that white and black Americans differ fundamentally in their use and understanding of jazz as an African American cultural resource, and moreover, that these differences are linked to racial developments in the social, economic, and political spheres during this era. Before I delve into the history of this period and offer my analysis of the images themselves, I will sketch out the theoretical and methodological concepts that underpin my approach to the topic.

Many recent cultural critics of the 1950s have empathically emphasized the symbolic distance traveled by progressive white Americans to the stigmatized cultural territory of black Americans; I, however, choose to underscore the gap that remained after they had traveled this symbolic distance.[1] My purpose is not to excoriate white people for their misappropriation of African American culture, nor to claim that black people have a purer, more privileged relation to these cultural resources. Instead, I seek to place race at the center of our understanding of the cultural exchanges that occurred during this period and to claim that the subordination of racial difference in previous constructions of progressive 1950s culture (even to achieve the goal of empathic understanding) has obscured and continues to obscure the centrality of racial power and experience in the making of both racialized identities and, more generally, U.S. culture. Because I use many terms and ideas that are still contested by scholars and lay people, I want to clarify my meanings—specifically, my definition of culture and my perspective on race, racial difference, and the historical constructions of "whiteness" and "blackness." In chapter 1 I will use these terms to characterize the significance of race in postwar U.S. culture.

Most critics writing in and about the recently emergent field of "cultural studies" have noted that the field is unified, paradoxically, by its broad range of methodologies and topics of study. This plurality of approaches has left the field with overlapping but different definitions of the key word "culture." As Raymond Williams suggests, even before the development of "cultural studies" culture was an extremely difficult term to define (1983: 87). A number of scholars doing research under the cultural studies rubric have influenced my approach to culture in this work, but my specific definition of culture borrows from Williams by way of Edward W. Said. The large framework for my definition comes from Williams: culture is a signifying system related to but not the same as the signifying and social systems we identify as the political or the economic (1995: 207–27). Williams thus makes a distinction between those practices, institutions, and works that we traditionally think of as "cultural"—artistic and intellectual activities—and other practices and institutions that are similar (in that they too have a signifying system or "language") but not identical. He says, moreover, that these different realms are linked (or, in his terms, "embedded" in each other), but not as the cause nor the effect. The virtue of this framework is that it enables me to make connections among these various systems without relinquishing my focus on the strictly cultural. Similarly, while my analysis concentrates on racial "discourse," I am also interested in showing how this discourse is influenced by and influences the material conditions of people in the United States. Like Edward Said's study of culture and empire, then, my work places at its center "all those practices, like the arts of description, communication, and representation that have relative autonomy from the economic, social, and political realms and that often exist in aesthetic forms, one of whose principal aims is pleasure" (Said 1993: xii).

Althusser's notion of "relative autonomy" (which comes through Williams) is important to the structure of my work. According to Williams, one of the implications of culture's "relative autonomy" from the social, political, and economic is that within any developed "social system" a variety of cultural producers may develop. Many, if not most, of these cultural producers will be "attached" to the dominant social group—that is, they will produce culture that supports their dominance. However, "some kinds of cultural work are deliberately produced in and more or less consciously attached to a subordinated group" (1995: 218). This "subordinated" cultural work, which may or may not "oppose" the dominant culture and society, is contained within an entire system that is "commanded" by the dominant group. In other words, the system described by Williams offers a model of culture that is fragmentary, uneven, and connected to the overall structure of society. Most important, Williams's model focuses our attention on structural power, hierarchy, difference, and conflict rather than on individualistic consent, opportunity, similarity, and consensus. So, for example, Edward Said offers an analysis of the relationship between imperialism and culture that comprises a dominant culture attached to Western imperialism and cultures of resistance that develop in response to that domination. Just as significantly, however, Said makes it clear that this system or process should not be seen as a conflict between "pure" cultures, but a hybrid in which these cultures and peoples—the imperial and the resistant—are linked together in the "insidious and fundamentally unjust" process of domination. Our task, he says, is to describe the process so that we can identify the "links" between those who dominate and those who resist (Said 1993: xxi–xxii).

In this work, I have translated Williams's and Said's ideas to fit the distinctive circumstances in the United States during the 1950s and 1960s. Although U.S. culture during this time was even more complex and hybridized (in terms of cultural power and influence) than the imperial culture described by Said, the postwar milieu certainly fits the general model theorized by Raymond Williams. Chapter 1 offers a more thorough narrative of the historical context of this era; for now, I should emphasize that I am reconstructing a U.S. culture stratified along a central racial axis. Thus, I argue that U.S. culture was dominated by a racial discourse, controlled by white Americans, that constructed rigid distinctions between "white" and "black" but obscured these differences behind a regime of what Ruth Frankenberg has called "color evasiveness" (1993: 14). Within this dominant racial discourse I identify various "subordinated" discourses, some white and some black, that challenge the assumptions, ideas, and representations of the dominant discourse. I am especially interested in the similarities and differences between these subordinated discourses, and their fit with the dominant discourse. I do not reductively characterize these discourses as good or bad, oppressive or liberating, true or false, authentic or appropriated according to the ascribed racial identity of the cultural producer; I do argue, though, that we can make distinctions between "white" and "black" discourses because the particular constellation of attributes attached to these discourses exhibit clearly different understandings and uses of a specific, significant African American cultural resource—jazz. Moreover, I argue that we *should* make these distinctions because they tell us something about the way oppositional racialized discourses have been and continue to be produced and recuperated by the dominant racial discourse: white discursive challenges are accommodated at the expense of black ones. Thus, for example, the well-intentioned but less racially subversive cultural work done by self-styled white outsiders like Jack Kerouac and John Clellon Holmes to contest the rigid boundaries set up around racial cultures had a greater impact on the U.S. cultural mainstream than did the work of such counterparts as John Williams and William Melvin Kelley. Beyond the relative success of individual writers, this cultural recuperation indicates the dominance of an ideology of whiteness that is hegemonic.

Parallel to this cultural recuperation is a similar recuperative process occurring in the economic, political, and social realms of U.S. culture. As I describe in more detail in chapter 1, the postwar era witnessed the recovery of a dominant, separate white U.S. society with such mechanisms as the government-funded rise of the racially segregated suburbs and the government-sponsored exclusionary practices of the major labor unions.[2] In addition, due to the overwhelming (and understandable) preoccupation with abolishing legal separation in the South, this era was characterized by a widespread inattention to the increasing racial segregation in the North. Thus, while such factors as the 1954 *Brown v. Board of Education* ruling, white support of the burgeoning black civil rights movement, and a racially transgressive (though subordinated) white cultural movement suggest that U.S. culture during this period was moving toward racial tolerance and integration, other elements suggest that the gap between white and black remained wide and perhaps even increased under the pressure from a widespread white retrenchment. I would even suggest that our current racial quagmire is connected to the fact that this retrenchment remained invisible or at least unmentioned until discussion of a "white backlash" began around the time Richard Nixon was elected president in 1968.

Fundamental to my interpretation of the cultural materials of this period is recent work that has identified, analyzed, and deconstructed "whiteness" in U.S. culture. Due largely to the pioneering work of such scholars as David Roediger, Eric Lott, Ruth Frankenberg, Michael Rogin, and George Lipsitz, the study of race in the United States has expanded to include a postmodernist shift in emphasis from the Other to "us." Rather than continue to mark African Americans, Latinos/as, Asian Americans, and Native Americans with the stigma of race, this approach to the study of race has theorized that "whiteness" itself is a racial entity with a particular history, particular identities, and even cultural content. This decentering of the racial subject has had at least five positive effects on our understanding of race in the United States.[3] First, it has given white people a stake in the solution to the "problem of race" by implicating them in its construction. Second, this work has unequivocally put the study of race in the social constructionist camp by illuminating the shifting historical relations between white and black people and between the native and immigrant white populations. Third, by focusing specifically on racial difference as a relational entity, this approach makes power relations a central feature of its analysis. Fourth, it follows the construction of whiteness into the present to show the continuing significance of race and racism. Finally, this project challenges white people to go beyond the domination and appropriation that have been integral to historical whiteness and to create what Ruth Frankenberg calls "a countercultural trajectory and identity" of whiteness— that is, a white history and contemporary white identities that are antiracist and otherwise politically progressive (1993: 232).

My work analyzes its cultural materials from this general perspective; it also borrows several specific theoretical ideas from previous work on whiteness. Eric Lott's examination of the nineteenth-century minstrel phenomenon has been especially valuable in its articulation of the cultural dynamic involved in the use of black culture by white men. Describing white male attraction to black men and culture as an ambivalent mixture of desire and fear, Lott profitably complicates a cultural relationship that has typically been characterized as a simple reproduction of society's racial hierarchy. Drawing on work (for instance, by such British scholars as Stuart Hall and Paul Gilroy) that theorizes culture as a complex, impure entity formed in a cauldron of competing categories and forces, Lott constructs minstrelsy as a cultural form that reveals much about the significance of race in nineteenth-century U.S. culture but not in its simple, traditional, reflective form: "we must now think of, say, the blackface mask as less a *repetition* of power relations than a *signifier* for them—a distorted mirror, reflecting displacements and condensations and discontinuities between which and the social field there exist lags, unevennesses, multiple determinations" (Lott 1993: 8).

Lott believes this unstable signifier carries not only meanings traditionally associated with it—racist ridicule, for example—but also meanings that had the *potential* (at least) to "transgress the color line" and forge alliances between white and black men. Although I am much less sanguine about the use of black culture by white men, I have tried to attend to Lott's assertion that blackface is a constructed, uneven, and contradictory signifier. Like minstrel performers and audiences during the nineteenth century, those white men around the mid-twentieth century who were attracted to black men and black culture expressed their attraction in images that announced simultaneously their indebtedness to and their mastery over black human and cultural resources. Moreover, as with the Civil War–era phenomenon, the cold war–era incarnation featured frequent appearances of such features as homosociality, romanticization, sexism, stereotyping, primitivism, economic appropriation and exploitation, and vicarious pleasure.

Along with Michael Rogin, however, I think Lott's own desire to prove the flexibility of race and to bridge the gap between white and black men by complicating blackface obscures power relations more than it clarifies them. Where Lott sees lost opportunities for interracial alliances—not only in the nineteenth-century minstrel shows, but also in later manifestations of blackface—I see only reassertions of white power accomplished partly through the recirculation of a signifier that is "flawed fundamentally in form" (Rogin 1996: 37). As Rogin explains, by promoting racist stereotypes, allowing only one-way cultural "permeability," and preventing African American performers from expressing their own culture and Euro American audiences from seeing African American culture, nineteenth-century minstrelsy had no chance of transgressing, much less erasing, the color line. While white men explored racial, sexual, and gender boundaries by putting on and taking off new identities, black people remained enslaved and excluded—materially and culturally. As I show in chapter 1, although the historical condition of both black and white people had changed dramatically between the mid-nineteenth century and the post–World War II era, the power relations between the races had remained much the same. Moreover, at both historical moments blackface functioned in a comparable way: to allow white people simultaneously to explore oppositional identities and to contain challenges to white supremacy.

Ch. 1

To avoid what I think is the postmodernist tendency to place too much emphasis on voluntary racial (not to mention gender and sexual) fluidity, I have chosen to follow the analytical models provided by David Roediger, Ruth Frankenberg, and George Lipsitz in their diverse work on whiteness in U.S. culture. While their work is no less attuned to the uneven and contradictory character of whiteness than is Lott's, these scholars do not bury the specific, integral, historical power relations of *race* beneath a layer of idealistic, constructionist possibility the way Lott does. In his analysis of the minstrel shows, for example, Roediger admits the theoretical possibility that blackface could have generated an interracial, oppositional culture based on class interests but forcefully concludes that, as a practical matter, it never did: minstrel shows were mostly all-white, "tended to support proslavery and white supremacist politics," and only allowed *white* people to play with their racial identity (Roediger 1991: 124–25). Like Roediger, Lipsitz (in some of his most recent work), and to some extent Frankenberg, I emphasize, even privilege, the cultural, political, and economic alliances that have promoted, maintained, and reinvented white solidarity over those that have opposed, resisted, and subverted it. Without denying that oppositional racial alliances and discourses have significantly contributed to historical progress in U.S. race relations, or that they have a pivotal role to play in the present and future, I agree with Lipsitz that "precise awareness of the present moment requires an understanding of the existence and the destructive consequences of 'white' identity" (1995a: 370). As Roediger makes clear, we will never displace our existing racial hierarchies until white people recognize that their identity, privilege, position, and power are based on a racial entity—whiteness— that consists of nothing more than domination and a paradoxical longing for and rejection of the cultures of other racialized groups (Roediger 1994: 1–17). My hope is that this recognition will enable and encourage white Americans to confront and solve the problem of racism instead of denying its existence by constructing notions of racial denial such as a "color-blind" U.S. society.

However, to solve the problem of racism, we must recognize that it is inscribed in the structure of our total signifying system. Therefore, any explanation of whiteness and its effect on racial equality must show how it influences both the way we think and the way we organize our society. As George Lipsitz accurately contends, too often studies like mine place too heavy a burden on the transformative power of culture: "Studies of culture too far removed from studies of social structure leave us with inadequate explanations for understanding racism and inadequate remedies for combatting it" (1995a: 371). Thus, I have tried to create an interplay between the material conditions during the postwar period and the complex signifiers—blackface, whiteness, blackness, jazz—that developed from and influenced those conditions. I discuss whiteness, for example, as a hybrid signifier that is influenced by, reacts against, dominates, excludes, and appropriates blackness. The existence of a variety of racially progressive and regressive social and cultural forces (and some that appear to be of one sort but function as another) during the postwar era requires the broadest possible approach to culture. If one were to examine postwar culture without noting developments in the social structure, for example, one might reasonably conclude (as many have) that the racial boundaries were being fractured much more severely than they actually were.

This tendency of cultural critics to exaggerate the permeability of racial boundaries during the postwar era is also due to the continued privileging of white cultural productions. Viewed from the vantage point of the Beats, or suburban bohemians, or the Abstract Expressionists, or amateur and professional followers of bebop, or Elvis and the emerging white rock and roll audience, or the mainstream and avant-garde makers of film and television programs, postwar culture would appear to have been making strides toward interracial borrowing, admiration, and respect. However, this apparent racial cross-fertilization was thoroughly in the control, under the domination, of white people. Thus, although there is interracial cultural activity occurring at these sites (as there had been in dominant culture continuously since at least the nineteenth century), it is a particular hybrid culture determined by the traditions, condition, needs, and desires of white people, and therefore it is qualitatively different from the hybrid culture that had and continued to emerge from the conjuncture of tradition, condition, needs, and desires of black people. My distinction here between whiteness and blackness in U.S. culture derives from my reading of Stuart Hall's approach to hybridity in "black" popular culture. (Because Hall theorizes a diasporic black popular culture this idea is not specific to African American culture.) According to Hall, black popular culture is no less "contradictory" an entity than white popular culture; especially in the twentieth century, during which popular culture has become hegemonic on a global level, authentic black cultural forms (if there ever were any) have been "compromised" by their commodification. However, within this compromised, contradictory form, black culture has retained what is distinctive about it: that particular combination of "cultural inheritance," forms from African culture, and diasporic experience, "negotiated" positions that derive from being a "subordinated" subject (Hall 1992: 21–33).

Believing that this construction of blackness has traditionally been used in ways that are essentialist—by marking traditions as mutually exclusive (black and white) it naturalizes and dehistoricizes blackness—Hall is finally skeptical about its usefulness in the inexorably inauthentic postmodern world. However, I have found this construction to be both useful and illuminating. At the very least, I believe this "strategically essentialist" notion of blackness is valuable as a heuristic: maintaining the boundaries between black and white in this way allows us to emphasize the differences between these signifiers, differences that typically have been (and still are) devoured by a whiteness that is, in Richard Dyer's words, "everything and nothing" (Hall 1992: 29; Dyer 1993: 142). Marking these differences in bold lines unequivocally illuminates the racial domination that has occurred (and continues to occur) on every level of U.S. society. Moreover, I do not believe my distinction between black and white signifiers is essentialist, since I am referring to cultures that have developed differently because of the long and homogenous history of racial separation in the United States.

To make this distinction between black and white texts, then, I counterpose a hybrid black signifier to the white hybrid signifier already discussed. Adapting Stuart Hall's model, I develop this notion of blackness as a combination of cultural inheritances and diasporic experiences. Just as whiteness developed unevenly and at times contradictorily, blackness is a complex signifier: for example, some expressions of it reveal more influence by the dominant culture in the United States, while others display a greater affinity with African traditions. Nevertheless, this unevenness, this diversity of black expression, is unified by the similarities within its difference. My conception here is similar to what Paul Gilroy says when he notes that the black diaspora is "connected" by "its logic of unity and differentiation" (1993: 120). Building on what he says are similar ideas in W. E. B. Du Bois's *The Souls of Black Folk*, Gilroy asserts that the construction of a diasporic "black" signifier must necessarily subordinate (although not erase) differences that have developed due to the distinctiveness of each particular cultural environment and as an inevitable result of cultural change. Thus, he says, although black music in, for example, England, the United States, and the Caribbean differs in many particulars—specific sounds, for instance—there are also similarities in such elements as structure—improvisation, the call-and-response pattern, or "radically unfinished form" (1993: 77–78, 105). Similarly, in the African American experience itself, black culture is not monolithic because its development was differently influenced by such factors as region, class, urban or rural location, and relative interaction with the dominant population.

The concept of blackness I will use, then, builds on this contemporary sense of hybridity and difference, but also reaches back to earlier work by Stephen Henderson, Houston Baker, and Henry Louis Gates to emphasize the structural and thematic unities that inhere in African American culture. Primary among these structural unities is the particular sense of improvisation described by Gates as "'nothing more' than repetition and revision." As Gates has demonstrated, improvisation inheres in most, if not all, "black vernacular forms," extending back to African culture and including African American forms such as "Singifyin(g), jazz—and even its antecedents, the blues, the spirituals, and ragtime" (1988: 63–64). Moreover, Gates's own use of the device—as "black intertextuality"—in his literary criticism suggests that this sense of improvisation is elastic enough to structure black forms that are not traditionally considered "vernacular." Toni Morrison has also said that improvisation is such an elegant, formal element that it organizes art in ways that are often not noticed. She says her goal in her writing, which is "informed" by black music, is to conceal "all the work that must go into improvisation so that it appears that you've never touched it." Morrison links this specific understanding of improvisation with "black art": "The major things black art has to have are these: it must have the ability to use found objects, the appearance of using found things, and it must look effortless. It must look cool and easy. If it makes you sweat, you haven't done the work. You shouldn't be able to see the seams and stitches" (Gilroy 1993: 78).

Along with improvisation and other structural elements such as call-and-response (or what Gilroy calls antiphony), black culture has typically been characterized by vernacular language (what used to be called Black English) and traditional themes and tropes. While I will use all these elements in my analysis of black texts, I will place particular emphasis on themes and tropes that distinguish black from white texts. This emphasis derives from the greater power of these elements as against language to mark differences between black and white texts. Perhaps because of the demands of the marketplace on black culture, the appeal of black vernacular speech to white writers, or other reasons, language use is less revealing of the differences between white and black culture because of its variability: many black and white texts are comparable in the frequency of their use of black vernacular speech. However, white texts tend to use a minstrel-like caricature of black vernacular speech (in both form and content), while black texts' use is more subtle and judicious. The use of traditional themes and tropes, on the other hand, reveals vast divergences between black and white texts. Among the factors that contribute to these divergences are the encoded nature of black culture (dating from slavery, when African cultural elements and strategies of resistance to oppression were hidden or masked in burgeoning African American culture) and the hegemonic influence of dominant culture's different themes and tropes (which influence white peoples' interpretation of black culture) on white texts.

Wrapped up in the meaning and significance of these cultural elements traditionally thought of as "ethnic" is race. Among ethnic cultures and identities in the United States, blackness is exceptional because of the particular history of racism and racial oppression experienced by African American people. Thus, there is a relational element to blackness as much as there is to whiteness; however, whereas this relational element in whiteness manifests itself as attraction to and appropriation of blackness, in the black signifier it reveals itself as a resistance to and dissatisfaction with the limitations and invasiveness of whiteness. Although this relational tension often manifests itself in political opposition and resistance to racism (especially during the period under study here), it also surfaces in other forms, including an ambivalence about interracial relationships, a rejection of competitive individualism and unfettered acquisitiveness, and a temperate contempt for white people with a penchant for black culture.

Jazz was one field on which the assaults, responses, exchanges, challenges, inversions, and rejections between blackness and whiteness were launched, issued, and played out during the postwar era. Although jazz never reached the mass popularity achieved by minstrel shows during the nineteenth century, it achieved its greatest popularity and had its most profound impact on U.S. popular culture during this period. Especially during the late 1940s and early to mid-1950s, jazz attracted Euro and African American bohemians, intellectuals, artists, young people, and other progressives to its music and to a burgeoning subculture in urban centers like New York City. From the mid-1950s to the mid-1960s, jazz had become so widely known among the public in the United States that jazz music, musicians, and the entire subculture enlivened popular magazines like *Time* and *Life*, movies like *The Benny Goodman Story* and *Too Late Blues*, and television programs like *The Twilight Zone*. Intertwined with the period's racial politics, economics, and social relationships, the jazz nexus offers myriad pathways to explore in search of the key to our continuing racial conundrum.

My strategy in this book for exploring jazz as a contested cultural resource is to compare the various constructions of it in white and black texts, to follow the trail of these constructions as they migrate from subordinated white and black cultural productions into the mainstream, and to connect these developments to the overarching social, political, economic, and cultural context. Among the specific uses of jazz, jazz musicians, and the jazz subculture I examine are the construction of a jazz tradition, the depiction of jazz heroes, the link between the music and peoplehood, portrayals of interaction between performer and audience, the definition of jazz artistry and craft, and the nature of improvisation. Although there is unevenness and variability among the uses of these elements in both white and black texts, I develop a framework in which the differences I have outlined between whiteness and blackness emerge. In the most general terms, white texts tend to romanticize the jazz musician's experience, stereotype jazz heroes, dehistoricize and decontextualize the development of the music, and emphasize competitive individualism over any sense of community. Black texts, on the other hand, tend to present the jazz musician as an admirable but complicated figure; set the development of the music in a clear tradition that is continually repeated and revised; make connections between the music, the musician, and social experience; and inextricably link the accomplishments of the individual with the success of the community.

This is not to suggest, however, that audiences have invariably received these texts as I interpret them in this study. In fact, most African American audiences probably received the Euro American texts I include in a more world-weary, subversive, and healthful way than I do. As Richard Dyer notes, "people do not necessarily read negative images of themselves as negative" (1993: 2). Instead, Dyer says, people who are used to seeing themselves represented negatively become inured to these depictions and often even take pleasure in subverting them into positive images. African American writer Al Young, for example, dismisses the significance of Jack Kerouac's racist caricatures by explaining that, unlike Euro Americans, African Americans can compartmentalize this aspect of his work: "Black readers were always aware of that [racist] tendency in Kerouac, but it was no different than when I would go with white friends at college to see a Marx Brothers movie and you'd have a sequence where Harpo would go down into Niggertown and everybody'd be dancing and singing and he'd be playing the harp and all that. And my friends would say, 'Are you embarrassed?' And I said, 'No, I'm not embarrassed, because I know who's making this movie'" (in Young, Kart, and Harper 1987: 135).

Nevertheless, the fact that African American audiences have developed strategies for processing them does not diminish the power these potentially destructive representations have in the construction of racial ideology among Euro and African Americans. If anything, these strategies foreground the differences I identify in the construction of race by Euro and African Americans. To quote Richard Dyer again, "We are all restricted by both the viewing and the reading codes to which we have access (by virtue of where we are situated in the world and the social order) and by what representations there are for us to view and read" (1993: 2). The pervasiveness and rigidity of these images in postwar U.S. culture (as well as their connection to other racial discourses at the time) suggest that the Euro and African Americans of this era had vastly different constructions of whiteness and blackness.

Periodizing this project was a challenge. Though I have maintained (within a few years on either side) the periodization with which I began my research, my study of jazz and U.S. culture during the postwar period has convinced me that many other valid choices could have been made for the beginning and the ending of the era in which the images I describe occur. It is certainly true that I have neglected similar images that fall outside the chronological boundaries of my study, and that I have reduced somewhat the heterogeneity of the images that exist within those boundaries. Nevertheless, I have chosen these chronological markers to isolate an extended period during which there was a degree of continuity in both jazz and racial discourse and an articulation between the two spheres.[4]

Not only was jazz extremely popular among both Euro and African Americans during this period; it was also in a stage of continuous, productive change and experimentation, rapidly moving from bebop to cool to hard bop to free jazz. These two elements—widespread popularity and rapid change—unify the various schools and musicians active in jazz during this era. And each of the succeeding schools of jazz built on some key elements pioneered by the beboppers—including challenging audiences with their music and style, willfully subverting popular song structures, and emphasizing the intellectual element of their work.

During this time racial discourse was central in American culture (with the rise to prominence of the civil rights movement) and permeated with a liberal, integrationist ideology. However, though passions ran high among Euro and African Americans, racial discourse had not reached the intense power and sensitivity it would have during the late 1960s. We can see the reciprocal influence of jazz and racial discourse in the themes of many jazz pieces composed during the era (for example, Sonny Rollins's "Freedom Suite" and Charles Mingus's "Original Faubus Fables"), and in the rhetoric of jazz musicians in interviews and the involvement of jazz fans in the civil rights movement.[5]

Given these broad criteria, the specific dates I have chosen make sense for many reasons. The year 1945 is significant not only because it marks the formal end of World War II, but also because it marks the convergence of intensified and increasingly popular efforts by African Americans to establish their equality in American society and culture. On the social and political fronts 1945 marks the intensification of efforts by African Americans (many of whom were enraged and empowered by the hypocrisy made more explicit by the fight against international fascism) to achieve equality at home. On the cultural front, it also marks the recorded origins of the bebop movement, a movement that began explicitly to assert the African American's preeminent position in jazz. Although the prehistory of bebop stretches back to the Minton's Playhouse sessions of 1941, the period from 1944 to 1948 includes bebop's most notable early moments: Dizzy Gillespie and Charlie Parker began playing in Fifty-second Street clubs and recording in 1944 and 1945; Gillespie's recordings (without Parker) outsold every other jazz album released in 1946; and Gillespie's group (also minus Parker) appeared at Carnegie Hall in 1947 and traveled to Europe in 1948 (Charters and Kunstadt 1981: 319–27).

The ending date of my periodization, 1966, was also chosen because of the articulation of social-political and cultural events it contained. Although the dominance of the integrationist discourse of the civil rights movement began to deteriorate before 1966 (one could make a case, for example, that 1965—the year of Malcolm X's assassination and the Watts riots—was the turning point), the year is especially significant because it marks the symbolic break between Euro and African Americans working for civil rights. It was in that year that Stokely Carmichael, the new chairman of the Student Nonviolent Coordinating Committee, publicly announced his opposition to integration and his support of a "new" ideology of "black power." In a 1966 *New York Review of Books* article, Carmichael explained the logic behind his new public positions: "Integration speaks to the problem of blackness in a despicable way. As a goal, it has been based on complete acceptance of the fact that in order to have a decent house or education, blacks must move into a white school. This reinforces among both black and white the idea that 'white' is automatically better and 'black' is by definition inferior" (Sidran 1971: 132).

This new unabashed explanation of the *differences* between black and white rather than the similarities among Americans marks an end of sorts to an era of public discursive cooperation between progressive Euro and African Americans.

We can detect a similar kind of racial rupture at the same time in the attitudes of many jazz musicians toward their profession. In 1966, for example, pianist Cecil Taylor, undoubtedly influenced by changes in the political sphere, offered a proposal that clearly staked out the same kind of race-conscious, separatist rhetorical position Stokely Carmichael occupied:

> There should be a boycott by Negro musicians of all jazz clubs in the United States. I also propose that there should be a boycott by Negro jazz musicians of all record companies. I also propose that all Negro jazz musicians boycott all trade papers and journals dealing with music. And I also propose that all Negro jazz musicians resign from every federated union in this country that has anything to do with music. . . . We're no longer reflecting or vibrating to the white-energy principle. The point is: we know who we are. We have a whole history of music in this country. (Sidran 1971: 143)

By emphasizing this confrontational rhetoric I do not mean to imply either that all African American jazz musicians agreed with Taylor or that this statement reflected recently acquired knowledge. Clearly, many jazz musicians did not participate in this kind of separatist rhetoric, and most jazz musicians recognized long before

1966 that the business of jazz reproduced many of the exploitative relations found in American society. However, Taylor's views did coincide with those of a sizable segment of African American jazz musicians; more importantly, they coincided with a stage during which many Euro American fans refused to follow jazz into its most "out" manifestations. Even if these coincidentally occurring rhetorical and musical conflagrations cannot be linked causally (as David G. Such argues), 1966 represents a public break in the uneasy harmony between black and white in both the political-social and the cultural sphere.[6]

I have organized my materials according to what seemed the most significant elements and frequently occurring images. In the chapters that specifically analyze cultural representations of jazz (chapters 3 and 4), I have selected particular, representative texts from the many that are available. Because these chapters are organized around key, contested figures, some of these representative texts are included in both chapters.

Analyzing developments in national politics, cultural theory, literature, jazz, the popular media, and youth culture during the postwar era, chapter 1 presents the overarching discursive context for this study. The chapter traces the development and interaction of the competing racial discourses that provided Euro and African Americans with the definitions they used to discuss and represent jazz. I argue that "color-blindness" emerged from this period as the dominant racial discourse despite the power and popularity of the oppositional discourses that emanated from the civil rights movement and urban bohemias like Greenwich Village. I also argue that this dominance of color-blindness contributed to the material and cultural benefits reaped but not acknowledged by Euro Americans.

In chapter 2 I narrow my focus slightly by reconstructing and analyzing the social and cultural relations between Euro and African Americans in Greenwich Village during the immediate postwar period. The most recognized, celebrated, and productive avant-garde locus of this period, the Village was also the site of significant social and cultural interaction between adventurous and rebellious black and white youth. The three goals of this chapter are to establish the character of the material relations of the period's interracial avant garde; to elucidate the connections between the avant garde and the wider popular culture; and to embed my subsequent analyses of cultural discourse in material relations.

Next, I consider the various depictions of the legendary bebop saxophonist Charlie Parker. Revered and even deified by both white and black writers, artists, and intellectuals during this period, Parker appears in cultural texts as both an "actual" symbolic figure (i.e., "Charlie Parker") and a transmuted, but identifiable, fictional character. While Parker as an important symbol during the late 1950s and early 1960s obviously fulfilled needs of both black and white men, the differences in the needs of the two groups are striking. By Euro Americans, Parker was most often romanticized as the prototypical suffering, alienated, *individual* artist. White texts focus almost exclusively on his specific victimization by society and connect this to his artistic "genius." African American texts, on the other hand, also portray Parker as a musical "genius," but in addition emphasize that he is another in the tradition of African American musicians. African Americans also tend to isolate Parker's musical talent from both his self-destruction and his societal victimization. Finally, black texts portray Parker not as a victimized artist, but as another in a long line of race heroes and martyrs.

In chapter 4 I examine representations of jazz performance in cultural texts of the 1950s and 1960s. Because it is a music that depends for its greatest power upon the electricity generated by the spontaneous moment, jazz performed in front of a live audience in a nightclub setting has often been used metaphorically. Many Euro Americans during this period especially focus on the lone jazz soloist, casting him as the prototypical American individualist who works through his personal pain and suffering and achieves greatness. Other Euro Americans concentrate on the competition, or "cutting," that often occurs between jazz soloists during performances to show how this free market of musical ideas encourages the cream to rise to the top. Many African Americans, on the other hand, emphasize the unity and interdependence of the members of a performing jazz group, and connect this depiction to larger types of unity and interdependence—in the culture, in the community, in history.

In chapter 5 I analyze the various narrative strategies authors use to simulate or capture the sound and attitude of improvisational jazz. Euro American authors often attempted to imitate jazz rhythms or structures in obvious and direct ways, while African Americans typically aimed for a more innovative structural variation or a thematic representation of the jazz attitude or ethic.

My epilogue surveys a couple of recent developments related to race in cultural studies, and assesses the possibility at present for creating what Paul Gilroy has called "non-dominating social [and cultural] relationships" (1993: 79).

The Color of Jazz

1.

Blinded by the White

The Hidden History of Postwar Racial Politics

> Between 1940 and 1970, blacks made steady strides, moving from farm and non-farm labor to an array of blue-collar industrial jobs and white-collar jobs. As the result of a booming post-war economy, the ascent of black professional athletes, the popularization of black music, and victories on the civil rights front—including affirmative action and government set-aside programs—blacks made considerable economic progress. . . .
>
> In retrospect, it appears that African Americans built their advancement on a foundation of sand. Since "white over black" characterizes the job market and occupational structure, black economic prosperity will be tenuous at best. (Taylor 1995: 400–401)

Reassessments like this one by Henry Louis Taylor appear throughout recent scholarship on the progress of racial politics during the past forty years. These reassessments have in large part been provoked by the need to explain the continuation of social, political, and economic inequality between white and black Americans; the desire to incorporate developments in social construction theory; and the wish to decipher the recent movement by a wide segment of white Americans to discontinue the programs Taylor characterizes as "victories on the civil rights front": affirmative action and set-aside programs. Before these recent reassessments, historical scholarship on racial formation had emphasized—with some justification—the social, political, and economic progress made by African Americans during this era: integration of the Armed Services, the end of legal segregation in the South, voting rights, school integration, and federal civil rights and economic legislation.

These achievements of the African American civil rights struggle remain standing and speak for themselves. However, racism persists, and racial inequality has worsened. Following Taylor and others, we must look to the recent past to discover what has gone wrong. We must search beneath, behind, and beyond the achievements of the civil rights movement, and in both the material and the ideal realms. Our inability to eradicate racism and racial inequality derives in part from white Americans' unwillingness to recognize the ways they have been and continue to be racialized as white.[1] As I explain, the racialization of white Americans has occurred not only through the actions of government, businesses, and private individuals, but through the expression and circulation of ideas that enforced and influenced these actions. As George Lipsitz states, "An elaborate interaction of largely *covert* public and private decisions during and after the days of slavery and segregation . . . produced a powerful legacy with enduring effects on the racialization of experience, opportunities, and rewards in the United States" (1995a: 371). Lipsitz and others have begun to excavate these "public and private decisions" during the especially significant period between the New Deal and the present.

The New Deal era constitutes the significant, immediate prehistory of this study. During this time several pieces of federal legislation were enacted that helped create the material field on which the cultural contest I am describing took place. At about the same time, the large gap between politically progressive white Americans' racial rhetoric and their actions became institutionalized. Although the Roosevelt Administration's record on race is decidedly mixed, a few generalizations about its legacy are becoming increasingly apparent. First, during Roosevelt's initial term in office, several pieces of legislation were passed that have had an enormous impact on African Americans specifically, and on the shape of the American social, economic, and political landscapes generally. As historian Harvard Sitkoff and sociologist Jill Quadrano explain, during its first term the administration could not accomplish any of its economic goals without the support of Southern Democratic congressmen who were still completely within the sphere of the white planter oligarchy (Sitkoff 1978: 34–57; Quadrano 1994: 19–24). However, there is not much indication that the early Roosevelt Administration would have gone very far to demand civil rights for black people anyway. Sitkoff notes that Roosevelt "had never championed the Negro's cause. He had shown no concern for racial problems" (1978: 40). In even more general terms (and closer to my point), Lipsitz argues that "white supremacy was not a gnawing aberration within the New Deal coalition but rather an essential point of unity between southern whites and northern white ethnics" (1995a: 385). However, from either a liberal or a moderate perspective, the combination of pragmatic party politics and Roosevelt's continuing lack of interest in the African American cause ensured that the administration would sacrifice the civil rights of black people to the pragmatic goal of party unity.

Sacrifice African Americans the administration did, on such important pieces of legislation as the National Housing Acts of 1934 and 1937 and the National Labor Relations Act and Social Security Act, both of which were passed in 1935. Designed to ensure basic "social rights" to American citizens through a national welfare state, these federal programs achieved their goal primarily for white Americans. As George Lipsitz argues, "these policies widened the gap between the resources available to whites and those available to aggrieved racial communities" (1995a: 372). The Social Security Act provided old-age insurance and employment compensation to industrial workers, but not to farm workers and domestic servants—two categories of employment disproportionately filled by racial minority workers.[2] The National Labor Relations Act (also called the Wagner Act) gave workers the right to organize unions and bargain collectively with employers, but "permitted labor organizations to exclude African Americans, denied the status of 'employee' to black workers engaged in strike breaking, and permitted the establishment of separate racially segregated unions" (Quadrano 1994: 23). These two pieces of legislation are notable not only because of what we now recognize as their transparent racism, but because of the long-lasting effects of their unequal distribution of economic resources. Although the inequities institutionalized in these bills were rectified in the mid-1950s, the twenty-year period that had elapsed greatly exacerbated the economic gap between white and black Americans.[3]

The final Roosevelt Administration bills marking this racial field were the National Housing Acts of 1934 and 1937. In effect, these bills "reinforced patterns of racial segregation through housing policy" (Quadrano 1994: 23; Lipsitz 1995a: 372–73). They established the Federal Housing Administration (FHA), which guaranteed private lenders against home buyers' loan defaults. This federal program enabled many Americans to become home buyers for the first time. However, the FHA's policies were thoroughly racist: its *Underwriting Manual* carried "the warning that property values deteriorate when Negroes move into predominantly white neighborhoods"; in the name of "economic soundness," it prohibited loans in "areas of cities considered risky for economic *or* racial reasons"; it would not guarantee mortgages on homes African Americans bought in white neighborhoods; and it built public housing projects with rental apartments "in racially segregated neighborhoods and selected tenants by race" (Sitkoff 1978: 50; Quadrano 1994: 23–24; Lipsitz 1995a: 372–73).

The pattern established by these bills is one in which increasing racial segregation and polarization occurred, especially during the 1950s, behind a mask of public rhetoric and public policy that declared itself democratic and racially progressive. As Richard Polenberg describes it, for all the progress occurring in the political and judicial spheres regarding integration—for instance, Truman's 1948 executive order requiring fair employment practices in the federal service and the Supreme Court's 1954 *Brown v. Board of Education* decision—American *society* in the 1950s was becoming increasingly segregated: "The process of suburbanization, it turned out, was strengthening the de facto basis for racial segregation even as judicial rulings, militant protest, congressional action, and executive intervention were weakening its de jure basis" (Polenberg 1980: 153). As whites "moved from cities to suburbs, black Americans, largely from southern rural areas, took their places" (1980: 150). This movement, then, increased the social distance that already existed between most black and white communities in the United States even as it increased the political power of African Americans by concentrating their population in urban enclaves.

Whether the coalition between Northern and Southern whites was one of mere political expedience or coincidence of interests, then, the result of these federal bills was to allow and even encourage white Americans to continue to think of themselves as better and more deserving than African Americans and other racial minorities. In the ideology of these bills, mainly white Americans were worthy of support in their old age and in their unemployment because they worked in jobs that were valuable to the U.S. economy and society; mainly white Americans were good risks for public and private moneylenders; mainly white Americans lived in neighborhoods that represented the success the federal government wanted to support. Black Americans, of course, were negatively represented in the ideology of these legislative acts.

More important for my purposes, this official hypocrisy legitimated a public discourse in which white Americans turned a blind eye to the significance and influence of race on the lives of *all* Americans while reaping the material and psychic benefits of their white privilege. In this way, whiteness was nurtured and allowed to prosper only by the marginalization and subordination of nonwhite (especially black) people. As I will describe shortly, this hypocrisy was reproduced in the cultural sphere of popular music beginning with the mass popularity of swing bands in the 1930s and 1940s. George Lipsitz recently coined the pithy phrase "the possessive investment in whiteness" to characterize this contemporary racialization process. Like Lipsitz, I believe this particular form of racism was newly created starting in the New Deal era and continues to be the predominant form of white racism in the United States today.

Within this period, scholars also identify an overlapping of dominant society's racial ideology, public policy, social patterns, and cultural production around the notion of "race-neutrality" or "color-blindness." As the dominant racial discourse or paradigm during this time, color-blindness has encouraged Americans to work toward the elimination of all racial difference under the idea that the natural tendency of all minority groups in the United States is to "assimilate." The basic components of this color-blindness paradigm were, beginning in the 1920s, conceived by sociologists and cultural anthropologists as challenges to the previously dominant racial discourse that constructed race as an essential, biological feature. Whereas the previously dominant paradigm of "scientific racism" contended that racial difference was not only biological but also determined the development of culture, the new color-blindness discourses argued that while physical, racial difference was biological, it had no influence on individual or group attributes. Culture, these new discourses asserted, emerges out of a group's sociohistorical experience. As such, culture reflects not essential, inherited differences between groups of people, but differences in the development of each group's history. Clearly, then, these new discourses were nominally relativistic: the cultures of Western and white people are not necessarily more sophisticated than those of African or Asian people—merely different because of different social and historical circumstances. Cultural differences between white and black Americans, then, were attributed directly to such historical forces as slavery, segregation, and poverty (thus social scientific thought of the early 1960s gave birth to the "culture of poverty" argument). Therefore, cultural differences (which were seen by color-blindness theorists as mostly negative when they deviated from the "norm") would naturally disappear when minority groups assimilated (Omi and Winant 1986: 14–16; Frankenberg 1993: 13; Pascoe 1996: 52–55; Sitkoff 1978: 190–94; Steinberg 1995: 29–33).

Much of the empirical research that yielded the various structural predictions included in these theories of color-blindness emerged out of sociological analysis of the American experience of white Europeans from the second great wave of European immigration. Making predictions about the future assimilation of all Americans from the experience of white immigrants, then, these theorists viewed race as an obstacle (albeit a large one) to the inevitable progress of nonwhite Americans. They believed that African Americans, for example, had not progressed as far as Jewish or Irish Americans in their structural assimilation because slavery and segregation had delayed their inexorable march toward that goal. Furthermore, they viewed racism as a problem in the beliefs white people had about black people rather than a structural lack of opportunity (Omi and Winant 1986: 16–21; Steinberg 1995: 44). Given these assumptions and predictions, then, the various discourses of color-blindness that emanated from the work of such scholars as Boas, Benedict, Myrdal, Gordon, and Glazer encouraged public policy makers to ignore race. Stephen Steinberg notes that the "leading sociological theorists (from Robert Park through Gunnar Myrdal to Talcott Parsons) avoided the issue of civil rights. Instead, they advanced theoretical models that projected racial improvement as part of an evolutionary process of societal change" (1995: 56).

As the dominant racial paradigm in the postwar era, color-blindness enforced a paradoxical approach to race. On one hand, sociologists like Myrdal recognized and deplored the fact that African Americans encountered severely limited opportunities in U.S. society because of racism. Moreover, they held white Americans accountable to a certain extent for perpetuating racism. However, because they theorized that assimilation was the inevitable and desirable goal of African American (or any minority group's) progress, they left the existing racial hierarchy in place: whiteness remained the *invisible* norm and standard of success, while blackness remained stigmatized as a deficient, primitive culture and identity. For this reason Ruth Frankenberg says that color-blindness involves "a double move toward 'color-evasiveness' and 'power evasiveness' ": it encourages us to ignore race and its effects on the distribution of wealth, power, status, and opportunity in society (1993: 14). The not-so-subtle message encoded in color-blindness, then, is that white and black Americans should begin to move away from the stigmatized category of blackness to the privileged, unmarked category of whiteness. The color-blindness discourse, in other words, builds the supremacy of whiteness upon a stigmatized but contained category of blackness.

We can see the influence of the color-blindness discourse in the mainstream press coverage of jazz music in the immediate postwar period. Although the conventional wisdom is that the mainstream press reacted to the development of bebop after the war as if it were the second coming of Nat Turner, the actual press response of the time was, as David Stowe explains, more complicated (1994: 207–10). Describing the polarized response to the new music—progressives loved it, "moldy figs" despised it—Stowe deempahsizes the racial specificity of this press reaction by setting it in the context of the era's recent history of media coverage of all jazz music. Those who most strongly condemned bebop, he says, were either conservative cultural critics who had also attacked white-led swing music a decade before using the same hysterical arguments about "juvenile delinquency, illicit drug use, sexual promiscuity, outrageous language and dress," or conservative jazz critics who feared they were losing their authority to set jazz tastes (1994: 209, 224). These critics, then, did not respond to the new music in knee-jerk racist fashion. Moreover, as Stowe makes clear, there were also many white writers in the mainstream music press who were ardent supporters of bebop, including such well-known critics as Leonard Feather and Barry Ulanov (1994: 226). Clearly, then, the press response to bebop cannot be characterized as wholly or even primarily influenced by racism.

However, we can locate the color-blindness discourse in both the critical and the supportive press responses to bebop. First, neither the positive nor the negative press reports on bebop that began appearing in the mainstream press during 1946 recycled the kinds of vicious, essentialist, racist rhetoric of earlier periods. In fact, overall this press coverage downplays race as the distinguishing feature of either the musicians' lives or the music they were creating. When race is mentioned, either verbally or visually, the emphasis is on the fact that the "bebop movement" has attracted both black and white devotees, implying that the significance of bebop— for good or ill—is that it is breaking down racial barriers. A *New Yorker* profile of Dizzy Gillespie from 1948, for example, notes that Gillespie's "followers, both white and Negro, often affectionately declare that Dizzy is 'it,' that he is 'real crazy,' 'a bitch,' and 'a killer'" (Boyer 1948: 26). In the notorious *Life* magazine feature on bebop, also published in 1948, photographs taken at the triumphant Hollywood engagement of the Gillespie band show singer Mel Torme and actress Ava Gardner enjoying the music. Although, of course, these photographs were newsworthy because of the celebrity of these white audience members, the fact that they are the only photographs of the audience in the magazine piece is also significant.

The positive and negative articles from this period also share a preoccupation with Dizzy Gillespie. He is so completely synonymous with bebop that the 1948 *New Yorker* profile of him is simply titled "Bop." On one hand, it is not at all surprising that Gillespie became associated more closely with bebop than any of his peers. None of the others who might have been deemed representative of the movement—Charlie Parker or Thelonious Monk, for example—had the kind of temperament that would have enabled them to do the endless promotion Gillespie did and still retain their good humor. As has often been noted, Gillespie good-naturedly obliged the mainstream press's desire for a cartoon image of the bebopper with his beret, horn-rimmed glasses, and ostrich leather shoes. Whatever his reasons for participating in his own glorification and marginalization (and I will return to Gillespie and the politics of bebop shortly), he provided the color-blind press with the ideal representative of this potentially threatening subcultural movement. Despite his criticism of what he saw at the time as Louis Armstrong's "Uncle Tomming," Gillespie himself was willing to act the clown in front of the white press. Moreover, unlike either Parker or Monk, for example, Gillespie seemed to lack an edge of any kind, although he had experienced and understood the kinds of experiences to which the press attributed the "erratic" behavior of his more notorious colleagues. In fact, these articles cast Gillespie in the role of anthropologist (a participant/observer) or intellectual, explaining or interpreting the seemingly inexplicable actions of beboppers like Parker and Monk. In the *New Yorker* article, for example, Dizzy interprets the "widespread" Islamic conversions of jazz musicians: "Dizzy's eyes filled with tears. 'They been hurt,' he explained, 'and they're tryin' to get away from it'" (Boyer 1948: 30). Of course, in these articles the specific causes of their pain remain unspoken; given the publicity surrounding jazz musicians at the time, the public was more likely to assume as causes drug and alcohol addiction, the "hard life" more generally, or artistic rejection, rather than racism.

In these mainstream articles, the highest form of compliment for bebop musicians is comparison with a white composer or artist, or a mention of their interest in European culture. This is not to suggest either that there is no legitimate connection between a jazz musician and a classical composer or that bebop musicians were not interested in European culture. However, I am suggesting that the use of these comparisons and quotations as the primary point of reference functioned to obscure the distinctiveness of jazz as an African American aesthetic tradition, and instead enclosed jazz and jazz musicians securely within the orbit of white, European American culture. Thus a *Saturday Review of Literature* introduction to bebop in 1947 admits that bebop "is an acquired taste," but says "the same is true of Stravinsky and Shostakovitch" (McKean 1947: 18). Typically, these early mainstream press reports—even those appearing in "jazz" columns—subordinate explanations of the music itself to these defensive claims that the new jazz is really no different from classical music. After explaining that the label "bebop" derives, in part, from a band leader's preliminary instructions to his musicians— "bee-bobba-doe-bobba-doe . . ."—this same *Saturday Review* article heads off its readers' expected objections: "Lest you carp too quickly and brand these effusions as childish, remember that Sir Thomas Beecham and countless other symphonic conductors clarify difficult passages vocally during rehearsal for the benefit of the orchestra. If put to paper these mounting would seem as bizarre as the passage transcribed above" (1947: 18).

Similarly, articles that characterize jazz musicians by comparing them to white cultural icons or by noting the musicians' interest in elements of acceptable (if not canonical) dominant culture do so as the primary means of legitimizing their subjects' artistry and sophistication. Thus, the *New Yorker* notes that "many of the Negro adherents of bebop . . . take a subsidiary interest in psychoanalysis and abstract art," and quotes Thelonious Monk as saying, "We liked Ravel, Stravinsky, Debussy, Prokofieff, Schoenberg and maybe we were a little influenced by them" (Boyer 1948: 27–28). A 1956 tribute to Charlie Parker by jazz critic Whitney Balliett legitimizes Bird's tragic but creative life by comparing him to Dylan Thomas: "Both had about the same amount of talent. Both were in their thirties when they died. Both were modified revolutionaries. Both had a maximum and highly daring creative approach to the basic *content* of their particular mediums. Both had damaging twists in their personalities that were bathed in either dope or alcohol. Both gave overgenerously of themselves in their work. Both loved and hated their homes, their families, and their work." Certainly there are comparisons to be made between Thomas and Parker (not least of which is that they died approximately sixteen months apart in the same city from the same dissipating habits). However, we must also note that this comparison fulfills the demands of color-blindness by simultaneously recognizing Parker's artistic achievements and universalizing his experience (not to mention that the first sentence is extremely patronizing).

The era bracketed by this study witnessed the absolute ascendency of the color-blind discourse. Stephen Steinberg asserts that the cultural challenges (what I have been grouping together as "color-blindness") to scientific racism constituted a "liberal orthodoxy" that held sway over social scientific and public thought about race until the late 1960s (Steinberg 1995: 50–67). During this time, however, there were also many "subordinated" discourses that challenged the legitimacy of this liberal orthodoxy's racial discourse. Some of these challenges were launched by white Americans and some by black Americans, with varying degrees of success. Some of these challenges were in the manner of "subculture"—which Dick Hebdige has defined as "the idea of style as a form of Refusal" (1987: 2)— while others challenged the dominant discourse on less rarefied ground—civil, social, and political rights. In the remainder of this chapter I present and analyze three of these subordinated discourses. First, I look at the discursive strategies holding together the bebop insurgency during the late 1940s and early 1950s and those propelling the early black civil rights movements of the mid- and late 1950s. Next I look at the discourse that emanated from the mostly white countercultural movements of the 1940s and 1950s. I am using "countercultural" here to designate both the individuals (most of whom remain anonymous) who participated in such oppositional social and cultural movements as the "Beat generation" (on both the East and the West coast) and those more famous people who produced texts that were oppositional, but who may or may not have been involved in the movements themselves (like Jack Kerouac and Norman Mailer).

To say, as David Stowe does, that "bebop's politics resist assimilation to any clear-cut political model" (1994: 232) is to be unduly coy and to adhere to the most prosaic notion of what constitutes politics. Clearly bebop musicians were not self-conscious politicians, traditional or otherwise; but, just as clearly, the bebop movement was rooted in social and cultural contexts that nurtured its positioning as an oppositional or subversive discourse. As Eric Lott says, "Brilliantly outside, bebop was intimately if indirectly related to the militancy of its moment. Militancy and music were undergirded by the same social facts; the music attempted to resolve at the level of style what the militancy combatted in the streets" (1988: 599). The founding bebop musicians, all of them black men, lived in the postwar historical moment I have already described. Although they found a somewhat more congenial atmosphere inside most of the clubs they played, outside these locales most of them faced the same violence and terror confronted by the typical black man of the era. In one of many similar situations in his autobiography, for example, Dizzy Gillespie vividly recalls an incident that occurred around 1944 in which he and bassist Oscar Pettiford were attacked by white sailors outside the Onyx Club on Fifty-second Street because the sailors thought (erroneously) the musicians were with a white woman (Gillespie 1979: 210–11). The "social fact" of American racism these musicians experienced, combined with such contemporary factors as the ill treatment of black soldiers they witnessed and the sense that they were being exploited by white businessmen in the music industry, contributed to the creation of new music that, as Gillespie says, "reflect[ed] the way we felt" (1979: 141). To echo Eric Lott, you can hear the tumultuousness of the times in the rhythm and tempo of solos by Monk, Parker, Gillespie, and others (Lott 1988: 599).

While it is true, as David Stowe cautions, that retrospective constructions of bebop as a full-blown forerunner to the cultural nationalism of the 1960s is presentist and romantic, any way you look at bebop—as music, style, subculture—its politics challenged the status quo. In his biography of Louis Armstrong, James Lincoln Collier says bebop "had been developed by a new generation of aggressive young blacks, who were not only making a revolution in jazz music but were openly bitter about the position of blacks in America and scornful of the white society, which they saw as hypocritical, shallow, and lifeless" (1983: 304). It is not necessary to construct these musicians as "black nationalists" or to reduce their complex music to a single dimension to hear and feel the anger and resentment in their music and life stories. Musically, bebop played itself off against the slower, more rigid, less complex compositions of swing and other older styles of jazz. Part of the revolt of bebop certainly concerns the typical artistic reaction to the "anxiety of influence." To this extent, bebop was simply that latest evolutionary development in jazz, the "newest thing," and the form of the music was simply a response to the form—swing—that preceded it. However, according to Max Roach, race played a part in at least one aspect of bebop's innovation: "When we got downtown, people wanted to hear something they were familiar with, like 'How High the Moon,' 'What is This Thing Called Love?' Can you play that? So in playing these things, the black musicians recognized that the royalties were going back to these people, like ASCAP, the Jerome Kerns, the Gershwins. So one revolutionary thing that happened, they began to write parodies on the harmonic structures. Which was really revolutionary. If I have to play it, I will put my own particular melody on that progression, and people would ask, 'Say, what is that?' " (Gillespie 1979: 209).

While Stowe is certainly correct, then, in identifying a significant generational break between swing and bebop, the racial element was the most prominent oppositional element in the bebop discourse. Music historian Samuel Floyd says, "The new music expressed the emotional realities of musicians in the midst of a powerful verisimilitude—swing music—that they felt repeated and encouraged the same suppressions and denials that black musicians had been experiencing since the ascendance of ragtime" (1995: 138). Correctly or not, bebop musicians considered swing to be yet another white appropriation of black culture, and saw almost exclusively white musicians and businessmen making money from it. However, bebop's racial critique was not limited to musicians with white skin; it extended to black musicians who seemed to be acting "white." Thus, even the beboppers' antipathy toward Louis Armstrong was expressed in terms of race.

Gillespie recalls: "I criticized Louis for other things, such as his 'plantation image.' We didn't appreciate that about Louis Armstrong, and if anybody asked me about a certain public image of him, handkerchief over his head, grinning in the face of white racism, I never hesitated to say I didn't like it. I didn't want the white man to expect me to allow the same things Louis Armstrong did" (1979: 295). Although Gillespie later said that he had "misjudged" Armstrong's behavior, this *racial* criticism of the legendary trumpeter was well known at the time.

The resurgent movement for black civil rights provided the postwar period with its most potent oppositional discourse. Although the black struggle for freedom and equality had been waged continuously since the settling of the United States, its spirit and moral righteousness were greatly energized in the twentieth century by the fight against fascism in World War II. The international conflict had brought racism in the United States into stark relief for African Americans, and had given them the moral and pragmatic belief that the federal government could no longer deny them equal rights. In defiance of the dominant discourse of color-blindness, African Americans were no longer willing to wait until white people were *ready* to grant them rights; they demanded they be given now.

An early sign of what was to come in succeeding decades was A. Philip Randolph's threatened March on Washington in 1941 to protest discrimination against African Americans in the U.S. defense industry and armed forces. Despite pleas by white leaders for national solidarity in the war effort, Randolph and other African Americans refused to back down. As excitement for the proposed march spread among African Americans across the United States, white politicians and leaders including President Roosevelt, Eleanor Roosevelt, and New York Mayor Fiorello LaGuardia scrambled to avoid the massive international embarrassment a march on the nation's capital would cause. However, no entreaties could dissuade Randolph from persevering, and finally, on June 25, 1941, rather than face a massive African American protest march President Roosevelt issued Executive Order 8802 calling for an end to discriminatory practices by defense contractors and set up a committee to investigate complaints. Although the committee had little power and, in the end, precious little effect on discrimination in the defense industry, African Americans glimpsed the potential of their collective power (Franklin and Moss 1988: 388–89; Polenberg 1980: 33–34).

This early skirmish in the modern black civil rights struggle is emblematic for several reasons. First, it shows the renewed spirit behind African American demands for freedom and equality even as it demonstates the link, in the person of A. Philip Randolph, between the modern civil rights movement and earlier struggles for African American civil rights. As Walter Kalaidjian suggests, Randolph's contributions to the theorization of the "new negro" in the 1920s constitute an important early source for later acts of African American resistance (Kalaidjian

1993: 75). Second, the 1941 showdown demonstrates the federal government's reluctance to take risks to fight racism: even Eleanor Roosevelt tried to persuade Randolph to call off the march for the good of African Americans (Franklin and Moss 1988: 388). Third, it hints at the federal government's inability to provide adequate solutions to the problems of race in the United States.

During the fourteen years following Randolph's stand against the Roosevelt administration, this dynamic was repeated several times, most notably in the NAACP's role in eliminating the legal basis for segregation on interstate buses and trains, in state universities and graduate schools, in Washington, D.C. stores and restaurants, and, finally, in public schools in the celebrated *Brown v. Board of Education* case of 1954. In each of these conflicts NAACP lawyers (including Thurgood Marshall) fought hard and won their cases on sound principles only to see state governments in the South circumvent federal law, and white moderate to liberal politicians in the North accommodate the Southern racists. Even after the *Brown* decision, for example, "Democratic leader Adlai Stevenson urged that civil rights be approached cautiously, with moderation" (Jezer 1982: 299). As this example demonstrates, even on the progressive side of the U.S. political spectrum there was not an ideological consensus on the appropriate approach to civil rights. Moreover, this division generally followed racial lines. As James Gilbert says,

> Although the movement allied itself to liberalism frequently during the 1950s and 1960s and black voters most often cast their ballots for Democratic candidates, the relationship remained a coalition rather than an agreement on principles. The demands of black Americans for social justice constantly pushed against the confines of liberal politics. Liberals supported many of these demands, but not all of them, and with differing degrees of fervor and urgency. (1981: 246)

Just as importantly, the prevalence of compromise (or coalition) between the white liberal establishment and the black middle-class establishment, represented by the NAACP, during the mid- to late 1950s widened the gap that already existed between the black establishment and other black Americans. Though black Americans recognized that these judicial victories were extremely important both as momentous legal precedents and as national events that "added historical momentum and political legitimacy to black struggles against racism," their ultimate failure to change social reality convinced many black Americans that more militant, grass-roots action was needed (West 1984: 44). Thus, Southern black women, religious people, college students, and others began to take direct action in what Cornel West calls "a revolt against the perceived complacency of the 'old' black petite bourgeoisie" (1984: 47).

Taking the form of civil disobedience in such acts as a bus boycott, sit-ins, and freedom rides, this revolt added a new strand of oppositional discourse to that contained within the judicial and legislative agenda of the black middle-class establishment. Even more so than the legal action taken by the NAACP and other groups, the revolt constituted a distinctive African American oppositional discourse, rising as it did out of Southern black churches and, as Cornel West says, taking the "form of a critique of everyday life in the American South" (1984: 49). For more than one hundred years before the start of the modern civil rights movement, black churches had been the indispensable hub of African American social, cultural, political, and economic life. Despite the many schisms over those years that split black congregants, black churches promoted group identity and self-help by educating members, teaching literacy skills, providing for the community's welfare, and offering black people opportunities they could not get otherwise in an American society controlled by white people. Of course, one of the most significant figures to emerge from the black churches historically was the preacher (Stuckey 1987: 61). Formed in the crucible of community need and fierce competition among ambitious black men, the preacher was capable of fiery rhetoric he could use to unite and mobilize his congregation. Out of the historical functions fulfilled by the black churches and around the central figure of the black preacher arose the initial stage of the modern civil rights movement. Although the cultural discourse generated in the African American church and catalyzed by the civil rights movement differs significantly from that constructed by jazz during this period (for example, in terms of the difference between the sacred and the profane), similarities between the two are more profound and substantial: both renegotiated Africanist cultural elements like the "ring shout," relied on the charismatic work of strong male figures, offered trenchant critiques of white power, and provided powerful means for unifying African American people.

In contrast to the morally charged political resistance of African Americans, the major form of white social and cultural rebellion or opposition in the postwar period was what Marty Jezer has called a "revitalized bohemian life" (1982: 263). Well publicized and mythologized since before World War I by such luminaries as Eugene O'Neill, John Reed, Max Eastman, and Walter Lippman, bohemian life, especially in Greenwich Village, began to attract an increasing number of new, young immigrants beginning in the late 1940s. Young Americans like writer and activist Michael Harrington were drawn out of their middle-class existences in cities and suburbs by the desire to participate in the artistic or political avant garde, to experiment in living, and/or to escape from a dominant culture that seemed stifling, boring, and excessively materialistic (Jezer 1982: 263; Jacoby 1987: 20).

Harold Cruse's description of Greenwich Village migrants in the 1920s fits the postwar generation as well: "They were deeply disturbed and agitated over the way America was developing into a nation without soul. In coming to Greenwich

Village from the hinterlands or from universities, they were escaping the real America they had grown up in" (1984: 28). A similar characterization can be found in Wini Breines's description of the motivation for female dissatisfaction and rebellion during the 1950s: "Girls' discontent was articulated, as it was by others in the society, as a longing for meaning, for something more real than the middle-class lives set out for them" (Breines 1992: 137). The legend of bohemian life, well established by this time, promised these refugees from middle America fulfillment on a couple of levels. According to Ronald Sukenick, "Any moderately well informed kid around 1950 knew about the going romance of Bohemia, with its peculiar mix of both pleasure and salvation so attractive for kids in pre-sixties puritan America" (1987: 12–13). On the West Coast as well as the East, young people migrated to places like Venice Beach in Los Angeles, where they "lived in cottages, sheds, garages, warehouses, and empty stores, observing a cheerful and offhanded ethic of noncompetition, nonacquisition, and disrespect for established values, however or by whomever established" (Maynard 1991: 47).

It is perhaps true, as Dan Wakefield says, that the migrants of the immediate postwar period needed the freedom of the Village even more than did those of earlier times, because the United States during the late 1940s and the 1950s had become even more oppressive in its demand for conformity to the ideals of capitalist, consumer society: "If the mood of the country was to force everyone to conform, to look and dress like the man in the gray flannel suit, surely it was all the more important to have at least one haven where people were not only allowed but expected to dress, speak, and behave differently from the herd" (Wakefield 1992: 121). Or as Sukenick describes the conflict between bohemian and mainstream values: "The spiritual geography of the underground describes a promised land of freedom, illumination, and excitement beyond the provincial ego, the constrictions of social class and ethnic heritage, beyond the conventional altogether" (1987: 16).

Whether or not American society demanded more conformity in the 1940s and 1950s than during earlier eras, questions about American values and character in an age of increasingly corporate and suburban society became prevalent enough then that they were the focus of such sociological works as *The Organization Man*, *Growing Up Absurd*, and *The Lonely Crowd*. And whether or not the rebellion of this time was one specifically against the conforming constraints of American capitalism, the overwhelming sense of present-day historians and sociologists is that the many rebellions that flourished then were challenges to the *numerous*, strict boundaries (those that defined the cold war, Jim Crow, and the suburban exodus) that divided American society and culture. Wini Breines says, "Literal and figurative boundaries were important in the fifties, a period in which distinctions between 'them' (foreigners and deviants) and 'us' flourished" (1992: 9).

One of the strongest of these boundaries was the symbolic, if not the actual, boundary between "black and white." During the immediate postwar era, not only were African American people absent from the white suburbs that began to develop in the United States; African American images were rarely projected anywhere in dominant American culture. Breines writes: "The America presented by movies, television, magazines, and advertising was white. Black people were practically nonexistent in the dominant mass media" (1992: 15). The only avenues most young white people could find leading into African American culture were in a few bohemian enclaves like Greenwich Village or in media related to music: black radio stations and, later, records by "white Negroes" whose appropriation of African American culture hinted at the excluded culture and people that stood behind it (George 1988: 39–57, 59–70). Despite what has been argued in the past (primarily by white scholars and musicologists), however, neither of these avenues of cultural attraction led masses of Euro American admirers to uncomplicated, equitable relations with African American culture.

To elucidate this point, let us consider the example of Elvis Presley. Here was a popular cultural icon that brought African American culture to a youthful mass audience (primarily young, white, and middle-class) wearing a "black mask" that was more acceptable than the faces of African American rhythm and blues performers. For all their rebelliousness against the constraints of the middle-class culture of the 1950s, the curiosity of American teenagers about what Nelson George describes as "excluded cultures and behaviors" was satisfied by a white surrogate. Moreover, if, as George suggests, Elvis "codified white youth rebellion," then it is significant that "Elvis was just a package, a performer with limited musical ambition and no real dedication to the black style that made him seem so dangerous" (George 1988: 63). This indicates that while the symbolic barrier between "black and white" appeared to be breaking down (as evidenced by the popularity of Elvis's "black mask" among white teenagers), below the surface the two cultures were not significantly meeting or fusing.

This is not to say, however, that the young white outsiders who migrated to bohemian enclaves like Greenwich Village were not contesting the dominant racial discourses in society at the time. They were in some ways, and in others they were not. In their interest in and openness to African American people and culture, these white Americans were resisting color-blindness's dictates both to privilege the invisible white standard and to ignore racial differences altogether. Like their reverse migration from the suburbs to urban centers and their acceptance of interracial relationships, their rejection of dominant white culture for African American (and other marginalized) cultures was an explicit rebuke of dominant society's middle-class values. We should not underestimate the significance of these moves to the creation of a new white counterculture, nor the *potential* of these boundary transgressions for interracial contact.

However, when we probe the uses of African American culture by white people associated with these oppositional movements we too often discover that their reversal of the dominant discourse is merely the obverse side of the same racist coin. Recent analyses of the white youth or outsider attraction to African American culture during the 1950s and early 1960s have been careful to note, for example, that many of these appropriations now seem to be "primitivistic" or "racist." However, in these analyses there remains a desire to romanticize the attraction and the effect of it on the formation of American mass culture.[4] In her analysis of Greenwich Village in 1963, for example, Sally Banes defends the use of African American cultural resources by Euro American avant-garde artists this way: "And although these appropriations may now carry for some the taint of rip-off culture, for the Sixties avant-garde it signaled cultural respect, even envy. If the envy was there for the wrong reasons, and expressed in what now seems inappropriate ways, the respect was undeniable" (1993: 208). A similar and more sweeping defense is offered by Wini Breines: "Young people and bohemians in the fifties were learning about white culture by appreciating black culture; if they were racist in their objectifications as was, for example, Norman Mailer in 'The White Negro' (1957), they were also drawn to it respectfully" (1992: 20). The notion of "respect" in these characterizations is particularly interesting because it implies the exact opposite of what actually happened in the contest between black and white culture in the 1950s and 1960s. If we understand "respect" to connote not only esteem but also the kind of deference that prevents one from interfering with the object of esteem, then we cannot say that white youth and outsiders respected African American culture. It was precisely because these Euro Americans stood in a superior social and political position vis-a-vis African American culture that they could appropriate or exploit these resources.

Even in those recent studies of 1950s American culture in which scholars (most of them white) have specifically confronted the interest white outsiders had in African American cultural forms, the positive effects of this contact have been overemphasized, and the obstacles this discourse put in the way of racial understanding and equality have been underestimated. Searching for a historical construction that demonstrates that white America is not racist to the core, these studies create subterranean spaces of integrationist or miscegenationist activity. Thus, a scholar like W. T. Lhamon stresses the similarities between the cultural interests and production of white outsiders and African Americans during the 1950s by placing writers (in this case, Ralph Ellison, Jack Kerouac, and Allen Ginsberg) from each group in an ideological vacuum: "Clearly Beats and blacks were both on the same track in the fifties, both reaching to connect with an only apparently lost culture. Thus when Beats could not connect with white fathers—symbolically when orthodox mentors proved inadequate—they adopted black jazzlore" (Lhamon 1990: 70). It is misleading to suggest, as Lhamon does, that "Beats and blacks" traveled this road (or track) with the same knowledge, motivation, and interest and that both would be adequate caretakers of the "lore" they "adopted." An analysis like Lhamon's that primarily presents cultural relations between whites and blacks during the 1950s as a kind of fortuitous structural convergence misses (or at least minimizes) the important power struggle that is bound up in the sort of cultural contest where different meanings are attributed by members of different groups to the same material. As George Lipsitz writes, "struggles over meaning are inevitably struggles over resources" (1990: 621).

This particular lacuna in these studies results from the fact that they almost inevitably look at this cultural contact from the angle of what they call the "mainstream"—that is, whiteness. Thus, according to this view the self-proclaimed attraction of white outsiders to African American cultural material is significant because it signals a new and profound openness to the influence of values from this tradition. Lhamon, for example, writes:

> In fact, mostly unaware but all across America, whites had absorbed Negro culture long before the fifties. . . . The paradox that had propped up the shabby house of American racism, however, was the pre-fifties tenet that such ethnic cultures were somehow separable. This fiction was one of the most victimizing beliefs for Americans of all races. Belief in separability kept the largest two American racial cultures touching while allowing whites their fantasy of distance. . . . Mainstream citizens only started acknowledging their latent black values once they began sharing the doubts and began feeling the lack of control blacks had long known. (1990: 39–40)

While this construction of "unaware absorption" is attractive in its positing of a fundamental, inexorable cultural integration, it actually subordinates the process by which these "black values" were incorporated into "mainstream" American culture and dismisses the possibility that these values were altered during this process so that they conformed to the requirements of whiteness and Euro American culture. As we know from Edward W. Said's work on "orientalism" in Western culture, it is extremely unlikely that these black values were transmitted through Euro American outsiders into mainstream American culture without being fundamentally and ideologically altered by those Euro American mediators. As Said makes clear, although hegemonic systems do not precisely determine or limit what writers (or other producers of cultural texts) depict, they do interact dynamically with those ideological subjects to produce a variety of representations all of which promote the same ideological concerns (Said 1978: 14). This means that although the Euro American writers who used African American resources may have identified intellectually and emotionally with African Americans and African American culture, they still used representational strategies that resulted in the distortion and decontextualization of the object of their representation. We must, in other words, reconsider whether the work being done on the margins was truly counterhegmonic or whether Euro American youth and outsiders formed part of the "historical bloc" that maintained the hegemony of Euro American culture.[5]

It is for this reason that much of my analysis in this book probes the contours of individualism in marginalized white and black texts. One of the principal ways black cultural values were transformed in their transmission through white texts was to ratchet up the significance of individualism. Whereas the black texts I consider almost always seek and establish connections, like jazz itself, by setting individual desires, achievements, hardships, and genius in the context of the group—e.g., riffing on traditional themes, signifyin(g) on classic texts, carrying on the struggle, reaching out to "the folk," or generating joy amidst the pain—the majority of white texts focus instead on discontinuities between the individual and any sort of group. Ray Carney, for example, has observed that Beat culture "imagine[s] the individual either trapped inside established social forms and structures of interaction, or grandly (and nobly) alienated, existing beyond them in some state of pure awareness and being" (1995: 239). Thus in Norman Mailer's "The White Negro" we get a revolutionary program, intended to change the structure of American society, that borrows significant elements from African American culture (or at least Mailer's perception of it) but completely eschews any connection to other Americans—based, for example, on racial or class solidarity—in favor of a radical individualism. While some part of this anticollectivism was probably the result, as Thomas Schaub indicates, of the American Left's despair and disillusionment following their Faustian bargain with Soviet communism, another part was undoubtedly the white male's continued, unapologetic privileging of the dominant culture's individualistic ethic, from which he more than anyone else benefitted (Schaub 1991: 137–62).

Questions regarding the process of incorporation, and the form assigned these "black values" in that process, are especially important if we accept the established notion that the cultural production done on the margins in the 1950s influenced the participation of white, middle-class youth in the oppositional politics of the 1960s, the development of the counterculture of the 1960s, and, by extension, the formation of youth culture that followed. In a recent study of the 1960s, for example, Edward Morgan asserts that the decade's counterculture is linked to the oppositional culture of the 1950s by a shared "outlook profoundly alienated from the modern world of post–World War II America" (1991: 172). Morgan says, moreover, that "The foremost expression of that outlook in the United States, and the one with the most obvious parallels in the counterculture, was that of the Beats—the mad 'howl' of Allen Ginsberg, Jack Kerouac's existential vision of life 'on the road,' the political sensibility of Lawrence Ferlinghetti, and Gary Snyder's Zen Buddhism" (1991: 172). Additionally, W. T. Lhamon has written, "insofar as art can win anything, this insurgent culture [of the 1950s] won. Its styles, attitudes, and icons more deeply shaped the styles, attitudes, and art of subsequent decades than have other fifties strains, or even the Cold War authorities themselves" (1990: 6). In a slightly different context Andrew Ross has even suggested that there is a connection between the cultural work of the 1950s (much of which was actively antipolitical) and the political work of the 1960s.[6] In *No Respect* Ross states that the work of such "new underground bohemian intellectuals" as Jack Kerouac and Norman Mailer "had real and powerful social effects . . . for the white students in SNCC who participated in the struggle for civil rights, and who supported the black liberation movements of the sixties" (1989: 69). Todd Gitlin, a member of SDS during the 1960s, explains this seemingly paradoxical connection in his memoir of the era: "But even the antipolitical enclaves opened a space for later and larger oppositions, both the New Left and the counterculture, oppositions compounded—however, contradictorily—of politics and culture. The beats were the main channel; hostile to the postwar bargain of workaday routine in exchange for material acquisition, they devoted themselves to principled poverty, indulged their taste for sexual libertinism, and looked eastward for enlightenment" (1987: 28). The fact that these particular links between 1950s culture and 1960s culture and politics (and, to a lesser extent, beyond) are well-established and accepted seems to indicate the presence of ideological connections between groups in these two distinct eras.

As Gitlin's quote underscores, cultural and especially political radicals during the 1960s were selective and, to a certain extent, critical in their attitude toward their predecessors. That is to say, 1960s oppositional culture and politics were not fashioned out of the whole cloth of any one previous movement or ideological orientation; instead, the literate, knowledgeable, and sophisticated participants in the decade's avant garde adopted what seemed vital and progressive, and abandoned elements (like the Beats' "antipolitics") that obviously led to dead ends. However, as Gitlin's quote also illustrates, the characteristic 1950s white outsider position toward black culture was not one of the ideological orientations or positions that was rigorously interrogated or deconstructed. Instead, it seems clear, from the beginning of the 1960s on out through the other end of it, white political and cultural outsiders adopted the same ideology toward blackness and African Americans as did the Beats and others from the 1950s—a form of romantic racialization that elevated their own sense of self and identity. Of the Northern, middle-class, white students who journeyed to the South to participate in the burgeoning civil rights movement, for example, Edward Morgan says: "They embarked on a journey of personal liberation as well as political action, inspired by the 'high moral purpose,' adventure, and rich community they encountered in the project" (1991: 37). Although Gitlin puts this ideology into the larger context of "the romance of intellectuals for the poor and uneducated," he also notes that many white students who became civil rights radicals stereotyped blackness and African Americans. He quotes one of these students as writing in 1965 that "rural Negroes had 'a closeness with the earth . . . a closeness with each other in the sense of community developed out of dependence . . . the strength of being poor'" (Gitlin 1987: 164–65). This link between "generations" exists even though the Beats' ideology led to inaction and the 1960s outsiders' led to political and cultural activism.

This transmission of the Beat-era ideology to the 1960s counterculture through the popularization of the mainstream media effectively contained the most radical challenges to whiteness and racial difference. Although the 1960s would be seven years old before the final break between white and black oppositional forces, the die was cast by the coincidence of this particular bohemia and the birth of television in the 1950s. As Russell Jacoby notes, the Beats "carried bohemia into the age of suburbia where it spread and disappeared" (1987: 65). Like the white bohemia of the 1950s, the 1960s counterculture was a site dominated and controlled by white, middle-class youth. The rare black face that materialized, like Jimi Hendrix or Richie Havens at Woodstock, was constructed by white audiences as more flower child than Black Panther.

2.

Racing the Village People

Euro American and African American Cultural and Social Interaction in Greenwich Village, 1945–1966

From the late 1940s through the mid-1960s, the musical, intellectual, and artistic communities in New York City constituted what Mary Louise Pratt terms "contact zones": "social spaces where cultures meet, clash, and grapple with each other, often in contexts of highly asymmetrical relations of power" (1991: 34). Even moreso than in the heyday of the Harlem Renaissance during the 1920s, New York City in the immediate post–World War II period witnessed extensive, meaningful social and professional interaction between representatives of Euro and African American culture—most notably among musicians, intellectuals, and artists. Greenwich Village, in particular, was the geographic space in which black and white members of these communities worked and socialized during this era. Although Pratt uses (and possibly intends) this metaphor to represent the collision of *widely* divergent cultures (such as the seventeenth-century meeting between Spaniards and Incas she describes), the dominant Euro American culture and the emergent African American culture that converged in New York City during the 1950s were distinct enough that Greenwich Village could exist as a specific place (one of the only places, in fact) where representatives of the two immigrated, met, and interacted.

The existence of a mostly integrated Greenwich Village during this era was, in part, a result of the strength of prevailing barriers between Euro and African American culture elsewhere in the United States. African and Euro American youth (and others) who were intrigued but not satisfied by the limited cultural and social contact available to them in or on the margins of dominant American culture and society migrated, as they had for decades, to the Village in search of a more immediate relationship with each other. Their dissatisfaction with the racial component of the cultural "containment" enforced during this period was one factor that pushed them out of the suburbs and into the Village.[1] With its reputation as a center of bohemianism, avant-garde art, political radicalism, and young writers, Greenwich Village seemed to offer these refugees a better chance at experiencing those people and experiences denied them as participants (or soon-to-be-participants) in the established cultural and social system.

During the rather long period under study here—that is, between 1945 and 1966—the Village went through changes that altered its look and dynamic. Developments such as the spread of coffeehouses and jazz clubs, the increasing national notoriety of the Beat scene in the Village, and the gradual movement of the center of bohemian activity from the West to the South to the East Village affected the number and kind of people who inhabited and visited the area and the nature of the activity that occurred there. A sense of these changes is supplied by Terry Miller's description of the development of the Beat community:

> In May 1953 six artists and writers got together and opened Rienzi, a coffeehouse of their own at 107 MacDougal Street. . . . The idea caught on, partly because an artist-owned coffeehouse required no liquor license, no dealings with state bureaucracy, no payoffs for protection. The Rienzi and its successors became central to a burst of activity unlike anything the Village had known in thirty years. Folk music gave way to bebop and bongos, art exhibits to environmental interiors, poetry reading to performance art and cafe theater. The South Village became Beatnik Country, a world unto itself that achieved worldwide fame. (1990: 227)

Despite these changes, however, the fundamental structure of relations between Euro and African Americans remained constant throughout this period. The Village remained firmly under the control of Euro Americans, who owned not only the venues where black and white people interacted (the nightclubs, coffeehouses, bars, newspapers, magazines, and galleries), but also the symbols of that interaction: the discourse on jazz. Given the relatively static racial situation in the Village during this period I describe this "contact zone" as essentially unified.

Although they were certainly a minority among the bohemians and other outsiders in Greenwich Village in the 1940s, 1950s, and early 1960s, African Americans, like their Euro American counterparts, came there to escape. For many of these migrants, the Village had a reputation not only as a haven for artists and other nonconformists, but also as a refuge from white racism and the deleterious effects of racism on black communities. James Baldwin, for example, started working at after-school jobs in the Village in 1939 partly to get away from the oppressive ghetto Harlem had become in the late 1930s and partly to put distance between himself and the problems he was having at home. According to biographer

David Leeming, on his forays into the Village Baldwin met "bohemians" who "on the surface . . . seemed less concerned with being 'colored' than did white people elsewhere" (1994: 37). In addition, Baldwin, looking for mentors, struck up a friendship with black artist Beauford Delaney, who had lived in the Village since 1929 (Leeming 1994: 32–36).

Baldwin's example is instructive: to a certain extent there were overlapping reasons for Euro and African American (especially from the North) migration to the Village—artistic and nonconformist proclivities, family problems, dissatisfaction with American life as it was. A later African American migrant to the Village from a Northern urban area, Amiri Baraka says that when he first came to the Village he "could see the young white boys and girls in their pronouncement of disillusion with and 'removal' from society as being related to the black experience" (Baraka 1984: 156). Elaborating on this similarity, Baraka notes that "the young Negro intellectuals and artists in most cases are fleeing the same 'classic' bourgeois situations as their white counterparts—whether the clutches of an actual black bourgeoisie or their drab philosophical reflectors who are not even to be considered a middle class economically" (1963: 231).

However, Baldwin's example also reminds us that unlike Euro Americans there was another level to the migration for African Americans: an escape from white racism and its effects, including Southern segregation, the rampant poverty and unemployment experienced in Northern ghettos, and, later, the white backlash to civil rights gains in the South (Franklin and Moss 1988: 415–24). Even for those African Americans who, like Baraka, claim similar motives for fleeing and similar aspirations as their Euro American counterparts, the motive force of racism made their escape different from, and perhaps of more consequence than, that of all Euro Americans. Amiri Baraka recalls, "I think that was the tone of that circle [the African American artists and writers in the Village during the 1950s], in fact perhaps a whole generation or two of black intellectuals, who, seeing segregation and discrimination as the worst enemy, sought a more open contact with the world" (1984: 129). When James Baldwin left the Village for a short while in the early 1940s to work at an industrial job in New Jersey, he discovered that the white people he worked with considered him "uppity" and lacking in "respect." He felt traumatized by his experience there, especially when he contrasted it with the more liberal attitude of his white friends in the Village, and left as soon as he possibly could (Leeming 1994: 38). As Wini Breines suggests, the inexorable daily experience of African Americans with racism gave their life decisions a dimension that was lacking in those of Euro Americans: "Black people in postwar America could not afford to submerge their awareness of the contradictions built into American society. The disparities between facade, or rhetoric, and actuality were more oppressive for blacks than for whites" (1992: 14–15).

Furthermore, as with Euro American bohemians, there was by this time a pattern for alienated or disaffected African Americans to follow, part of which included, at least, contact with the Village's more enlightened Euro American bohemians. According to Harold Cruse, during the 1920s "Carl Van Vechten, a music critic, novelist, photographer and art patron . . . was the first to establish a link between the Harlem and Greenwich Village artistic movements" (Cruse 1984: 26). In addition, according to Amiri Baraka, "the Village has had a legacy of black music, both the show biz and gambling club variety, as well as the more blues-oriented music that was created when the great waves of black immigrants came north after the Civil War in the latter part of the nineteenth century" (Baraka and Baraka 1987: 183). The intersection of "black music" and the freedom associated with artistic communities, says Baraka, gave the Village a privileged place in the American social and cultural history among many African Americans: "The Village had been identified as early as the twenties with this nonconformity and openness that black music always suggests in relationship to the formal culture of America or its official highbrow and lowbrow music" (Baraka and Baraka 1987: 184).

Whatever the previous legacy, however, the pattern was firmly established by the late 1940s and early 1950s when some of the beboppers, most notably Charlie Parker, began to travel down to the Village, initially to meet people and party, later to play in private residences and at clubs that were offering the latest developments in jazz to the hipper Village denizens. This, according to Baraka, increased the attraction of the Village for African Americans: "Bird was probably the patron saint of the generation preceding mine, as he was an arch-bohemian in the downtown Villagey sense" (Baraka 1984: 129). Baraka believes that by leading African American musicians downtown, Parker also helped change the direction of modern jazz: "The musicians [of the early forties], also, generally lived in those ghettoes (which is what I meant by 'a natural reference' to the folk origins of the music). But Charlie Parker, during the later forties and fifties, used to frequent New York's Greenwich Village, traditionally a breeding ground of American art and open-air fraternity house of a kind of American Bohemianism" (Baraka 1963: 232).

Charlie Parker's participation in Village society was crucial to the establishment of the downtown area as a hospitable place for progressive African Americans because his legend as "the patron saint" of bohemians (both Euro and African American) provided the highest avant-garde endorsement of the Village. Parker's seal of approval not only attracted knowledgeable bohemians; it also provided even more reason (that is, to witness what was then the most vital music around— that by Bird and other beboppers—performed in a socially freer, more integrated environment) for "important" artists, writers, and musicians who were on the verge of success (for instance, the Abstract Expressionists and the Beats) to live, or at least spend much of their time, in the Village.

The Bowery bar called the Five Spot, for example, became a central Village location members of almost every artistic avant garde frequented between the mid-1950s and the mid-1960s. Characterizing the Five Spot as a "nerve center" where "the arts became democratized," Greenwich Village historian Terry Miller says that "a new underground formed here, and painters, writers, and jazz musicians joined forces to stage an assault on the very definitions of art, music, theater, and literature" (1990: 259–60). As musician David Amram remembers, the interaction of these vital artists, writers, musicians, and others had a beneficial effect on all of them: "The painters not only made the Five Spot grow from a Bowery bar into a jazz center, but they also created its atmosphere. They were genuinely interested in the music and they felt that what we were doing was serious music. They were not like most jazz fans, who just wanted to come in to pick up chicks or make the scene. They actually liked the music. They were open-minded to any kind of music" (Amram 1968: 264). In a description that combines the most promising aspects of the Village's developing social and artistic trends, Dan Wakefield says that the Village during the 1950s was "a time of hope, of new beginnings, of colors mixing and complementing one another, as in the new abstract expressionist paintings being done in lofts down in the Bowery by Franz Kline" (Wakefield 1992: 111).

However, the dawn of harmonious interracial relations in the Village alluded to by Wakefield—"colors mixing and complementing one another"—never came close to realization. Despite the optimistic rhetoric and high expectations, the achievement of an integrated Village community occurred only in relatively superficial interpersonal relationships and myth. In fact, the Village community—including its social, political, cultural, and economic dimensions—remained predominantly separate and unequal during the period under study here. Though James Baldwin, for example, had many romantic and platonic relationships with white women and men in the Village during the late 1940s, his closest, most supportive group of friends were the other few African American artists and writers there at the time. According to David Leeming, Baldwin's relationships with white people, men and women, were tainted by racial "prejudice" (1994: 45). More important, though, than the structure of these personal relationships was the fact that almost every important institution catering to artists, writers, and other bohemians—from coffeehouses and bookstores to newspapers and magazines to clubs and theaters—was owned and operated by white people. Largely, African Americans' participation in these institutions depended, as it did elsewhere in the United States, on the good will of white people.

Even as late as 1963, according to Sally Banes, the artistic avant garde in the village remained a network that was firmly controlled by Euro Americans. Even James Baldwin, who by this time was well known and respected, had problems with the Actor's Studio production of his play *Blues for Mr. Charlie* that he interpreted as racial (Leeming 1994: 232–33). Baldwin's almost unique power among African Americans at the time enabled him to emerge victorious from these production battles. Analyzing the larger picture, Banes writes, "despite the rhetoric—both verbal and artistic—of equal rights and equal opportunity, very few African Americans or other people of color systematically played a part in most of its arenas" (1993: 110–11). Moreover, Banes supplies a total picture of interracial relations in the Village at this late date that actually included very little integration. Instead what she uncovers in the racial dimension can be reduced to two elements: the nascence of "a renewed separate search for aesthetic identity by African American artists"; and the "African American tradition of musical improvisation . . . translated into theater, dance, and other artistic practices of the white avant-garde" (145, 157). The first category of activity included plays such as LeRoi Jones's *Dutchman* and *The Toilet* and James Baldwin's *Blues for Mr. Charlie*, while the second included the Living Theater's production of Jack Gelber's *The Connection* (which incorporates jazz musicians as part of its cast), Shirley Clarke's film *The Cool World*, and various dance performances that used improvisational techniques. Banes's portrayal offers very little to suggest that there was any interracial interaction beyond the occasional use of an African American musician, dancer, or actor by the Euro American avant garde and the continuing Euro American attraction to and appropriation of such African American resources as improvisation.

Another indication of the paucity of interracial interaction in the Village at the time is the organization of the Umbra group of African American writers, musicians, and artists on the Lower East Side (also known as the East Village). "The core of what became known nationwide as the Black Arts Movement," Umbra gathered a diverse group of African Americans who were interested in avant-garde art expressing "racial themes" (Thomas 1993: 576). Attracted to the Lower East Side because of its established reputation as a haven for the social and cultural avant garde, many of these African Americans settled there because of its cheap rents and demographically varied population. Poet and Umbra cofounder Tom Dent says, for example, that "the early sixties was a time when we, like many other aspiring black artists, emigrated from various sections of the country to New York, which was considered a mecca, and then to the Lower East Side, which had cheap rents and was an amazingly varied and vibrant community" (1993: 597). By all accounts the general environment created in the East Village was different, and better, than that in the better-known parts of the Village because the East Village's lower public profile attracted fewer newcomers. According to poet Lorenzo Thomas, "people who found their way there were already—for various reason—headed into the newly emerging networks of alternative media, a diverse politics of liberation, and the arts" (1993: 574).

However, even in this generally hospitable avant-garde environment, African Americans say that race was a (if not the) primary element structuring their relationships and work. Although the East Village was "a historically more progressive and diverse zone [where] Black men ventured free with their white female partners," African American avant-gardists there were subject to the same forms of racism that existed outside the Village at the time (Ismalli-Abu-Bakr 1993: 585). Novelist Sarah E. Wright, for example, remembers the hostile opposition of some East Village residents to her occupancy of an apartment there:

> Though far from a palace, my building was nevertheless off limits to people of color. But some progressive white friends had through a subterfuge obtained a lease for me, and I was safely ensconced in my small apartment before the landlord realized his mistake, something to which the tenant directly below me could never resign herself, throwing open her window from time to time in the middle of the night and screaming her protests to the streets below, "Nigger whore! Nigger whore!" Ultimately, she and more than half the other tenants in the building would unsuccessfully attempt to have my husband and I evicted on trumped-up charges that my writers' meetings were actually wild orgies. (1993: 593)

Moreover, as in other parts of the Village, most of the stores and gathering places were owned by Euro Americans. Calvin Hernton remembers a particular coffeehouse because "it was the only such place where one of the owners was a black man. But very few blacks were there; often I was the only one" (1993: 579).

It was because of these factors that these African American avant-gardists decided to band together to form Umbra, a social and cultural collective. Scholar Calvin Hernton says that the original idea behind Umbra "was that the blacks on the Lower East were very few in number—particularly the writers and artists— and we should do something about the isolation and anonymity we felt. We could at least come together and get to know each other" (1993: 580). However, this gathering of progressive African Americans developed out of more than their small numbers; their common experiences were also a factor in their association. Sarah E. Wright explains, "I was not alone among the writers of our workshop in enduring the injuries of racism. And it was a frequent topic of our conversation— not just the crude bigotries, but particularly the paternalistic racism of liberal whites who prided themselves on what they thought to be their cosmopolitan and enlightened views" (1993: 594).

Wright's last point is particularly interesting because it suggests the extent to which race was a significant factor (for African Americans) in this apparently progressive and integrated sub-society. Though African Americans like Wright had some positive experiences with "progressive white friends" (like the ones who helped her get an apartment) and may even have "excluded them from the justifiable rage they might have harbored toward others," they still looked to each other for support and friendship rather than to Euro Americans (Thomas 1993: 577). Thus, though the members of Umbra "consisted of people who were as different as any group of people could possibly be—in background, education, temperament, sexuality, color, talent, and flaws," they still found more in common with each other than with the Euro American artists in the community (Hernton 1993: 581).

Unlike the Euro American avant-gardists, who were mostly satisfied with the kind of community created when social and cultural outcasts congregate in a small spatial location, the African American writers, musicians, and artists felt compelled to merge themselves with a smaller communal configuration. Who these African Americans were as artists and writers was bound up in their mutual association as African Americans. As Tom Dent explains, the needs of African Americans differed from those of Euro Americans, who seemed satisfied with the status quo of Euro American bohemian life: "It was there that our lives intersected in the quest to grow as artists. For us, from different backgrounds and histories, it was a time of intense companionship and sharing which provided us with a sense of 'we-ness' that tempered the 'I-ness' prevalent in so much of American literature and art" (Dent 1993: 597). Out of this association came work that was received as "controversial" because it was "militantly race conscious and outspoken" (Thomas 1993: 576). Also created at the time were allied nationalist institutions such as the Negro Ensemble Company that "served as a home to Black playwrights, actors, directors, and arts administrators for years" (Ismalli-Abu-Bakr 1993: 588). Working together, as Sarah Wright says, African Americans "managed to create a kind of Harlem Renaissance downtown, reverberating to the rising struggles of the Civil Rights and Black Liberation Movements around the country" (1993: 593).

The relations illustrated by the experiences of African Americans on the Lower East Side did not change until 1965 when many African Americans who lived there began to leave the East Village (and other parts of the Village) and their frustrated hopes of an ideal, integrated community behind. Having long and quietly endured the feeling that their integrationist dream was a denial of "real" race relations even in the Village, these African Americans reached the point at which they could no longer "mak[e] an idealist evaluation of reality" and left for places such as Harlem where they believed they could establish zones of noncontact that would be of greater benefit to them and other African American people (Baraka 1994: 153). Sally Banes notes that LeRoi Jones's "departure in 1965 from Greenwich Village and its somewhat integrated avant-garde was paradigmatic of the shift by African Americans to political and aesthetic separatism" (1993: 146–47). Fittingly, however, this "shift" caught many Euro Americans in the Village by surprise. Even those Euro Americans who believed they had close and strong relationships with individual African Americans had difficulty understanding the anger that fueled the schism. Thus, artist Larry Rivers describes a particularly personal and vitriolic verbal attack by his friend LeRoi Jones and musician Archie Shepp one night at a Village Vanguard symposium as an "ambush." Moreover, after this experience, Rivers and Jones did not see each other socially for twenty years (during which time, Rivers says, he came to understand Jones's position in this incident) (Baraka 1984: 189; Rivers 1992: 431–32).

Sally Banes's analysis of Greenwich Village in 1963 is, however, typical of both contemporary and retrospective accounts in its inability or unwillingness to puncture completely the myth of racial integration in the Village. Despite the description of an artistic community in which there is little evidence of equitable or integrated material relations between African and Euro Americans, Banes generalizes that

> Greenwich Village was already a place where blacks and whites could mingle socially. The Beat Generation of the late Fifties was an integrated one in which not only white and black poets met, but also, as Norman Mailer pointed out in "The White Negro," white writers and other hipsters appropriated elements of black cultural style, from marijuana to sexual freedom to jazz prosody. Furthermore, the tolerance of much of the Village population for nonconformity in general attracted interracial couples— artists and nonartists. Although the white ethnic population in the Village might (and sometimes vociferously did) object, it was well-known by 1963 that "at a time when the attention of the world is focused on racial strife in America, Greenwich Village and few other Bohemian strongholds are the only communities in the country where interracial couples can live comfortably." (Banes 1993: 146)

Again, it seems a romanticization and an overstatement to classify as "social mingling" such contacts as white and black poets meeting and the white "appropria[tion] . . . of black cultural style." Moreover, the idea that the existence of interracial heterosexual couples in itself and necessarily signifies anything progressive about interracial relations in the Village is fallacious. First it should be noted that the quotation that Banes uses at the end of this passage comes from the Introduction to a "guidebook" to Greenwich Village published in 1963. This kind of "boosterish" literature is hardly a good source of evidence for an accurate characterization of interracial relationships in the Village. More important, however, this superficial description neglects the power dynamics that inhered in many of these relationships. It is interesting, moreover, that according to a 1955 *Ebony* magazine article Greenwich Village was not even the most congenial place in New York City for interracial couples. The article, "Where Mixed Couples Live," notes that Harlem was the choice for most interracial couples in New York City.

A brief inquiry into their nature will suggest that these interracial heterosexual relationships in the Village were plagued by many of the same unequal power dynamics that troubled the other social and cultural interactions I have surveyed.

The most widely cited examples of the interracial heterosexual relationships that existed in the Village were those between African American men and Euro American women. Almost certainly these particular relationships were most notable in this context because of the historical prohibitions against them: the ultimate sign of the "progressive" racial attitudes allegedly held by Euro Americans in the Village was their acceptance of these previously proscribed romantic/sexual relationships between black men and white women. Nevertheless, according to Hettie Jones there were still very few "steady interracial couples" in the Village at the time (she says there "weren't a half-dozen" around 1957) and still a great deal of hostility on the streets. However, she says the hostility mostly consisted of dirty looks or "jeers" and that while these experiences unnerved her with their threat of greater danger lurking below the surface, it was "only later that I realized we might have been hurt, or *killed*—and him more likely—had we been out of New York City" (1990: 37). Thus, for Jones the Village offered, if not a completely supportive public atmosphere for her relationship, at least a haven from the more violent reactions to interracial romances.

Also, in the Village the increasing number (or at least visibility) of interracial relationships between black men and white women prompted the appearance of "a hip new bar in the Village called Johnny Romero's [that] . . . had a smoldering kind of illicit sexual excitement about it, for the place was supposedly a rendezvous for white girls to meet black men" (Wakefield 1992: 160). For white males, Johnny Romero's had, according to Ronald Sukenick and his informants, "its happy side and its sinister side" (1987: 105). On the one hand, because of its hospitality to interracial relationships the bar was "a place [Euro Americans] went to to support. . . . You were glad that this was what was happening in America. . . . It became a political gesture to go there." On the other hand, some of the white males who frequented the bar did not feel comfortable being there. Some, for example, were self-conscious about their appropriation of "black cultural style"—"Most white cats including myself spoke a spade musician's lingo and it was (embarrassing) strange, me talking to some spade cat imitating his jive. Hi man, gimme some skin!" (Sukenick 1987: 106). Other white men assumed a lot about the African American men based on their own fear:

> I'd never been in a place up to that point in my life that looked more dangerous. Wooo! Especially to an innocent Jewish kid from New Jersey, I'll tell you. And the Black guys in there did not look like they were fooling around, either. I mean they looked like they'd just as soon cut you up. They looked like guys fresh out of Harlem who heard that you

could get white girls and they were there, but they didn't care about the Village, reading books, they didn't care about anything, they were there for poontang. That's what they were there for. (Sukenick 1987: 107)

According to an article written in 1963 by the African American novelist John A. Williams, white women in the Village were also prone to view the African American men in their midst stereotypically: "In Greenwich Village there is known to exist a certain group of white women who will sleep—to use a euphemism—only with Negroes who, in the middle of the act (it has been related often enough to give some basis for truth), have been put out to hear themselves addressed as 'black prince' or, at the extreme end of the range of racial epithets, 'dirty, black nigger'" (Williams 1973: 26). According to David Leeming, James Baldwin also had this kind of experience twenty years earlier with white women who "were intent on having their 'Negro experience' in the Village, forcing him into the central role as they played out the myths of black sexuality" (1994: 45).

These examples of the white perception of interracial relationships in the Village suggest that the mere evidence of their existence does not necessarily indicate that the people involved in these relationships (much less those in the community who allegedly sanctioned them) did so in an uncomplicated or "comfortable" manner. Similarly, African American men who established romantic and/or sexual relationships with white women did so with the encumbrances that accompanied *all* interracial relationships at the time. Moreover, some African Americans in the Village established these relationships as symbolic statements of their rebellion, or because they were part of the "uniform" of African American bohemianism. Amiri Baraka, for example, remembers that his sexual attraction to white women "seemed to me part of the adventure of my new life in the village. The black man with the white woman, I thought. Some kind of classic bohemian accouterment" (1984: 142). Like the other claims of integration in Greenwich Village's bohemian community, those surrounding interracial relationships are much more complicated than the myth suggests.

The trajectory of social and cultural integration in Greenwich Village is represented, largely, in the record of the Beat movement of the mid- to late 1950s. Members of the Beat scene living around Greenwich Village saw themselves as a new, racially integrated sub-society, not an ingredient of *either* of the racially constituted parts of New York City (i.e., black Harlem and white elsewhere). Describing the difference between what she still (when the book was published in 1990) sees as the difference between the Beats' interest in African American culture and that of previous generations of white bohemians, Hettie Jones says, "But it's important to the particular history of what would later be called the New Bohemia that going to the Five Spot was not like taking the A train to Harlem. Downtown was everyone's new place. . . . And all of us there—black and white were strangers at first" (1990: 34). Although Jones depicts herself as rather naive upon first arriving in the Village (especially concerning race), she portrays the Village bohemian scene as remarkably free of not only the sicknesses of the dominant society (e.g., racism) but those ascribed to hipsters by the likes of Norman Mailer: "That summer [1957] *Dissent* magazine published Norman Mailer's essay 'The White Negro.' There I read that jazz was orgasm, which only blacks had figured out, and that white 'hipsters' like me were attracted to the black world's sexy, existential violence. But the only violence I'd ever encountered, the one time I'd heard bone smashing bone, had been among whites in the South. The young black musicians I met didn't differ from other aspiring artists. And jazz music was complicated, technically the most interesting I'd heard, the hardest to play" (1990: 35). In fact, contrary to Mailer's theoretical stance, Jones's overall depiction of the Village in the late 1950s is one of an open, youthful community full of optimism and goodwill. Remember too that Dan Wakefield described the Village during the 1950s as a "haven where people were not only allowed but expected to dress, speak, and behave differently from the herd" (Wakefield 1992: 121).

Similarly, Lawrence Lipton justifies the Beats' use of the descriptive term "spade cat" instead of "Negro" by appealing to the notion that the relationship between these hip whites and their black counterparts was outside what had been typical in American society: "The holy barbarians, white and negro, are so far beyond 'racial tolerance' and desegregation that they no longer have to be polite about it with one another" (Lipton 1959: 317). It is significant that Lipton places the relationship between "white and negro" bohemians outside what was the most radical race politics of the time—"desegregation"—as well as what could be called more polite, middle-class politics—"racial tolerance."

Corroboration of Lipton's and Hettie Jones's characterizations of hope at the initial stages of the association of people in the Village comes from Allen Ginsberg and from Jones's friend, Joyce Johnson, and Jones's ex-husband, Amiri Baraka. Through his developing friendship with Amiri Baraka during the late 1950s, Allen Ginsberg went to parties attended by African American jazz musicians, trendy patrons of the Cedar Street Tavern, and painters such as Willem de Kooning and Franz Kline. About this era Ginsberg has said, "An acme of good feeling. A lot of mixing, black white hip classic" (Miles 1989: 252). Describing this period even more optimistically, Joyce Johnson says, "In the excitement and hope of that moment [1957]—in what was real and strongly believed and truly lived out, as distinct from fad—there seemed the possibility of enormous transformations. It seemed entirely possible that newness and openness expressed in the poems, the paintings, the music, would ripple out far beyond St. Marks Place and tables in the Cedar, swamping the old barriers of class and race, healing the tragic divisions in the American soul" (1983: 216). Although Baraka is, predictably, less charitable than Johnson in his retrospective assessments of this gathering of bohemians, he does admit that he "came to the Village thinking the people there, those vaunted intellectuals and artists, could not possibly be 'prejudiced' because that was dumb shit" (1984: 132). Moreover, he says, "I could see the young white boys and girls in their pronouncement of disillusion with and 'removal' from society as being related to the black experience. That made us colleagues of the spirit" (1984: 157). Above all, Baraka describes his relationships with the Beats as being an affinity of rebelliousness against the prevailing political, social, and cultural conservatism. Together, he says, they formed a "people's front of opposition to certain dead ideas of the society" (1987: 131–32). And it is important to remember that black and white migrants to the Village were similar in that they envisioned and were trying to create a new kind of community that would be a haven from the conformity of American middle-class culture and the terror of the nuclear age.

However, the social and cultural idyll hoped for and suggested by the potential of African and Euro American outsiders living and working in the Village during the 1950s was more of a reality, predictably, for the Anglos in the mix than for the African Americans. Many contemporaneous and retrospective accounts of Village life during this time report racial tension and even attacks on African Americans. Most of the violence, it seems, was perpetrated by the youth of what was the neighborhood "white ethnic" (mostly Italian and Irish American) population. This is not surprising given what we know about the intense social and cultural pressures on "white ethnics" (especially first- or second-generation youth) to prove their "whiteness" by distinguishing themselves from black people; very often this is done through violence. In a piece describing the later Beat scene in 1960 Ned Polsky reported that "Most of the violence is directed against Negroes and much of it is focused in and near the main beat crossroads, Washington Square Park" (1967: 158). Ronald Sukenick remembers that "the Italians were very insular, Tribal. Hoods loafing around storefront social clubs directing dead deadly looks at Bohemian interlopers, especially if they seemed to be gay or, in their view, worse, were like Ted Joans, Black. Pre-civil rights America" (1987: 20). In an even more dramatic memory, Dan Wakefield recalls, "It was not the racial millennium, understand . . . Baldwin himself was beaten up at an Irish bar in the Village because he was sitting in a booth with two white friends, one of them a woman" (1992: 111). Amiri Baraka has described the state of race relations in the Village during the late 1950s as "dangerous" and said that "the general resentment the [Village] locals felt toward the white bohemians was quadrupled at the sight of the black species" (1984: 133). Finally, in an article from 1963 John A. Williams characterized a subtler, more pervasive racism that existed in the Village at the time: "Two summers ago, citizens, rich and poor, who lived near Washington Square Park in New York's Greenwich Village, complained vigorously that the folk singers who gathered near the fountain to play guitars and sing were bawdy and disturbed the weekend peace. In the ensuing meetings with city officials, it became apparent that what was opposed was not so much folk singing as the increasing presence of mixed couples in the area, mostly Negro men and white women" (1973: 22). Obviously, these negative social forces external to the formation of a bohemian community in the Village made that community much less a racial paradise for African Americans than for Euro Americans.

This is not to deny or even minimize the fact that many bohemians (not just the Beats) in the Village were genuinely interested in achieving some degree of racial harmony. As I have noted, part of what pushed many migrants out of their middle-class communities into New York City and the Village was their dissatisfaction with the social barrier set up between white and black Americans. However, the Beats' interest in forming a community without racial problems remained more of a desire than a reality. As Ned Polsky says, "Nowhere is there greater disparity between beat theory and practice than in the role that Negro beats, wittingly or unwittingly, are forced to play for white beats" (1967: 181). Polsky describes a range of racial problems that existed among the Beats, from an opposition by white Beats to black male/white female relationships (although the reverse was acceptable) to limitations on the roles in which white Beats would accept black Beats (1967: 184).[2] This may have been true for most of the Beats Polsky interviewed, although Hettie Jones reports that Jack Kerouac was "pleased" when he learned of her relationship with LeRoi Jones, even forcing the two into a three-way bear hug when he first learned of their "connection" at a party (Jones 1990: 70).

There was, however, a general undercurrent of racial tension between most African and Euro American bohemians that only occasionally rose to the surface. Dan Wakefield, for example, remembers getting into an argument with James Baldwin that ended with Baldwin saying something "in anger . . . that hung like a sword over all interracial friendships: 'You're just like all the others.' It meant, of course, the other whites, the ones who didn't understand. It meant: I thought you were different but I was fooled again, deluded again, you are one of Them after all" (1992: 112). For the most part, this racial tension seems to have been caused by African Americans' lingering or renewed distrust of Euro Americans and Euro Americans' racial naivete (to put it nicely). That is, some African American bohemians never completely believed that their Euro American counterparts had thoroughly divested themselves of the racism that was part of the culture in which they grew up, nor that they understood the profound effects the experience of racism had on African American people. Other African Americans thought their Euro American friends had made a break with dominant culture's racism and then were disillusioned when they realized, often because of a confrontation, that they had been mistaken. As Baraka and even Joyce Johnson (but not Hettie Jones) recognize (even if for slightly different reasons), the hope that the relationships between white and black Beats would be free from America's racist disease was *only* a hope, *only* illusion. Using Hettie Jones herself as her example, Johnson attributes this false hope to the idealism of youth that obscured the social facts of the period: "Children of the late and silent fifties, we knew little of political realities. We had the illusion our own passions were enough. We felt, as Hettie Cohen Jones once put it, that you could change everything just by being loud enough" (Johnson 1983: 216).

Baraka remembers that though he felt a "spiritual" connection with these white outsiders, he never quite felt that he fit in—their ultimate concerns were not his and vice versa. Finally, he was an outsider "even inside those 'outsider' circles" (1984: 157). Characterizing, for example, his differences with other Beat writers, Baraka says that "the unique position of being black in that situation is that you might think that [you are just a poet who is not interested in politics], but you are so constantly and blatantly affected by politics beyond and above what other members of that group might be, so that the whole question of making political definitions a reality became much more of a consistent problem for me" (1987: 134). Interestingly, Baraka also attributes his discomfort with "bohemianism" to his "lower-middle class craving after order and 'respectability'" (1984: 156–57). That is, he portrays himself as more inhibited by these "mainstream" values than the middle-class whites with whom he associated.

Euro Americans, on the other hand, typically came to the Village having known few, if any, African Americans, and thus were not aware of the depth and extent of racism in American society at the time. Ronald Sukenick illustrates this point with a story about a trip Amiri Baraka took to Washington, D.C. with Allen Ginsberg and Gregory Corso. Driving into the city for a reading, Baraka crawled under the back seat of their car, surprising both Corso and Ginsberg. Baraka explained his fear to the pair—"Don't you understand, I'm in Washington, D.C., I'm in a place where they don't like Blacks." Retrospectively, both Ginsberg and Corso say that, before this incident occurred, they did not realize the hatred and fear that existed but that they now recognize that Baraka "was right at the time" (Sukenick 1987: 20). Nevertheless, this story reveals a lot about the gap in racial understanding that existed during the late 1950s between African Americans and even the most sympathetic Euro American social outsiders.

Another dimension of this kaleidoscope of mostly positive black/white social engagement was the meeting of African and Euro American culture in the form, most notably, of African American music—jazz—and writing and Euro American writing. The formation of the bohemian community in Greenwich Village during the 1950s was catalyzed, in no small part, by jazz and the response to it by artists, writers, and intellectuals. If the characterization of the Euro American/African

American *social encounter* as a "contact zone" is appropriate, then, it is even more so if we limit our analysis to the social and symbolic community revolving around the thriving jazz scene of the time. Because the jazz music scene itself was unbelievably vibrant and sprawling from the 1940s to the early 1960s (with the innovation and development of bebop as well as the spread of jazz music clubs first from Harlem to midtown Manhattan and then to the Village), it attracted a wide range of the pool of self-selected bohemians, rebels, and outsiders who had migrated to the Village. In the early 1940s Jack Kerouac followed his high school buddy Seymour Wyse to Harlem to hear jazz at such legendary places as Minton's, the Savoy, and the Apollo Theater. Kerouac became so inspired by these journeys that he began a music column in his high school paper in which he wrote about jazz (Nicosia 1983: 65–66). In the early 1950s, Kerouac introduced new Village migrant Ted Joans, black poet, to the remaining jazz scene in Harlem (Knight and Knight 1987: 273–74).

Although bebop specifically and jazz generally became much more commercialized as the 1950s began, they still attracted a following among bohemians in the Village. As Dan Wakefield says, "Jazz was *the* music of New York in the fifties, at least of literary and artistic New York" (1992: 304). Ronald Sukenick confirms this observation: "the uniquely native American art form, jazz, became, through the fifties, more central than ever for underground artists of all kinds" (1987: 58). Ned Polsky, finally, verifies both the importance of jazz to Beats and its biracial appeal: "Insofar as most beats, whites and Negroes alike, can be said to have a dominant intellectual interest, it is jazz music. And the jazz world is the single non-beat segment of American society that often attracts beats" (1967: 175).

Jazz is important for understanding the avant-garde society of New York City not only because the incredibly vibrant and creative music inspired similar creativity among writers, artists, and others, but also because it brought whites and blacks into closer contact in jazz clubs. As early as 1938 individuals looked to Greenwich Village as the place to open integrated jazz clubs. In that year Barney Josephson opened his club Cafe Society, "determined," according to Terry Miller, "to end the racial barriers in every club from Midtown to Harlem" (Miller 1990: 34). Growing up Jewish in Trenton, New Jersey, Josephson says he learned about prejudice firsthand and through the experiences of an African American classmate whom he "made a point of befriending." This friend introduced Josephson to jazz and kindled in him the dream of opening "a club that would bring audiences and good music together and to hell with these racial barriers" (Miller 1990: 34). Thus it was that "in 1938 I decided to give it a try. I picked Greenwich Village purposely. I figured I'd have better luck finding an audience ready to accept what I wanted to do. Also, rents were low and I only had $6,000 in borrowed money. I decided an interracial club would have to look stylish to be accepted but couldn't really afford much" (Miller 1990: 34–35).

Although Josephson closed Cafe Society in 1950, other clubs offering jazz music to integrated audiences opened in the West Village during the 1950s. Writing about the racial composition of jazz audiences at these and other New York area clubs at the time, jazz critic Nat Hentoff asserted, "Jazz clubs, however, have become islands of at least acquaintanceship between Negroes and whites" (1975: 22). Hentoff's limited claim for the effect of jazz-inspired integration is probably an indication that minimal *contact* was about the extent of the black/white interaction here.

As with Euro and African Americans who were involved in interracial romantic relationships, however, the existence of mixed audiences at jazz clubs does not necessarily signify that these jazz fans occupied racial positions or participated in racial discourse that were ultimately more progressive than those of Americans who lived outside Greenwich Village. In fact, even in their retrospective accounts, Euro American members of these audiences characterize their participation not in terms of racial interaction but in terms of their rebellion against the more established segments of American culture. Thus, for example, Ronald Sukenick recalls that "digging Bop is one of the main ways subterraneans can express their cultural radicalism—if you want to hear Dixieland go to Eddie Condon's on Eighth Street with the fraternity boys" (1987: 84). Being in the audience at a bop performance, in other words, was significant to white outsiders because it helped distinguish them from the mass of the American population. Writer Gilbert Sorrentino has a similar recollection about the meaning of bop for him: "We wanted a music of our own, something removed from school dances, the Hit Parade, and 'long-hair,' which, when I was in my teens, was something I associated with the 1812 Overture, period" (1972: 125). In these reminiscences the racial element of this experience— i.e., white youth becoming "worshippers" of expressive forms of African American culture—is erased. Similarly, these jazz fans characterize the significance of African American musicians in terms that are devoid of racial connotations:

> While the pre-bop musicians had removed themselves from nice society with their roughness, drinking, and lack of formal education, the bop musicians removed themselves even further by becoming identified with that contemptible segment of American life, the *intelligentsia*. Yet at the same time, they lived hard, wild lives, identified themselves with the liquor (or, beginning with the boppers, the narcotics), the women, the night living, the vagrancy, the poverty, the insularity of the older musicians. Thus, they were twice-removed from the respectable, and so (hopefully) were we who adulated them. (Sorrentino 1972: 129)

When these writers do acknowledge racial differences they do so without being fully self-conscious of their own position as white jazz fans:

There were many uptown clubs, but neither my friends nor I ever went to them. The reasons for this were complex, but essentially it was because we were afraid to go, as whites, to all-Negro clubs, in all-Negro neighborhoods. Nobody relished the idea of getting caught in a strange neighborhood by a non-white gang that didn't care whether one was "hip" or not. Underscoring this was the fear that we would be taken for square white kids who were "slumming" in Harlem. The fear of being thought square was almost as great as the fear of being jumped. (Sorrentino 1972: 133)

Though this quotation acknowledges one limitation of whiteness with its recognition that some African Americans may not attach much meaning to a white youth's "hipness," its humor cannot disguise the fact that Sorrentino believes the most important distinction is between different kinds of white—"hip" and "square"—and not between white and black. All agency is stripped from African Americans as this spin casts them into the role of "obstacle," simply preventing these cool white beboppers from expressing their difference from uncool whites.

Among Euro Americans in the Greenwich Village jazz community, the sense of ownership expressed by Sorrentino (in an earlier quotation)—"a music of our own"—is an essential part of their relationship to jazz. It is this sense, in fact, that obliterates any recognition that there is anything specifically African American about the music, the performers, or the tradition of which they are a part. Sorrentino says, "The whole damn thing was *our* music. The musicians were absolutely aware of this feeling. . . . We were members of the same cult as the musicians" (1972: 132). Apart from its obvious arrogance (which can be attributed to white privilege), this perspective is notable because it blinded most white jazz fans to the significance of jazz as a specifically African American expressive form. Thus, when African American musicians, emboldened by their success, began asserting their authority as *African American* artists, white jazz fans misinterpreted their behavior as some sort of "sell-out": "the musicians lost all touch with the audience . . . the musicians began to change. They all started in on the by-now classic Miles Davis attitude, a combination of fear, disgust, and contempt . . . looking as if he [Charlie Parker] was worried he'd do something wrong: all this in front of an audience of kids in sunglasses. . . . Now, it was something ugly and vulgar" (Sorrentino 1972: 132–33). Through it all, then—worship and rejection—white jazz fans like Sorrentino and friends positioned themselves as more outside and more hip than the jazz musicians they followed.

As Mary Louise Pratt makes explicit in her definition of the contact zone, the relations of power in this kind of cultural encounter are most often not equal. So it was with the Euro and African Americans meeting along the axis of jazz music. That is, though the Euro Americans on whom jazz had the greatest impact defined themselves (and were defined by others) as social and artistic outsiders, they still maintained positions in society that guaranteed that their relation to and perspective of African American music and musicians would support the dominant Euro American racial ideology in ways that those of African Americans would not.

3.

Caging Bird

Charlie Parker Meets the Postwar Construction of the Jazz Musician

People sit and tell you Bird stories for hours. That is true, but probably half of them never happened, because I've heard people tell me some fantastic stories that, comparing the time and place, I know didn't happen. (Reisner 1977: 172)

More than any critic or biographer, it would more likely be a novelist, a black novelist, who might eventually illuminate those parts of the cold inner darkness that finally took over all of Bird. (Hentoff 1976: 194)

A study of any aspect of jazz in the 1950s would be incomplete without an extended investigation into the life and legend of Charlie Parker. Although he was given very little press coverage by the mainstream media during his life or immediately after he died in 1955 at the age of thirty-four, he was *the* living, then dead, legend among jazz musicians, jazz fans, and hipsters in the immediate postwar period. These friends and fans have been responsible for spreading the legend of Charlie Parker in books, recordings, and films for the past forty years. Chances are that if a person today knows anything at all about the history of jazz they know about that mythical figure nicknamed Bird who was a prototype of the self-destructive modern musician, whose death so shocked his followers that they scrawled "Bird Lives!" on walls and subways in New York City and elsewhere.

As with most phenomena of this kind, the explanation for the Parker legend is complex and can only be hinted at by citing historical causes. Nevertheless, before beginning the work of analyzing Parker's representation in postwar American culture, I want to recount briefly the commonly accepted causes. First, more than any other single musician, Parker was and still is credited by the jazz cognoscenti with the musical innovations that created the revolutionary style of jazz known as bebop. In the most recent biographical account of Parker, for example, Gary

Giddins says that "Parker, like Armstrong before him, engineered a total shift in the jazz aesthetic" (1987: 10). This is believed so although Dizzy Gillespie (and perhaps Charlie Christian, Kenny Clarke, and Thelonious Monk) were also indispensable in the creation of the sound of bebop, and although Gillespie received and accepted the lion's share of attention during Parker's lifetime. Moreover, unlike Gillespie, Parker is a Gatsby-like figure (springing full-blown from an image of himself) in the development of his bebop style. While Gillespie's early experimentation with the bebop sound occurred in the after-hours Minton's Playhouse lab with nurturing allies—Monk, Clarke, and others—Parker's early development is somewhat of a mystery. By the time he came to New York and started playing with Gillespie and others at Monroe's in Harlem and other places he was already playing an early form of bebop. According to the legend, Parker developed his early style while "woodshedding" in the Ozarks as a teenager playing in a road band.

Next, Parker lived long enough to establish a significant body of work (unlike, for example, guitarist Charlie Christian) but not long enough to evolve out of his bebop style (like Gillespie or Miles Davis).[1] Thus, like actor James Dean's screen image, Parker's musical image is perpetually youthful, rebellious, and vital. His extramusical image also contained the excesses associated with youthful experimentation (especially in the postwar era): by most accounts he had huge appetites and typically indulged them. Ross Russell says that Parker's "appetites went unchecked. He could drink and he could eat like a horse and run after all of the women that interested him" (1996: 140). Also, because Parker was not prominent during his lifetime in media reports on bebop, there is less public documentation of his life and even his music than that of many of his contemporaries. Thus, most of what we know about Parker's life comes from the often exaggerated, often conflicting myths about his life told by people who knew him and claimed to know him. Parker's sudden and tragic death—transgressive not only because it was due to his overindulgences but because it occurred in the apartment of a wealthy white woman—seemed to confirm his rebelliousness and alienation and establish his claim (desired or not) to martyrdom.

Another reason for the growth of the myth is undoubtedly the specific cir-cumstances of the time in which Parker lived. As I describe in some detail in the first two chapters, Parker's rebellious image provided disaffected Americans with an icon, a totem of their alienation. Parker's impact on alienated writers and intellectuals in particular during this era is not surprising, considering that bebop was received by many jazz musicians and critics as a "revolution" in the sound of jazz. Typically, these artistic and intellectual admirers of Bird were also people who saw themselves as fighters in one "revolution" or another (i.e., against the literary or artistic establishment, against middle-class conformity, against society's racism, and so on) and so could identify with the beboppers' revolutionary spirit. Parker's significance for these bohemians and rebels of the post–World War II generation was enhanced by his centrality to a musical revolution that was also "the core of a set of social ideas" that emphasized resistance and nonconformity (Collier 1978: 360). Hipsters, Beats, and others, then, seized on Parker as their "high priest" of rebellion because of the sound of his music, because of his air of mystery, because of his seeming refusal to conform.

Finally (and I have placed this cause last for emphasis) there is his music: listening to it forty years later, especially given what most jazz of the time sounded like, one understands, almost instantly, why his playing affected listeners so powerfully. Fast and dynamic but also bluesy and melodic, Parker's alto solos are continually amazing, surprising, and inspiring. Even in groups filled with other supremely talented musicians—Gillespie, Miles Davis, Max Roach, and Bud Powell—Parker's playing stands out. Notwithstanding all I know about Parker's place in the African American tradition—his direct and indirect influences—and the contributions of the musicians surrounding him, it is hard *not* to hear his electrifying musical performances as the product of a transcendent musical genius.

Despite (or maybe because of) the Parker legend that was developing during his lifetime, the popular media ignored Parker. Giddins notes, for example, that "when, at the peak of his influence *Life* ran an article on bop, Parker wasn't discussed. When *Time* cast about for a cover story on the new jazz, it turned to a white musician with a 'classical' education, Dave Brubeck" (1987: 20). Moreover, Giddins says, Parker won few awards from the jazz press, was usually billed second to Gillespie when they played dates together, and was barely noticed in newspaper obituaries when he died (and those few papers that ran stories got vital information, like his name and age, wrong). Even during his lifetime, Parker and others (more after he died) claimed these slights were explicitly racist, and without a doubt there is something to this assertion. The fundamental white racism alive and well in the United States during the 1940s and 1950s unquestionably infected the music industry. However, some of these slights were more likely due to Parker's particular personality and the effects of it—for example, his uncompromising artistic vision and discipline, mental instability, drug addiction, lack of interest in self-promotion, and general unreliability. The *Life* magazine story on bebop, for example, featured full-page photographs of Gillespie, Chano Pozo, and other black musicians in Gillespie's group. However, the article demeaned the bebop movement in its emphasis on ridiculous and exaggerated subcultural elements like Gillespie's secret greeting, and secured Gillespie's tacit agreement to do this (which he later regretted). It seems unlikely that Parker would have submitted himself to this kind of treatment. One of Parker's contemporaries, trumpet player Howard McGhee, has said, for example, that Parker disapproved of Gillespie's antics during performances: "He was very unhappy with Dizzy 'cause he didn't like the way Dizzy acted on the stage. He said

Dizzy was a Tom" (Gitler 1985: 172). Whatever the cause, however, Parker was completely neglected by the mainstream media and treated shabbily by the popular jazz press.

In light of Parker's low visibility in the contemporary media, it is interesting to examine the popular image of the jazz musician circulated in the 1950s by Hollywood movies and its connection to the color-blindness discourse that predominated during this decade. Mostly, this popular image was offered in a series of movies that told versions of the life stories of actual jazz musicians: *The Glenn Miller Story* (1954), *The Benny Goodman Story* (1956), *St. Louis Blues* (1958, about composer W. C. Handy), and *The Five Pennies* (1959, about cornetist Red Nichols). It is not coincidental that the 1950s, a decade in which there were "recurrent rumors of a [swing] revival," erupted with a rash of movies depicting the lives of successful, mostly white, jazz musicians from earlier eras (Stowe 1994: 242). Although it is perhaps true, as Krin Gabbard has recently assumed, that the typical moviegoer in the 1950s did not differentiate between these "white jazz biopics" and other contemporary motion pictures about white entertainers, the similarities among the jazz-specific movies nevertheless tell us about the popular construction of jazz musicians in this decade (Gabbard 1996: 77).

Given that there is always lag time—though it is becoming shorter and shorter—between subcultural trends and their appearance in the mass media, it is not surprising that these movies do not use Charlie Parker, Dizzy Gillespie, or any other actual or fictional bebop musicians of the 1950s for their lead characters, instead using musicians from the swing era and before. Nor is it surprising that these Hollywood productions lavish their attention on white musicians and composers (except, of course, for Handy) who achieved moderate or enormous financial and popular success by adapting black music to white tastes. However, it is significant that the characters and plots in these movies reproduce the color-blindness discourse that was dominant in the United States at the time.

These movies do this primarily by discursively reproducing the central dynamic of color-blindness: Euro American culture's ascendancy is established on, and even authorized by, the containment of African American culture. Thus, in each of these movies the musician and the music itself move away from the black source toward the white mainstream. This movement occurs, for example, in the development of the narrative: as the musicians become increasingly successful they take the music from its local source—Harlem nightclubs, African American workingmen, New Orleans riverboat musicians—to the established venues of American culture—Carnegie Hall, the New York Philharmonic, European concert halls, even the U.S. military. Also, in each of these movies the individual musician (white except Handy) is represented as taking the music beyond where it could have gone if it were left in the hands of African American musicians. The music's development from a kind of African American "folk music" (in the sense of "folk art"—a collective craft passed on and modified by naive artists) to a successful and esteemed popular art is implicitly connected to the *white* musician's ability to imagine and practice a distinctive, sophisticated, individual variation on the jazz music that preexists him. Glenn Miller (played by James Stewart) and Benny Goodman (played by Steve Allen), for example, are shown to be driven in their musical ambitions by the "sound" only they hear but for which they cannot get any financial or musical support. Moreover, this "sound" is elevated above music made by African Americans because it is presented as more sophisticated, not only because it is positively called "arrangements" and "compositions" when created by white musicians but because the musicians are shown to play easily in the improvisational style of black musicians; more listenable because it achieves greater popularity and is more danceable; and more artistic because it is the product of one individual's creativity rather than the result of a group's cultural experience.

Following the liberal color-blindness ideology, the distinction between black and white culture is made without unduly diminishing black culture or being explicitly racist. In fact, the movies implicitly recognize the worth, although limited, of black culture by showing that it is powerful enough to attract young, ambitious white men to it. As Amiri Baraka has explained, even this limited recognition "served to place the Negro's culture and Negro society in a position of intelligent regard it had never enjoyed before" (1963: 151). Each of these movies, then, acknowledges the black source of jazz music by bringing the white musician in contact with an earlier, more primitive producer of jazz music. Benny Goodman, for example, derives his passion for jazz from hearing Kid Ory and his band play aboard a Mississippi River steamboat. However, each movie uses a black musician only to propel the development of the white musician and his career. Thus, Glenn Miller and Red Nichols are shown playing in Harlem nightclubs with Louis Armstrong at points in the narrative when their musicianship or morale needs a boost. As Krin Gabbard points out, the narrative function of the black musician as a source of power for the white protagonist is emphasized by the associations made between musical and sexual virility (1996: 82–87). These associations also foreground the "prurient" aspect of jazz in the black locale. Although Armstrong's entertaining musicianship in these scenes is allowed to stand on its own, the movies further emphasize the illicit nature of the black source of jazz by shooting these scenes through colored filters, marking off these Harlem clubs as fundamentally different (read, more base) places of entertainment than the ballrooms and concert halls where white musicians play and aspire to play.

The movies create agency for their white musicians and revoke it from black musicians by scripting scenes in which black musicians baptize and legitimize the white jazz musicians by offering them their approval and support. This is accomplished most effectively by using an actual musician. In both *The Five Pennies* and *The Glenn Miller Story*, for example, Louis Armstrong fulfills the role, while in *The Benny Goodman Story* Kid Ory, Lionel Hampton, and Teddy Wilson play important, authenticating, supporting roles. Ory is especially important because he is Goodman's initial inspiration and, later in the movie, comes to a Goodman gig in Chicago to tell the clarinetist that his band is the best one he has ever heard. At other times this legitimation is accomplished with an actor playing an actual musician. Thus, for example, in *The Benny Goodman Story*, Fletcher Henderson (played by Sammy Davis, Sr.) makes a special trip to see Goodman to express his appreciation and admiration for the clarinetist's music and success. Finally, in each of these movies the white musician is shown to be properly deferential to black musicians—Miller and Nichols both say they do not play as well as Armstrong—but the movie's narrative subverts this verbal deference by plotting the white musician's transcendence of the black musician's popularity and financial success.

Even *St. Louis Blues*, starring Nat King Cole as black composer W. C. Handy and featuring such renowned African American performers as Mahalia Jackson, Ella Fitzgerald, and Pearl Bailey, reproduces the color-blindness ideology by using the same central elements that appear in the other "white jazz biopics." That is, the same movement from stigmatized black source to the privileged white establishment is reproduced in *St. Louis Blues*, although it is (only) slightly complicated by the fact that the protagonist himself is black. Handy's main black inspiration is shown to be the secular worksongs he hears sung by black workingmen in the streets of Memphis when he is a child. The movie makes it clear, by creating a rigid distinction between these worksongs and the church music Handy's father—a preacher—wants him to write, that "black" music is less sophisticated and more primitive in its form than music—like that played in church—that has been fused with white music. Moreover, like Goodman, Miller, and Nichols, Handy is presented as a superior, individualized artist, because he is a composer, one who makes something more (read better) out of this promising raw material. The result of Handy's individualistic talent are "blues" songs that are, as Samuel Floyd says, "Tin Pan Alley-type songs into which the structural and expressive characteristics of the blues were carefully set and integrated" (1995: 109).

The movie's denouement offers viewers a scene comparable to those in the movies about white jazz musicians: Handy's music is performed by the New York Symphony at Aeolian Hall in front of an audience filled with stodgy old white people. This scene effects a reconciliation between Handy and his father, who is finally convinced of his son's worth and success because the symphony's world-famous conductor has endorsed his sophisticated compositions. Although the scene changes the convention slightly by showing Handy (and Eartha Kitt's character) singing with the symphony, it is clear that Handy and his music are only there because the white conductor has found Handy's compositions to be worthwhile. The scene even includes a kind of white authentication of Handy's music in the form of the conductor's speech to the audience endorsing jazz as "America's only pure art form" and describing the positive audience responses he received when he played "St. Louis Blues" for audiences in Europe (who mistook the song for the "Star Spangled Banner").

For the most part, the popular images of jazz musicians in these films stand in stark contrast to the contemporary images (popular and subcultural) projected by bebop musicians like Charlie Parker and, to a lesser extent, Dizzy Gillespie. In these movies, Benny Goodman, Glenn Miller, Red Nichols, and W. C. Handy are all depicted as serious, respectable, ambitious, moral, conservative family men. Though they come in contact with some of the more prurient elements (which are limited in these stories to bootleg liquor, late hours, and sexy women) of the jazz world in Harlem nightclubs and Memphis speakeasies, they remain little more than bourgeois white men (except, of course, for Handy who, although black in Memphis around the turn of the century, appears to live a stable, uneventful middle-class life—his father is a preacher) who earn their livings unconventionally.

One element these pre-bop musicians do share with their 1950s counterparts, however, is a degree of social alienation. Around the edges of these popular constructions are signs that even these middle-class jazzmen are at odds with American society because of their inexorable pursuit of their art. Goodman, Miller, and Nichols, for example, all experience professional setbacks—being fired from or forced to quit bands—economic insecurity, and social ostracism because of their preoccupation with realizing the idiosyncratic "sounds" they hear in their heads. This social alienation—they are, at times, estranged from friends, family, and even less creative jazz musicians—is presented as a constitutive part of who they are. When pianist Teddy Wilson, in *The Benny Goodman Story*, tells Goodman he is crazy for wanting to start his own band, the clarinetist replies, "I can't help being the way I am." In these films, however, this alienation is presented conventionally as resulting from their artistic temperament or personality and not, in the end, from anything peculiar to being a jazz musician. One does not get the sense, except in the most superficial ways, that these musicians have been cast out of mainstream American culture because they are attracted to jazz music. The only exception, and it is a partial one, is W. C. Handy (strangely enough), whose primary social isolation occurs because his father, the preacher, thinks any kind of secular music is "devil's music." This association is shown to be a product of a defect in the father's character, however, when near the end of the movie Handy's Aunt Hagar and his friend, the singer Gogo Germaine, chide the preacher for being "prejudiced against jazz." Properly rebuked, the preacher accompanies the women to the Aeolian Hall to hear Handy's music performed by the New York

Symphony, where he and the audience pay Handy proper respect for the music he has created.

For all these musicians, then, jazz is, finally, what connects them to American society: how they make their money and become successes, express their individuality, reconcile with estranged family members, aid the war effort, bridge the generation gap, and make their families happy. In this way, the popular construction of the jazz musician is a fitting metaphor for the color-blindness discourse: in it, African American culture is acknowledged as a fertile though base source of modern American culture; individuals who engage it and combine it with their own idiosyncratic artistic genius can reap financial, personal, and public success.

A variation on this metaphor is Dorothy Baker's portrayal of trumpeter Rick Martin in her 1938 novel *Young Man With a Horn*. Although this novel was published several years before the period bracketed by this study, it is significant enough to discuss for two reasons. First, Baker's romantic variation on the white jazz musician reverberates in the representations found in Jack Kerouac's and Ross Russell's novels in the 1950s and 1960s. Second, Baker's novel was adapted into a movie produced in 1950, in the process changing her story in ways that reveal ruptures in the white representation of jazz musicians. Baker's novel, although essentialist in its portrayal of African Americans, inaugurates a tame white challenge to the popular construction of the jazz musician and to the optimism of color-blindness: her white jazz musician creates beautiful music but, in the end, fails tragically, in part because of his proximity and attraction to African American people and culture. Although she claims her story is inspired only by "the music, but not the life, of a great musician, Leon (Bix) Beiderbecke," Baker bases her portrayal of the jazz musician in *Young Man With a Horn* on what James Lincoln Collier has said was the contemporary "legend" of Bix Beiderbecke: "the sensitive artist killed by the insensate crowd" (1978: 168). This legend was widely disseminated in a 1936 *New Republic* article by Otis Ferguson. Not incidentally, during his life and even more so after his death Beiderbecke became (and to some extent still is) a cult hero to white jazz players and fans who imitated his solos note for note and kept his name alive. Beiderbecke's more "lyrical" sound was seen by many white players and fans as an attractive "alternative" to the bolder style of Louis Armstrong (Collier 1978: 161, 173).

Baker establishes and emphasizes the cliché of the doomed artist in the "Prologue" to her novel in an attempt to elevate the position of the jazz musician from that of a popular entertainer playing for audiences interested merely in dancing to that of an "artist" motivated by the most exalted desires. Using the Thomas Mann character Tonio Kröger as an example of the driven, creative human being to whom trumpeter Rick Martin can be compared, Baker's narrator explains, "Now these are strong words and should surely apply much more truly to a poet like Tonio Kroger than to the man who played hot trumpet in Phil Morrison's band. But I don't think they do, and that's the thing about Rick's story that moves me. The creative urge is the creative urge, no matter where you find it" (1961: 4). Baker represents Martin as a tragic figure (though her narrator specifically declines to describe his story as "a grand tragic theme") who destroys himself with alcohol *because* he is unable both to resist the demands of the crowd and to pay as much attention to his life as to his art: "Our man is, I hate to say it, an artist, burdened with that difficult language, the soul of an artist. But he hasn't got the thing that should go with it—and which I suppose seldom does—the ability to keep the body in check while the spirit goes on being what it must be. And he goes to pieces, but not in any small way. He does it so thoroughly that he kills himself doing it" (1961: 6). Although the third-person narrative voice used here is purposely understated (to heighten the tragedy of Rick Martin's story), the basic idea of Baker's "Prologue" is clear: in life artists suffer because of their genius and very often they pay for their gift with their lives.

Even more important for our purposes, though, is the fact that Baker develops this depiction of Rick Martin as the suffering, sacrificing genius against the portrayals of African American jazz musicians in the novel. Though Baker populates her story with several admirable, worthy African American musicians (one of whom is Martin's best friend and two of whom give Martin his initial jazz training), none of them are explicitly or implicitly called "artists." Instead, African American jazz musicians in Baker's book are presented as having an inherent connection with the music: Martin's friend Smoke Jordan, a drummer, is described as having "rhythm in his ears all the time"; Jeff Williams, the reigning jazz piano giant, is "a natural piano player; he just picked it up by himself"; and Jeff Williams's quintet "were so many gold mines as far as the pure vein of natural music is concerned. They came equipped with their racial heritage despite the fact that they had been put down in Los Angeles, of all places, and not, as Nature must have intended, in New Orleans or Memphis" (1961: 23, 29, 38).

The image of the jazz musician developed in this novel, then, is similar to those offered in later movies about actual musicians like Goodman, Miller, and Nichols. White jazz musicians are (or, at least, can be) born "artists" who use whatever materials are available (even those from black sources) and, because of their innate genius, can transform those materials, including such previously degraded forms as jazz, into Music. Black jazz musicians, on the other hand, are born *jazz* musicians, with a racial inheritance rather than a learned skill or individual gift, and so are less capable, or at least less likely, to develop much beyond the level of a pure, primitive musician. Unlike in the movie depictions, however, Baker's novel develops the underside of this story: instead of succeeding finally like Goodman and Miller (and, to a lesser extent, Nichols), Rick Martin (like the real-life Bix Beiderbecke) dies before achieving mass success. Although the novel spreads the blame for Martin's early death among several causes (including his artistic temperament, naivete, and the dangerous milieu of the jazz musician), the overall trajectory of his character suggests that the white person's engagement with jazz (and by extension with African American culture) is potentially more serious, more threatening than the discourse of color-blindness would lead us to believe. Of course, the novel raises this challenge only by trafficking in racial stereotypes and risking accusations of hysterical racism, but as we will soon see these are typical problems with this kind of white cultural challenge.

The nature of this challenge to or rupture in the dominant construction of the jazz musician in postwar culture is revealed by changes made to Baker's novel when it was adapted into a movie in 1950. The movie (starring Kirk Douglas as Rick Martin) alters Baker's novel to bring it closer to the image of the jazz musician found in the later white biopics and to the strictures of color-blindness. Eliminated from the narrative in the movie version is any sense that African American culture—in the form of jazz or jazz musicians—is responsible for the problems encountered by Rick Martin. To accomplish this, the movie erases two of the major black characters—Martin's friend Smoke Jordan and pianist Jeff Williams—from the story. Instead, the movie focuses on a single black character—Martin's trumpet mentor Art Hazard—whose relationship with Martin better exemplifies the "proper" power relations between black and white culture. In the movie, Hazard teaches the young, orphaned Martin how to play the trumpet and remains the white musician's idol and model throughout his life. The movie chronicles an uncomplicated (though, as Krin Gabbard expertly argues, humorously Freudian [1996: 71–2]), Dreiseresque transfer of power in which Martin inexorably rises as the best trumpet player in the United States (presumably) while Hazard declines and finally dies.

This dual trajectory enables the movie to reestablish the unmarked supremacy of white over black culture. This idea is emphasized in a speech Hazard gives after Martin's initial bandstand "triumph" over his mentor. Hazard tells the audience, "I taught him how to hold that trumpet he just played for you. But I didn't teach him how to play it. Not the way he does. That's something that you can't learn. You've got to have it." This idea is also reinforced by the movie's ending, which brings Martin back to life after he nearly dies from alcohol abuse. Driven to alcoholism by his inability to hit that "high note" he hears in his head but cannot play, Martin is brought to recovery through the help of his white friends (the ones who were black in the novel) and the realization that "You can't say everything through the end of a trumpet, and a man doesn't destroy himself just because he can't hit some high note he dreamed up." Although this movie, then, offers a more qualified success story than the white biopics—Martin apparently never plays that high note or succeeds on his own terms—it does offer a much more optimistic story than Baker's novel.

Another significant but ambiguous white challenge to the dominant construction of the jazz musician is found in the 1946 autobiography of Mezz Mezzrow, *Really the Blues*. Mezzrow, a white, suburban, middle-class Jew from the northwest side of Chicago, grew up during the early twentieth century admiring the music and "character" of African Americans who lived on Chicago's South Side. Because of his admiration of what he identified as African American culture as well as his friendship and professional association with the respected white jazz musicians who came out of Chicago's Austin High School, Mezzrow established a career of sorts in jazz music. Although by all accounts Mezzrow's historical significance has more to do with his engaging personality, knowledge of African American vernacular, and selling of marijuana to jazz musicians than with the music he made, he is also responsible for an autobiography that has been enormously influential on subsequent white bohemians (Collier 1978: 333; Gillespie 1979: 333; Gates 1988: 69–70; Mezzrow 1990: vii–viii).

Mezzrow's contribution to the subversion of the dominant white racial construction of the jazz musician lies in his almost complete romanticization of black culture and black life. Like the hipsters who imitated him, Mezzrow turned the invisible racial hierarchy of color-blindness upside down: blackness is the ideal, whiteness is stigmatized. Throughout his autobiography, Mezzrow represents himself as being completely absorbed with the task of learning not only how to play jazz like a "black man" (because, of course, they instinctively know how to play jazz) but also how to *be* a "negro." Mezzrow's subversion, in other words, depends, like Baker's (and other white writers' before her), on the stereotyping of African Americans as "natural" folk musicians (even those who did not, technically, *play* music are said to possess musical ability):

> Everything the Negro did, we agreed, had a swing to it; he talked in rhythm, his tonal expression had a pleasing lilt to the ear, his movements were graceful. Was it this quality in him that made the white Southerners resent him so much, and was this why they kept him oppressed? Were they afraid that if the Negro was really set free he would make us all look sick with his genius for relaxed, high-spirited, unburdened living? . . . We could see that every move he made was as easy and neatly timed as anything Mother Nature had put down on this earth. His laughter was real and from way down inside. His whole manner and bearing was simple and natural. He could out-dance and out sing anybody, in sports he could out-fight and out-run most all the competition, and when it comes to basketball don't say a word, just listen. (1990: 146)

Of course, this positive stereotyping of African Americans was not new or surprising. As George M. Frederickson explains, some abolitionists sought to rouse passions against slavery by informing white people about the "redeeming virtues and even evidences . . . of superiority" in African Americans that they believed were "tragically lacking in white American civilization" (1987: 101, 108).

However, Mezzrow's positioning of himself as a white man who agrees, even downright demands, to subordinate himself to the "natural" glories of blackness is a new wrinkle.[2] In contrast to the relation of white to black in the dominant representation of the jazz musician, Mezzrow does not present himself as the imperialist invader who wants to raid African American music for its riches and then dissociate himself from blackness; he wants to lose (or find) himself in blackness. Throughout the book Mezzrow distances himself from those white musicians who would put themselves in any other position vis-à-vis African American music: he labels as unacceptable not only those who would steal without attribution or those who claim that the history of racial division also prevents any "cultural" mixing, but also those who want to develop another kind of jazz altogether—a "whitened" jazz, as it were. Mezzrow demands, instead, that the white musician who is committed to *jazz* must become a "negro" jazz musician: "To be with those guys made me know that any white man, if he thought straight and studied hard, could sing and dance and play with the Negro. You didn't have to take the finest and most original and honest music in America and mess it up because you were a white man; you could dig the colored man's real message and get in there with him" (1990: 53). When Mezzrow, however, says "studied hard," he does not mean to imply that jazz is a cultural entity on the level of classical music— that is, one requiring years of formal study (perhaps this accounts, to some extent, for his widely reported lack of skill playing jazz). Instead, he means that the white aspirant should study the people, the way of life, and the total experience of being black in America:

> I never believed that you had to practice and study a hell of a lot to play real New Orleans. The secret is more mental than technical. If you want to play real jazz, go live close to the Negro, see through his eyes, laugh and cry with him, soak up his spirit. That's the best way to prepare for a recording; it's what I always do. If you're not prepared to do that, then okay, play your own music but don't pretend that it has anything to do with jazz. Make up a new name for what you're doing, just to keep the record straight. But if you're humble enough, and strip off all the prejudices that are a barrier between you and the source, you'll make it. It takes a lot of living and loving, among the right people. The rest comes easy. (1990: 353)

Although his earnestness and humility are admirable, these observations suggest rather explicitly that Mezzrow considers black culture to be a basic, primitive entity. Rather than considering African American music the creation and revision of particular aesthetic forms the way, for example, critic Albert Murray does, Mezzrow seems to believe that jazz derives *directly* from life—that is, from living as a black person in America: "The colored man doesn't often get sullen and tight-lipped and evil because his philosophy goes deeper and he thinks straight. Maybe he hasn't got all the hyped-up words and theories to explain how he thinks. That's all right. He knows. He tells about it in his music. You'll find the answer there, if you know what to look for" (1990: 14).

Moreover, Mezzrow represents it as possible for a white man to have this experience, to learn this experiential "philosophy" and thus to play jazz the way a black man can simply by virtue of being a black man. This is why in his life and in his autobiography Mezzrow continually puts himself in the position of the African American. Mezzrow achieves this position literally in some situations; for example, as Barry Gifford explains in his introduction to *Really the Blues*, "when he was jailed on Riker's Island for two years for selling marijuana, Mezz insisted on being classified as a Negro inmate and considered it a great honor to be housed in the Negro section of the prison" (Mezzrow and Wolfe 1990: viii). Mezzrow, however, also achieves this African American position discursively when, in *Really the Blues*, he concludes that, at age forty-six, he has achieved his goal of "soak[ing] up [the African American's] spirit"; of "fighting to get back to the source" (1990: 353). According to his coauthor, Bernard Wolfe, Mezzrow's belief that he had returned to "the source" did not refer simply to his musical prowess, nor was it metaphorical: Mezzrow, Wolfe says, "came to believe he has actually, physically, turned black" (1990: 389). Thus what is comprised by his autobiography is "really the blues."

As Wolfe's observation suggests, Mezzrow's self-presentation is the product of an enormous "personal mythology" (1990: 390). As such, *Really the Blues* is an engaging, even compelling performance. Its blend of personal mythology, entertaining anecdotes, and knowing slang demonstrates a hipster celebration of a life lived in the interstices of mainstream American society. However, like Norman Mailer's clearly derivative "The White Negro" (1957), Mezzrow's autobiography is a performance of the alienated white man's search for a simpler, more elemental relation with his own self, his own body, his particular and different (from African Americans) place in the American social and cultural order. And unlike similar narratives written by more savvy and political personalities like Johnny Otis, for example, Mezzrow's autobiography is all lack and all desire untempered by any awareness that it is his very privilege as a white man in America that enables him to perform the relation between white and black as he does. There is no indication in *Really the Blues* that Mezzrow recognizes the truth in what George Lipsitz writes about the contemporary incarnation of the "white negro," Johnny Otis: "Of course, he has always known that there are some dimensions of the

African American experience that he cannot feel; that his biological makeup has always allowed him the theoretical option of living as 'white'" (Otis 1993: xix). Although Lipsitz continues by noting that Otis's "absorption in Black culture has become such an internalized part of his experience that he finds it impossible to think of himself in any other terms," and although Otis himself repeatedly calls African Americans "my people," there is not the same sense of desperation, of self-aggrandizement, of *fantasy* in Otis's performance that there is in Mezzrow's. Otis is clearly as committed to the difficult task of participating meaningfully in his community as he is to the joy of experiencing its culture.

The positioning of the white jazz musician offered in Mezzrow's self-portrayal in *Really the Blues*, then, is different from the one inscribed in the dominant culture image in Hollywood movies and the slightly different one presented in *Young Man With a Horn*. Unlike Dorothy Baker, Mezzrow does not position the white musician above and outside of the black musician. Instead, Mezzrow seemingly subordinates the white jazz musician to the black one. In fact, Mezzrow apparently believes that "blackness" is essential to successful jazz musicianship.[3] Of course, it is true that Mezzrow's performance in his autobiography can be characterized (and dismissed) by contemporary readers, as John Szwed does: "as in the minstrel shows, the medium is a white man boasting of his competence in black culture by taking observers on a guided tour, complete with a glossary of native hip terms" (Szwed 1980: 587). There is no denying that despite his protestations to the contrary, Mezzrow *was* a white man who worked extremely hard in his personal life and narrative to apply the metaphoric black paint to his visage. However, while I think Szwed's characterization is on the mark insofar as it minimizes Mezzrow's understanding of African American experience, people, and culture, it misses the significance of Mezzrow's unintended construction of whiteness, especially for the time it depicts and the time it was published. That is, the absence of racist ridicule in his self-representation suggests that this was a model for an alternate white identity that had jettisoned pejorative minstrel conventions. Certainly, as Allen Ginsberg indicates, Mezzrow's narrative struck a chord for white bohemians in the 1940s and 1950s. Those who, during this time, already believed they were outside of American society or even simply wanted to portray themselves as being on the outside took up this particular strand of outsiderism—which Norman Mailer finally popularized as "the white negro."

The particular representations of Charlie Parker one finds in work by Euro Americans during the postwar era trace their lineage back through Mezz Mezzrow and, to a lesser extent, Dorothy Baker's Rick Martin. As such, these representations are a combination of subversive or oppositional ideas and ideas that tend to support the dominant construction of race and racial difference. Like Mezzrow's self-presentation, the Euro American uses of Charlie Parker emphasize the bankruptcy of dominant white culture and celebrate the greater spontaneity and emotional-ity of black culture. These representations also use Parker's life and music to symbolize the personal freedom that many in the immediate postwar era saw as an alternative to the conformity enforced by the seemingly engulfing corporate, middle-class culture. However, by staking their flag of rebellion on the turf of "personal freedom" these representations very often ended up offering support for the ideological priorities—competitive individualism over collective action, for example—of the establishment against which they were fighting. Schaub says: "At the same time that analysts of developments in Italy, Germany, and Russia wanted to explain the rise of totalitarianism, they also wished to prevent its spread, and this complementary reflex naturally led to a renewal of essentially romantic values and assumptions about the autonomy of individuals and the virtues of 'spontaneity,' and to conventional oppositions between self and society, nature and civilization, rebellion and conformity" (1991: 148).

In part, this self-sabotage was due, as Schaub says of Norman Mailer, to the political and cultural Left's fear of and retreat from collective identification and action after the catastrophe of Stalinism (1991: 141). Turning away from collectivism, the political and cultural Left (one represented by Mailer and the other by Kerouac) elevated individual subjectivity—their own feelings of alienation and repression, their own desire for freedom and rebellion—into a revolutionary program. Although the terms of their programs differed depending on their specific interests—Mailer's in politics and social order, Kerouac's in art and literature—the result was the same: individualism and subjective psychological states were privileged over collectivism and social or economic condition. Thus, when they looked for symbols of their rebellion and found them in groups in American society whose "psychological types, states, and qualities" they believed reflected their own situation and desires (African Americans), they substituted the part for the whole (Schaub 1991: 145). That is, they distorted African American rebellion to fit their own psychological, political, and cultural needs. Thus, for example, we find this passage in Mailer's "The White Negro":

> The Negro has the simplest of alternatives: live a life of constant humility or ever-threatening danger. In such a pass where paranoia is as vital to survival as blood, the Negro has stayed alive and begun to grow by following the need of his body where he could. Knowing in the cells of his existence that life was war, nothing but war, the Negro (all exceptions admitted) could rarely afford the sophisticated inhibitions of civilization, and so he kept for his survival the art of the primitive, he lived in the enormous present, he subsisted for his Saturday night kicks, relinquishing the pleasures of the mind for the more obligatory pleasures of the body, and in his music he gave voice to the character and quality of his existence, to his rage and infinite variations of joy, lust, languor, growl, cramp, pinch, scream and despair of his orgasm. (1981: 302–3)

In this stereotyped formulation, jazz emerged as the vehicle by which white rebels could find and express their own rebellion in apparent sympathy with African Americans: "For jazz is orgasm, it is the music of orgasm, good orgasm and bad, and so it spoke across a nation, it had the communication of art even where it was watered, perverted, corrupted, and almost killed, it spoke in no matter what laundered popular way of instantaneous existential states to which some whites could respond, it was indeed a communication by art because it said, 'I feel this, and now you do too'" (1981: 302–3).

Similarly, the version of Parker that appears in the work of Jack Kerouac is a white fantasy of a black self. Kerouac uses Charlie Parker (as well as other "real-life" jazz figures) by name both as a character and, more significantly, as a symbol. These jazz musicians, Parker most prominently among them, are more than merely "the furniture of Kerouac's fiction"; they are, because of their use and frequency, an integral part of the system of meaning constructed by Kerouac's writing (Kart 1983: 25–27). Whether or not he succeeds in "achiev[ing] his dream of a prose that shadows the chorus structure of an improvising jazz soloist" (Kart 1983: 27), Kerouac uses jazz not only for its ideal of improvisation but also for its status as a music and subculture that is outside what is traditional and accepted. In contrast to Mailer, Kerouac's use of African American people and culture has less to do with any interest in rebelling against the political establishment than with his rebellion against the cultural and literary establishment.

Kerouac's *The Subterraneans* is a novel in which Charlie Parker figures prominently. Occurring early in *The Subterraneans*, the following scene describes the night the narrator (a Kerouac substitute named Leo Percepied) first meets the young African American bohemian Mardou Fox and they go with some friends to hear jazz (more specifically, Charlie Parker) at a club called the Red Drum: "and up on the stand Bird Parker with solemn eyes who'd been busted fairly recently and had now returned to a kind of bop dead Frisco but had just discovered or been told about the Red Drum, the great new generation gang wailing and gathering there, so here he was on the stand, examining them with his eyes as he blew his now-settled-down-into-regulated-design 'crazy' notes" (1971: 18–19). A couple of elements in this passage are both significant and characteristic of the way Kerouac depicts and attributes meaning to jazz. First, Kerouac's focus on Charlie Parker is, of course, on his victimization—"been busted fairly recently"—and, just as importantly, on Parker's emotional response to his position as a suffering black jazz musician—solemnity; perhaps indicating a certain amount of resignation to his social victimization and his martyr-like status among the jazz faithful (certainly the religious connotation of the word "solemn" cannot be ignored, especially as the scene is further developed by Kerouac). Of course, Kerouac is neither the first nor the last to emphasize the notion that Parker (especially, but really *all* black jazz musicians are typically included) suffered at the hands of society, or that he was resigned to his victimization. For example, in Elliott Grennard's fictionalization of the infamous Dial recording during which Parker had a breakdown, there is a passage that includes a very similar description of Parker's face while he is playing: "and the expression on his face was just about the saddest expression I've ever seen. It made you think he wanted to cry inside, only he had tried and found he couldn't" (Grennard 1947: 421). However, this is, and remains, Kerouac's major use of the Parker image in his work. Moreover, Kerouac's reference to the cause of Parker's victimization is characteristically universal and individualistic—a drug arrest. It is, in other words, a martyrdom that could be had by any social rebel.

In a subsequent characterization of Parker, found in the late choruses of his *Mexico City Blues*, the same themes—victimization and Parker's resignation to his Christ-like status—are emphasized. This time Kerouac compares Parker to another religious figure, the Buddha, but again focuses on the quiet resignation on his expressive face:

> And his expression on his face
> Was as calm, beautiful, and profound
> As the image of the Buddha
> Represented in the East, the lidded eyes,
> The expression that says "All is Well"
> —This was what Charley Parker
> Said when he played, All is Well. (Kerouac 1990: 241)

In this Chorus (239), Kerouac's focus, again, on Parker's victimization by his followers takes the following form,

> —Charley burst
> His lungs to reach the speed
> Of what the speedsters wanted
> And what they wanted
> Was his Eternal Slowdown. (1990: 241)

In this poetic yoking of Parker's death and the demands of his thrill-seeking fans, Kerouac perhaps reveals a hint of his fear of his own "Eternal Slowdown" at the hands of those who saw him as living, through his art, the life they wanted to lead. In any case, the image of Parker in this excerpt is universalized enough to make him a martyr with whom any rebel can identify.

From the previous scene in *The Subterraneans* we find another imaginative use of Charlie Parker:

returning to the Red Drum for sets, to hear Bird, whom I saw distinctly digging Mardou several times also myself directly into my eye looking to search if really I was that great writer I thought myself to be as if he knew my thoughts and ambitions or remembered me from other night clubs and other coasts, other Chicagos—not a challenging look but the king and founder of the bop generation at least the sound of it in digging his audience digging his eyes, the secret eyes him-watching, as he just pursed his lips and let great lungs and immortal fingers work, his eyes separate and interested and humane, the kindest jazz musician there could be while being and therefore naturally the greatest— watching Mardou and me in the infancy of our love and probably wondering why, or knowing it wouldn't last, or seeing who it was would be hurt, as now, obviously, but not quite yet, it was Mardou whose eyes were shining in my direction, though I could not have known and now do not definitely know. (1971: 19–20)

As with the earlier passage, this one glorifies the image of Parker in a way that is at odds with the depiction of the bebop legend by musicians, like Miles Davis, who knew and worked with him. Although the portrayal of Parker in Davis's autobiography as "greedy" and not at all likable is perhaps an exaggeration, many of the musicians who contributed to Robert Reisner's oral history about Bird recall that he was, at best, a difficult, erratic person. Describing Parker, then, as "the kindest jazz musician there could be while being and therefore naturally the greatest" diminishes Parker in a couple of ways. First, Kerouac patronizingly reduces this undeniably complex human being to a single characteristic—kindness—that belies the tumult of his life. More important, the association of kindness (especially its connotations of a natural gentleness and helpfulness), Parker's musicianship, and "nature" evokes elements traditional in minstrel and minstrel-like depictions of black people. In addition, this passage again emphasizes the eyes as the locus of emotion and interaction, and suggests that the audience is somehow able to sense something about Parker's life and his strategy for living that life by gazing into his eyes. The total effect of this representation, then, is to erase or obliterate Parker's particularlity as a symbol.

The obliteration of Parker's symbolic specificity is especially significant because Kerouac uses this rhetorical strategy, finally, not to say something about Parker or jazz musicians overall but to enhance his own image as a kind, humane but suffering, victimized artist and man by connecting himself to the already established image of the exploited jazz musician. The passage begins and ends with the narrator making an intimate connection with the jazz performer: Percepied sees Parker not just looking at him and his "date" but looking at them very meaningfully.[4] Percepied imagines that Parker connects with him from the bandstand as a fellow artist: "looking to search if really I was that great writer I thought myself to be as if he knew my thoughts and ambitions." As with many of Kerouac's self-aggrandizing assessments of his talent, this comparison of himself and Parker is ambiguous. Although Percepied's comparison is undercut somewhat by his introductory warning in the novel that he is an "egomaniac" (1971: 1), one gets the sense from the very fact that this "big word construction" has been "erected" (1971: 23) that the "author" takes his artistic talents very seriously indeed. Similarly, in a later piece, "The Origins of the Beat Generation," Kerouac reveals the conflict (without any seeming awareness) between what he knows to be real—the jazz musicians' ignorance of him as an artist and person—and what he wants to be true—a human connection between fellow suffering artists. He says, "when I first heard Bird and Diz in the Three Deuces I knew they were serious musicians playing a goofy new sound and didn't care what I thought." However, in the next sentence Kerouac continues, "I was leaning against the bar with a beer when Dizzy came over for a glass of water from the bartender, put himself right against me and reached with both arms around both sides of my head to get the glass and danced away, as though knowing I'd be singing about him someday" (1961c: 72).

In this scene, Percepied also imagines that Parker connects with him as a sad, doomed, suffering individual: "watching Mardou and me in the infancy of our love and probably wondering why, or knowing it wouldn't last, or seeing who it was would be hurt as now, obviously, but not quite yet it was Mardou whose eyes were shining in my direction, though I could not have known and now do not definitely know." The effect of this narrative strategy—linking himself with the jazz performer—on his depiction of Charlie Parker is to romanticize and stereotype even further the image of Parker specifically and the jazz musician more generally. Parker becomes more than simply a saxophone player; he is a seer, a savant, a psychic—able to see (what the narrator himself is blind to at that moment) in the one look that Mardou directs at Percepied that she is going to hurt him. Perhaps more importantly, at the same time Parker becomes less than a full-fledged character in the novel—he simply remains a static, stereotyped symbol. As with most nonwhites in Kerouac's work Parker never speaks for himself; his silence is necessary to maintain the focus on Kerouac's (and his cohort's) experience as American outsiders.[5]

While Kerouac uses the image of Charlie Parker fairly straightforwardly to enhance his own position as a social and cultural outsider, other Euro Americans used Parker in ways that are more ambiguous. If one looks, for example, at *The Sound* (1961), a novel written by noted Parker record producer Ross Russell, one finds a fictionalized Charlie Parker character, Red Travers (transformed from an alto saxophonist into a trumpet player), whose position as a victimized artist is again foregrounded but who is not unconditionally glorified for it. Russell is notable not only because he produced many of Parker's recordings (for Dial Records), but because he wrote a biography of Parker in 1973, *Bird Lives!*, that, according to James Lincoln Collier, simultaneously is "one of a tiny number of truly first-rate jazz books" and contains "occasional romanticisms" (Collier 1978: 362). As Richard Albert notes, Russell's novel displays "his first-hand knowledge of the jazz scene during the bop period" and "is a veritable catalog of jazz musicians and styles and a lexicon of jazz jargon" (Albert 1990: 4–5). Travers is characterized by the classically-trained white musician Bernie Rich (the novel's narrator) as a musical genius on a par with such modern European composers as Arnold Schoenberg: " 'I studied with Schoenberg for two semesters. He was much the same [as Red]—broke all the rules, and made new ones as he went. I guess there's just one word for it—' 'Genius, Bernie' " (Russell 1961: 205–6). However, unlike Schoenberg, Travers's individual gift is described as both part of his natural, racial heritage and connected with behavior that leads to his self-destruction. Russell specifically, even if tentatively, links Travers's individualist genius—"breaking all the rules" in music—to his tendency to transgress social and physiological rules as well:

> He breaks every rule in the book. Maybe that's where he gets his inspiration. Then again, maybe he had it with him all along. Look at his sex life. He doesn't run true to form. Junk kills the sex drive in most people. When I was on I didn't care about the most beautiful chick that ever lived. I heard once how in Chicago Red shut himself up in a hotel suite with a supply of Horse and five women, and just balled for three days and nights! The average junkie has no appetite for food. Look at Red! That man eats like a dockhand. One night I was in the Stage Door Delicatessen when he devoured six club sandwiches, one after the other, then gave the counterman hell because he hadn't built them big enough. (1961: 205–6)

This passage suggests that there is a connection between Travers's musical genius and the way he lived his life: artistic rebellion and personal rebellion are conflated. It is not significant, for our purposes, that the characteristics and situations described here derive from Charlie Parker's life.[6] There is no dispute that Parker was a musical genius, nor that he had enormous appetites. However, the use that is made of this raw material is significant because it suggests, in the fashion of Norman Mailer, that the ultimate jazz musician—in the figure of the fictional Charlie Parker—creates inspired, beautiful music out of some primitivistic rejection of "the sophisticated inhibitions of civilization."

Moreover, Ross Russell never attributes the emotional content of Red Travers's music to Travers's experience of racism in America. If a case were to be made that jazz comes from experience, one would expect that racist oppression would figure prominently in that experience. However, in *The Sound*, the arguments made by those explaining the desperation that drives Travers to self-destruction involve only his genius and his experience of economic squalor and depravity. Travers's white girlfriend places his problems in the context of the misunderstood, mistreated "artist":

Did you ever think of the price Red pays for his gift? He can't play a pop so the squares can understand it. Red's got to twist it around and put it back together his own way. Kid it and pull it to pieces, all the time he's making impossible things on the horn, that nobody else in the business can touch. Red couldn't ever be a big popular success. What he puts down is strictly for other musicians. Then it gradually works down to the hip dance bands like Jimmy Vann's. They're the cats that coin all the gold, with Red's ideas, dig? It will be years before they catch up with what Red's putting down today. (Russell 1961: 175)

Travers's genius, in this perspective, is responsible for both his unparalleled artistic expression and the desperate situation that leads to his incredibly self-destructive behavior.

The other perspective offered is one that attributes both characteristics to Travers's ability to survive an upbringing in which "his own old man turned him on to pot at twelve," and he "had to sleep on the floor . . . listen to drunken Saturday-night brawls in the next room . . . starve . . . lie and steal just to live" (1961: 174, 206). Travers's upbringing is contrasted not only with white musicians who "came from respectable middle-class homes," but with black musicians who did as well. By implication, hardship of any kind—but not specifically racism— can generate the kind of life that leads one to supreme expression in jazz music. Russell creates this type of character though many of those who know Parker claim that he was very sensitive to the social problems he faced because of his race. In a revealing quotation, for example, jazz promoter Robert Reisner says, "He had a big thing about race. He was not paranoic about it, but he never made a real adjustment to it. Bird partially solved this problem by becoming one of the greatest musicians who ever made sound" (1977: 19). Ten years after publication of *The Sound*, Russell himself, in a book on the development of jazz in the Southwest, wrote, "Charlie Parker, inwardly seething with anger over segregation, outwardly calm and beguiling, many times carried his baiting of racist types to the threshold of disaster. If Lester Young was the first hipster in jazz, Charlie Parker was its first angry black man" (Russell 1971: 199). Changing his Parker character as he does in *The Sound* is another way of universalizing jazz expression.

This is not to suggest, however, that in *The Sound* Russell is unconcerned with matters of race; he is. In fact, Russell's construction of race—both whiteness and blackness—in the novel is particularly interesting given that he does not foreground Travers's experience of racism. Instead, Travers's story—the story of *the* pioneering bebop jazz musician, in other words—is told from the perspective of a white musician, Bernie Rich, who admires Travers and aspires to play music like he does. Within this narrative structure, Russell develops a construction of blackness and whiteness that is remarkably similar to that found in Mezzrow's *Really the Blues*.

When Bernie first hears Travers's bebop the third-person narrator describes it thus: "Player and instrument seemed gathered together in the grip of some dark, primal force, beyond Bernie's ken; as remote from his own experience as the witch doctor's art lies from the practice of clinical medicine" (Russell 1961: 53). Obviously, the imagery used to characterize the music—"dark, primal force" and "witch doctor's art"—emphasizes the "naturalness" and "primitiveness" of jazz and gives it a "sinister" cast. More important, though, this passage sets up the essential racial tension played out in the novel's plot: jazz, more specifically bebop, is a music made by black people that is inaccessible to whites unless they "experience" what blacks experience. However, Russell's construction of African American experience in this novel is hollow and primitivistic because it refers not to anything specific to African Americans in American history—for example, racism or their musical tradition—but to the universal experience of the misunderstood and suffering artist and to the existing stereotypes about African American musicians. Representing this point of view is the novel's voice of reason and experience, big band leader Jimmy Vann, who says, "I found out a long time ago that my skin was the wrong shade. Benny [Goodman] was the greatest single jazz musician our race produced, and he never quite made it either. He was born on the wrong side of the gray issue, too" (Russell 1961: 214).

There are, moreover, other ways Russell develops the difference between white and black in relation to the Red Travers character. One way involves Charlie Parker's real-life inability/unwillingness to write down his music. The most famous stories about this part of Bird's life involve Parker coming over to Dizzy Gillespie's house in the middle of the night to get Gillespie to write down some new music Parker had been playing. Musician Trummy Young says, "now Bird, he didn't write music. But every time he thought of something, he'd come around to Diz to write it down. . . . So Diz would sit at his piano, and Bird would play it out in the hall, and Diz would write it down" (Gitler 1985: 148). According to Gillespie himself, Parker did not write music only because he did not want to take the time to do it: "I had been putting down Bird's solos on paper, which is something Bird never had the patience for himself" (Reisner 1977: 94).

In Russell's novel, however, all of this material is transformed in an interesting and revealing way. Parker's unwillingness to write music becomes a romanticized matter of strongly-held principle for Red Travers: "For Red Travers the act of committing sounds to staffed paper was a serious compromise of musical principle. As he viewed such matters, provided you could hear it, you certainly ought to be able to play it. And, if you didn't hear it, then you didn't really have any business trying to play it anyway. For him the act of musical creation was simply the extension of thought. For some time this had been the nature of his private quarrel with the school-trained performer, the sight readers, the academy, and the big bands"

(Russell 1961: 63). Again, this matter of principle is related to the notions that Travers is a musical genius while most other jazz players are simply hacks, and that black musicians create music while white musicians steal.

This latter point is reinforced with the "collaborative" relationship developed between Red Travers and Bernie Rich. Russell transforms the real-life, collaborative Gillespie-Parker relationship into one that displays an essential tension between black and white musicians. Whereas the real-life relationship was, as Trummy Young says, one in which Gillespie and Parker "really complemented one another . . . Diz got some things from Bird, and Bird got some things from Diz," Russell's fictional representation emphasizes the idea that black musicians were exploited by white musicians, composers, band leaders, managers, and so on (Gitler 1985: 148). At one point in their partnership, for example, Travers says to Rich, " 'I don't want no brain-picker with a music pen clipped in his coat pocket sitting at the piano in no band of mine. I don't want no dichty gray that thinks music is a lot of hen tracks put down on a piece of paper' " (1961: 217). This kind of exploitation is also used as an explanation for Red Travers's (and other jazz genuises') self-destructiveness. A white jazz musician, for example, compares Travers to Lester Young because both have had their ideas stolen from them without compensation and both wind up poor, unemployable alcoholics (1961: 163). Certainly, Russell's description of the institutional exploitation in the jazz music business is a valid and important point to make in the novel. However, Russell's transformation of this relationship has unintended effects on the construction of black and white in the novel. By transmuting Gillespie into a white man and by not creating any other African American character in the novel who transgresses the boundary between playing jazz and writing jazz, Russell makes *this* difference one between black and white. Thus, an essential part of blackness in the novel is improvisational jazz creation and playing without subsequent notation. Whiteness, on the other hand, is defined as blackness's opposite—lacking in improvisational creation but superior in synthesizing different jazz elements and preserving them on paper. Given the significance of literacy in the African American cultural tradition this distinction is not trivial.

This difference increases in importance because it contributes to the lack of agency in the depiction of African Americans, and the commensurate overattribution of agency in that of Euro Americans. Red Travers and the other African American musicians in *The Sound* are presented as being in control only of the creation of their music on the bandstand. Every other aspect of the music and the business is depicted as being in the hands of whites. Thus, while it may be accurate to fictionalize Parker himself this way, to represent *every* African American character this way is to ignore the example of people like Gillespie and to essentialize blackness as a pure position of victimization.

Furthermore, this positioning of black jazz musicians as victims also naturalizes the notion that making money (another form of maintaining control over one's creation) from the creation of jazz is not consistent with the kind of experience needed for creative jazz productivity. Although Red Travers realizes that he is being ripped off by managers, agents, band leaders, and club owners—" 'The owner is makin the money,' Red cried angrily. 'Booze ninety-five cents a drink and we're packin' the joint. This guinea is cleanin' up"—he is unable and unwilling to change because he fears that money and the security it will bring will sap his creativity (1961: 144).

This ethic is described in detail by another African American musician, the drummer Hassan, who explains to Bernie Rich the different attitudes black and white musicians have about money: "Well, the spade has it figured different. Take this movie loot now. To me it ain't worth while to stick around when my own true mind tells me it's time to head back. The spade figures money for something that comes and goes. Yes, man, I'm wise, we have to scuffle awful hard just to get enough to make out, but still we don't try to hold on to it forever. Maybe on account of we've had to travel second class so long we're used to getting our kicks out of common everyday stuff—food, and music and sex, and even religion" (1961: 101).

It is important that the character who speaks these words, Hassan, is depicted as one of the most reasonable, sober, reflective musicians in the novel—he has, for example, converted to Islam and is one of the only African American musicians who openly and warmly embraces a friendship with Bernie Rich. Thus, Red Travers's "irresponsible" behavior with money is portrayed not as idiosyncratic or aberrant, but as part of a pattern that is rooted in experience and can be intelligently articulated by the musicians themselves.

The white musicians, on the other hand, are represented not only as "realistic" about money and music—seeing jazz primarily as a business while also being unconcerned about the possibility that money will defile their artistic integrity— but also as genuinely and paternalistically concerned about the financial well-being of their black colleagues. After Bernie Rich, for example, "inadvertently" steals one of Red Travers's unpenned compositions, Rich voluntarily gives Travers "composer credit and royalties" and offers to form a writing partnership with him, saying: " 'You have a fortune kicking around in your head but it isn't worth a dime until somebody helps you mine it. Why, anybody else would have gone right ahead and stolen "The Chase" and been done' " (1961: 189). However, even in this regard Euro Americans are represented as different and "smarter" than African Americans because they are more hardheaded about money, friendship, and music. Bernie Rich is only willing to help Red out for so long and with so much money. After a certain point, Bernie decides that the best thing he can do for himself *and* for Travers is to sever ties with him and quit "enabling" him. The African American musicians, on the other hand, continue to help Red with money, drugs, or their company even past the point where it is good for them. While one could interpret this simply as loyalty, the novel encourages us to identify and agree with its central consciousness, Bernie Rich, who takes the "tough love" approach to Travers.

Of course, neither Kerouac's nor Russell's narrative strategy vis-a-vis Charlie Parker is fundamentally different from that used by earlier Euro American writers to depict African Americans generally. As Ralph Ellison explained in a 1946 essay on twentieth-century fiction, "they [Euro American writers like Faulkner] seldom conceive Negro characters possessing the full, complex ambiguity of the human. Too often what is presented as the American Negro (a most complex example of Western man) emerges an oversimplified clown, a beast or an angel. Seldom is he drawn as that sensitively focused process of opposites, of good and evil, of instinct and intellect, of passion and spirituality, which great literary art has projected as the image of man" (in Ellison 1964: 25–26). However, the depiction of Parker as a one-dimensional symbol is especially ironic since, by all accounts, one force motivating Parker and the other beboppers to create new jazz music *and* new jazz symbols was a desire to counter the image created by Louis Armstrong. Thus, in contrast to the stage personas created by such jazz stars of the 1920s and 1930s as Armstrong, Calloway, and Ellington, who emphasized their roles as entertainers *of predominantly white audiences* by "mugging . . . wearing a white satin suit . . . and white collar and tie, satin lapels, and a satin stripe down the leg," the beboppers made "a deliberate attempt to avoid playing the role of flamboyant black entertainer, which whites had come to expect" (Collier 1978: 360).

However, as Ralph Ellison suggests in his perceptive 1962 review article "On Bird, Bird-Watching, and Jazz," the effect of Parker's response to Armstrong's assumption of the clown role was to become a one-dimensional figure himself—that is, "a sacrificial figure whose struggles against personal chaos, on stage and off, served as entertainment for a ravenous, sensation-starved, culturally disoriented public which had but the slightest notion of its real significance" (1964: 227). This was especially true, Ellison notes, for the "educated white middle-class youth" who formed a cult around Parker in an expression of their dissatisfaction with American society and in a search for greater feeling and meaning in their lives. The Parker image we find in Russell's or Kerouac's novels is probably close to the one created by these white fans. However, this Bird—the "suffering, psychically wounded, law-breaking, life-affirming hero"—that Ellison says "lives . . . because his tradition and his art blew him to the meaningful center of things" is predominantly a whitened Bird; his image for interested African American audiences is significantly different (Ellison 1964: 228, 231).

Of course, the African American audience at the time was not, as a whole, any more receptive to the new music created by Parker and the beboppers than was most of the white audience. In *Blues People*, Amiri Baraka comments that "the willfully harsh, *anti-assimilationist* sound of bebop fell on deaf ears [among middle-class African Americans], just as it did in white America" (1963: 182). Or as drummer Art Blakey said when asked, after Bird's death, whether Parker had been important for African Americans during his life: "A symbol to the Negro people? No. They don't even know him. They never heard of him and care less. A symbol to the musicians, yes" (Reisner 1977: 51). However, those African American writers who did believe Parker was an important enough figure to fictionalize or refer to in their work constructed a significantly different image of the bebop legend than did their oppositional Euro American counterparts.

Before looking closely at the African American writing that presents images of Charlie Parker, I want to offer provisional explanations for the difference between the Parker figures portrayed in the work of African Americans and oppositional Euro Americans. Part of this difference is undoubtedly due to the increasing importance and urgency of political African American writing during the period under consideration. Although the period under study here was chosen specifically because it precedes the most intense and self-conscious political activity of the postwar era and thus limits the effect of this activity on writers, it is clear that the political developments during this period generally had a greater impact on the consciousness of African American writers than on that of Euro American writers (at least those who wrote about jazz). Later, as we approach and enter the early and mid-1960s, the work of many African American authors reverberates with a heightened concern for social and cultural separatism that suffused the nationalistic social movements of the time. These political forces affect the use of jazz in literature and, specifically, the depiction of Charlie Parker not only in the increased focus on these sources as *African American* cultural forms but also in the increased need to connect the music and musicians to political themes and goals. One of Ralph Ellison's contemporaneous criticisms of Amiri Baraka's 1963 book on African American music, *Blues People*—that it neglects the aesthetic elements of the music to emphasize the political and sociological elements—indicates the manifestation of these political forces in the writing about jazz during this period: "For the blues are not primarily concerned with civil rights or obvious political protest; they are an art form and thus a transcendence of those conditions created within the Negro community by the denial of social justice" (Ellison 1964: 257).

However, as part of a black oppositional discourse to color-blindness, these representations are more than simply isolated expressions of support for civil rights or of protest against white racism and social injustice. They are part of a fluid African American cultural process that expresses simultaneously a complex and valuable African American presence and an outspoken resistance to the obliteration of that presence by the dominant culture. As such, these representations help place an obstacle in the path of a dominant discourse that implicitly argues against the value and complexity of African American culture and the urgent need to change the relation of black to white in social and cultural relations. Moreover, the literary recognition that jazz and the jazz musician are an integral part of a larger group identity—African Americans—because they express ideas and emotions not expressed in Euro American culture is a notion that precedes the period under study here. As Nathan Huggins explains in his study of the Harlem Renaissance, Langston Hughes, virtually alone among his contemporaries, "took jazz seriously" as sophisticated cultural expression (Huggins 1972: 9–10). Hughes's essay, "The Negro Artist and the Racial Mountain" (1926), suggests the connections that are important to understanding postwar representations of jazz. Against those African Americans—James Weldon Johnson and Alain Locke, for example—who expected, under the sway of color-blindness, African American cultural forms like jazz to be transformed into something "better," Hughes argued that jazz was the real thing: "Jazz to me is one of the inherent expressions of Negro life in America; the eternal tom-tom beating in the Negro soul—the tom-tom of revolt against weariness in a white world, a world of subway trains, and work, work, work; the tom-tom of joy and laughter, and pain swallowed in a smile" (1926: 663). In a corollary to A. Philip Randolph's work in the social sphere, Hughes also insists in this essay that black poets should reject the black bourgeoisie's call to acquiesce to white society's unmarked standards of beauty and excellence but should instead bravely express and celebrate the forms that mark the difference of African American identity.

We can begin to confront the differences between African and Euro American representations of the jazz musician, I think, if we look at an African American source that is roughly contemporaneous with Dorothy Baker's novel and Mezz Mezzrow's autobiography but offers a significantly different representation of the jazz musician—a jazz portrait that has much in common with the later African American depictions of Charlie Parker. This source, Ann Petry's 1947 short story "Solo on Drums," offers a depiction of the jazz musician that does not reduce the musician's role to one that simply connects his musical vitality to his individualism and victimization. Instead, Petry creates a complex portrait that includes his individual pain and suffering but also focuses on his position as part of a historical and current community of people and traditions.

The main character in the story is a jazz drummer named Kid Jones who is about to take the stage for a performance as part of a jazz orchestra. As the story opens the reader learns, through an indirect narrative, that Jones is brooding on the fact that his wife has left him for the orchestra's pianist. Thus at the beginning of the story, Jones is represented as a victim and an individual who is mostly concerned about his own problems. As the story progresses and Jones accompanies the orchestra, he is transported back in time to remember a most personal incident: the morning hours when his wife told him about her affair with the piano player. The trumpet solo, especially, takes him back because it reminds him of his wife's voice: "He wanted to cover his ears with his hands because he kept hearing a voice that whispered the same thing over and over again. The voice was trapped somewhere under the roof—caught and held there by the trumpet. 'I'm leaving I'm leaving I'm leaving'" (1990: 54).

However, when the trumpet solo ends and "the spotlight shift[s] and land[s] on Kid Jones," his role shifts from the victimized, individually suffering husband into that of an undifferentiated, creative musical *force*: "The long beam of white light struck the top of his head and turned him into a pattern of light and shadow. Because of the cream-colored suit and shirt, his body seemed to be encased in light. But there was a shadow over his face so that his features blended and disappeared. His hairline receded so far back that he looked like a man with a face that never ended. A man with a high, long face and dark, dark skin" (1990: 55). Not only does Kid Jones seem physically to melt into his environment; he feels as though he is losing his identity to the music—"He began to feel as though he were the drums and drums were he"—and the audience too is enveloped in the flow of the music emanating from his drums: "The theater throbbed with the excitement of the drums. A man, sitting near the front, shivered and his head jerked to the rhythm. A sailor put his arm around the girl sitting beside him, took his hand and held her face still and pressed his mouth close over hers. Close. Close. Close. Until their faces seemed to melt together" (1990: 56).

As Kid Jones begins to become part of the music, he is taken by it through a series of ritual experiences that enable him to transform his painful, individual experiences into profoundly expressive music.[7] The series of experiences he has while playing are significant because of their sequence: his experience that morning with his wife leaving becomes simply one of several that contribute to the emotional intensity of his music. The narrator comments that "it was almost as though the drums were talking about his own life." Moreover, through the music and his performative dueling with the piano player, Kid Jones's painful personal experiences are also linked to the larger musical and cultural tradition of which he is a part:

> The drums took him away from them, took him back, and back, in time and space. He built up an illusion. He was sending out the news. Grandma died. The foreigner in the litter has an old disease and will not recover. The man from across the big water is sleeping with the chief's daughter. Kill. Kill. Kill. The war goes well with the men with

the bad smell and the loud laugh. It goes badly with the chiefs with the round heads and the peacock's walk.

It is cool in the deep track in the forest. Cool and quiet. The trees talk softly. They speak of the dance tonight The young girl from across the lake will be there. Her waist is slender and her thighs are rounded. (1990: 57)

Finally, all these experiences, from his personal life and from his cultural heritage, combine to create the emotional apotheosis of the music—that is, the point at which Kid Jones and his music are truly one: "He forgot the theater, forgot everything but the drums. He was welded to the drums, sucked inside them. All of him. His pulse beat. His heart beat. He had become part of the drums. They had become part of him" (1990: 58).

Yet, unlike the African American musicians depicted in Baker's novel or Mezzrow's autobiography, Kid Jones is not represented as a simpler, more carefree, happier man because he can express himself powerfully and emotionally in his music. Instead, when the performance is over, Kid Jones is portrayed as aware that his music is not only an art form in which his apparent catharsis is ritually enacted and temporary, but also that it is a commercial one, in which he exploits his own pain and suffering to entertain his audience: "When he finally stopped playing, he was trembling; his body was wet with sweat. He was surprised to see that the drums were sitting there in front of him. He hadn't become part of them. He was still himself. Kid Jones. Master of the drums. Greatest drummer in the world. Selling himself a little piece at a time. Every afternoon. Twice every evening. Only this time he had topped all his other performances. This time, playing like this after what had happened in the morning, he had sold all of himself—not just a little piece" (1990: 58). Petry represents Kid Jones as every bit as aware, complex, and entangled in modern social relations as would be any other American artist. The image of the African American musician presented in "Solo on Drums" encompasses the spectrum of roles or identities (and then some) that Euro American writers tend to differentiate by race: individual, community member, victim, opportunist, artist, innovator, primitive, and modern man. Blackness as a sign in Petry, then, is both specific and universal—specific because it refers to the traditional roles fulfilled by musicians in African American culture and by African Americans in American society, and universal because it refers as well to roles that could be fulfilled by white or black members of American society.

Of course, not every African American writer who fictionalized or referred to Charlie Parker in their work followed Petry's lead and represented Bird in every one of the roles fulfilled by Kid Jones. After all, these portraits were somewhat limited because Parker was an actual person. However, the roles Parker does fill in these writings differ from those ascribed to him by Euro American writers such as Ross Russell and Jack Kerouac. The most salient distinction between Euro and African American writers' representations of Parker is the emphasis placed on race, community, and culture. As we have seen, Euro American writers tend to deemphasize these concepts in favor of more universal notions such as victimization, the persecution and suffering peculiar to the plight of the artist, and artistic transcendence. As we will see (and saw in Petry), African American writers tend to integrate collective and universal themes in their representations of Parker. However, even when these writers engage the same universal themes as their Euro American counterparts they invest them with the concerns or interests connected to a common blackness shared with Parker.

This basic difference can be seen in two works that use Parker in a limited manner: James Baldwin's 1957 short story "Sonny's Blues" and Amiri Baraka's 1964 play *Dutchman*. Written only seven years apart, these works are nonetheless the products of two different political environments and perspectives. As Sigmund Ro and others have noted, Baldwin's story partakes of "the whole integration ethos of the first postwar decade," while Baraka's play marks the beginning of his and other African Americans' symbolic and physical break with white society (Ro 1984: 10). Despite these differences, however, both works use Charlie Parker as an explicitly racial and political symbol, as a symbol that marks both a distinction between blackness and whiteness *and* a blackness of a particular political orientation.

"Sonny's Blues" presents a conflict between two brothers, each of whom represents (among other things) a typical position of the African American male of the 1950s. The narrator is a former soldier in the U.S. Army, now a schoolteacher, who lives with his wife and children in Harlem. His younger brother, Sonny, is a jazz musician and recently recovering heroin addict who lives and plays music in Greenwich Village. Early in the story Baldwin develops each of these characters to emphasize the differences between them. Baldwin makes it clear that these differences are the result of a cluster of factors including "generation" (not only is there a seven-year gap between their ages, but the gap separates the more idealistic prewar generation from the more cynical postwar one), circumstance (when Sonny is only fifteen he loses both his adult male role models due to the death of their father and the narrator's departure for the Army), temperament (the artist and nonartist), and experience (as a musician Sonny is exposed to drugs, night life, etc.). However, the broader implication from early in the story is that the narrator, despite living in Harlem, has lost contact with his racial heritage (that is, his immediate and extended history, the people living in Harlem, the experience of racism) while his brother, despite having moved out of Harlem, has struggled and continues to struggle with this lineage. As Baldwin's biographer David Leeming notes, in many ways the brothers in "Sonny's Blues" closely parallel Baldwin and his own brother David (Leeming 1994: 135–36).

As critics have argued, these differences are encapsulated in the contemporary intracultural conflict suggested by Baldwin's association of the older brother with Louis Armstrong and the younger with Charlie Parker. The context of this comparison is an argument, told in a flashback, between the narrator and his brother. When Sonny tells his brother that he plans to be a jazz musician, his brother's response comes from the prewar black bourgeoisie: "I simply couldn't see why on earth he'd want to spend his time hanging around night clubs, clowning around on band-stands, while people pushed each other around a dance floor. It seemed—beneath him, somehow. I had never thought about it before, had never been forced to, but I suppose I had always put jazz musicians in a class with what Daddy called 'good-time people'" (Baldwin 1990: 110). Nevertheless, Sonny's brother tries his best to be supportive and to connect with Sonny by showing that he understands Sonny's ambitions:

> I suggested helpfully: "You mean—like Louis Armstrong?"
> His face closed as though I'd struck him. "No. I'm not talking about none of that old-time, down-home crap."
> "Well, look, Sonny, I'm sorry, don't get mad. I just don't altogether get it, that's all. Name somebody—you know, a jazz musician you admire."
> "Bird."
> "Who?"
> "Bird! Charlie Parker! Don't they teach you nothing in the goddamn army?"
> I lit a cigarette. I was surprised and then a little amused to discover that I was trembling. "I've been out of touch," I said, "You'll have to be patient with me. Now. Who's this Parker character?"
> "He's just one of the greatest jazz musicians alive," said Sonny, sullenly, his hands in his pockets, his back to me. "Maybe the greatest," he added bitterly, "that's probably why you never heard of him." (1990: 110)

This simple contrast is significant because it indicates a use of Parker that differs from those of Euro American writers. Baldwin's use is specific to a conflict within African American culture in the immediate postwar period between the older, black middle class and the "younger" generation of African Americans coming of age during and after the war. Parker, in this sense, is an important symbol of *African American* modernity, claiming independence, defiance, complexity.

Even more important, though, is the way Baldwin develops the Sonny character as the fictional equivalent of Charlie Parker. With the explicit connection between Sonny and Parker as well as the similarities—that both are heroin addicts, both make music because they suffer, and both are gifted musicians (though Sonny plays piano)—Baldwin's implication is clear: not only does Sonny admire Parker, but he is supposed to be like Bird. Although these initial, superficial similarities suggest that Baldwin's further use of Parker does not differ significantly from the Euro American use of him as a suffering musical genius, the development of the Sonny character hints otherwise.

Baldwin connects Sonny's suffering and his powerful music (and therefore Bird's) to many factors that are specifically African American. The most important of these is African American manhood. Sonny and his brother are linked in the narrative to their father and their uncle (their father's brother). Like Sonny, his uncle was one of those African American males who "gets sucked under" and was "always kind of frisky." One Saturday night, when Sonny's father and uncle were out going from one dance to another, the uncle was run over and killed by a car full of drunk, white men. Sonny's mother describes this incident (to Sonny's brother) as an important but not unusual event and an "accident": "They [the white men] was having fun, they just wanted to scare him, the way they do sometimes, you know. But they was drunk. And I guess the boy, being drunk, too, and scared, kind of lost his head. By the time he jumped it was too late." Furthermore, the mother says, "Your Daddy never did really get right again. Till the day he died he weren't sure but that every white man he saw was the man that killed his brother." Finally, the mother tells Sonny's brother, "I'm telling you this because you got a brother. And the world ain't changed" (1990: 107).

Concerning Sonny's character this connection is important because it locates him in a history of violence, victimization, and suffering that is specific to African American people—obviously at the hands of white Americans. This history or tradition becomes even more important at the end of the story when Sonny's performing reconnects the narrator with Sonny and this aspect of African American history. The music generally (labeled "the blues" by Baldwin), then, and Sonny's musical genius specifically (improvisational) are inextricably connected with this characteristically African American historical experience.

Moreover, unlike the Euro American construction of the African American jazz musician in which jazz allows the musician to express a natural "harmony" (Mezzrow) or a "kindness" (Kerouac), Baldwin's construction is linked to anger, brutality, and violence. That is, it is connected to not only the kind of violence committed by whites against blacks, but also the anger blacks feel as a response to the oppression they have experienced and continue to experience. Thus Sonny speaks of jazz as a way of "getting it out—that storm inside" and explains his need to play music in terms that frighten his brother with the intensity of the violence behind it: " 'Sometimes you'll do *anything* to play, even cut your mother's throat.' He laughed and look at me. 'Or your brother's.' Then he sobered. 'Or your own' " (1990: 123). This constructed connection between the jazz musician and the violence or rage that derives from their social experience is one of the main ways African American writers have tried to reclaim Charlie Parker from the universalists. Novelist John A. Williams, for example, says that "It is mere nonsense to believe that Charlie Parker existed his life and died his death as any other person might have done in America regardless of race or creed" (1973: 222). The universalists' strategy, he says, of transforming Parker into the stereotypical suffering artist is to misrepresent him: "Dividing the music from Parker's embattled Negro personality is schizoidal and ignoring the culture that produced both is ridiculous. But it was done" (1973: 230).

The construction of jazz as a violent and aggressive versus a joyful and ecstatic expression, then, is a significant contrast between the work of African and Euro American writers. As Lorenzo Thomas has recently argued in distinguishing the poetry of African American Beat Bob Kaufman from that of Kerouac, "Unlike Kerouac, Kaufman knew very well that jazz was not mere ecstasy, that it was as dangerous to ordinary American illusions as every beatnik's mother said it was. Jazz was an overdose of reality" (Thomas 1992: 295). The violence or aggressiveness that is used by African American writers to characterize jazz is part of what transforms the victimization and suffering of racial oppression into a positive, creative force. Thomas says that Kaufman, for example, "is not content to paint the jazz musician merely as a martyr sacrificed to jargon-spouting philistines in shades . . . the music also encodes a more aggressive response to the racially motivated humiliations that frame the jazz artist's life—and the lives of all Black people. Kaufman's musicians squeeze out notes as if they are hurling spears" (1992: 295).

The African American literary interest in and emphasis on violence and hostility increases, of course, as the 1960s progress. Amiri Baraka's 1964 play *Dutchman* not only provides a trenchant example of this trend but also displays remarkable similarities with Baldwin's linking of violence and jazz (in the figure of Charlie Parker) in "Sonny's Blues." Baraka's play comments harshly on the inability and unwillingness of white Americans, especially those who profess a "love" for African Americans, genuinely to understand the experience and position of black Americans. In a particularly intense, passionate monologue near the end of the play, Charlie Parker and blues singer Bessie Smith are cited as black cultural symbols whites have, to some degree, "accepted" and "appreciated" but not understood. As Kimberly Benston characterizes Baraka's construct, "White people believe they can penetrate the pure, pumping black heart by learning a few of black culture's symbols and venerating a few of its more obvious leaders" (Benston 1976: 166). Like the Parkeresque character Sonny in Baldwin's story, Parker's musical passion is characterized in *Dutchman* as the result of his need "to get it out—the storm inside." However, Baraka, unlike Baldwin, explicitly describes the storm inside as the storm of anger that is targeted directly at white people: " 'Charlie Parker? Charlie Parker. All the hip white boys scream for Bird. And Bird saying "Up your ass, feeble-minded ofay! Up your ass." And they sit there talking about the tortured genius of Charlie Parker. Bird would've played not a note of music if he just walked up to East Sixty-seventh Street and killed the first ten white people he saw. Not a note!'" (Baraka 1964: 35). This anger is characterized not only as the force that propels Parker to such great heights in music, but also as actually being in the music in coded form. As Baraka says about Bessie Smith in the same speech, "If Bessie Smith had killed some white people she wouldn't have needed that music. She could have talked very straight and plain about the world. No metaphors. Nor grunts. No wiggles in the dark of her soul. Just straight two and two are four. Money. Power. Luxury" (1964: 35). John Williams makes a similar observation about Charlie Parker when he says that after Bird's stay at Camarillo State Hospital "There was anger in his tone and lyricism more haunting and beautiful than before—as though what it symbolized could never be attained in life and thus had become more desirous" (Williams 1973: 228).

The "hip white boys" who "scream for Bird" and worship his "tortured genius" cannot decode this anger because they, like most white people, remain willfully ignorant of both the experience behind the anger and the cultural language used to express the anger and describe the experience. Similarly, the Euro Americans who write about Parker do not hear the anger or are uninterested in it. Perhaps part of this apparent deficit in Euro American writing has to do with the lack of agency given to African American characters and figures by white writers. This agency is necessary to transform suffering and victimization into anger, hostility, and violence.

A final interesting example of the difference between portraits of Parker by Euro and by African Americans can be found in the main character in William Melvin Kelley's 1965 novel *A Drop of Patience*. Although he seems to be a combination of a few different jazz musicians (Bud Powell and, especially, Lennie Tristano come to mind), Ludlow Washington's primary model is undoubtedly Charlie Parker. Washington is portrayed as a 1940s-era jazz pioneer who is considered, like Parker, to have "invented modern jazz" (Kelley 1965: 127). Furthermore, Washington is represented using some of the details of Parker's career: his jazz inventions are initially developed while he plays as part of a group in Harlem; other jazz musicians worship him and "can even play [his] solos note for note" (1965: 130–31).

What is especially interesting about Kelley's portrait, however, is his almost complete rejection of the standard depiction of Parker as a doomed, suffering genius. Kelley, in fact, almost reverses the Parker trajectory by depicting Washington as an unwanted, neglected, unappreciated child who finds himself and meaning in life through his interest in and talent for music. Moreover, whatever "genius" Washington has for jazz and whatever enjoyment he derives from the music are both unavoidably connected to the historical and contemporary community of African American musicians. While other people, for example, credit Washington with "inventing modern jazz," he and the dramatic detail of the novel suggest that his innovations are, more accurately, *contributions* to the evolution of African American music, and furthermore, that these innovations were developed in collaboration with other musicians.

In an "Interview" that introduces one of the novel's sections, for example, Washington says:

> What's all this mess about me coming to New York and inventing modern jazz? Right out, there are two things wrong with that.
>
> First of all, I don't think I invented it alone. I mean, lots of us did it. We all sat up in Harlem and put the new stuff together. It wasn't just me. I got things from them; they got things from me.
>
> And second of all, if I did invent it, like they say, I invented it back in New Marsails in Bud Rodney's band, or maybe even before that, in the blind home. Because all my life I been playing what I liked. Take Norman Spencer. He coulda been the one who invented it hisself. He was doing new things way back in the twenties. I only listened and played what I liked in him and that was that. I didn't decide one day—blam!—I'd play something new, because I been playing pretty much the same since I was thirteen, except now maybe I can play a little faster. But that ain't genius. That's just practicing. (1965: 127)

This construction is significantly different from the Euro American position that emphasizes the singular genius of a musician like Charlie Parker and foregrounds his *break* with tradition and his isolation from those around him. As Albert Murray suggests, the different conception of innovation embodied here is basic to an understanding of the entire blues idiom:

> The self-portrait (and/or the personal signature) that emerges from the music of Jelly Roll Morton, King Oliver, Bessie Smith, Louis Armstrong, Duke Ellington, Lester Young, and Charlie Parker is not primarily a matter of such egotistical self-documentation but rather of the distinction with which they fulfilled inherited roles in the traditional ritual of blues confrontation and improvisation. Incidentally, the revolutionary nature of their improvisations and syntheses was not nearly so much a matter of a quest for newness for the sake of change as of the modifications necessary in order to maintain the definitive essentials of the idiom. (Murray 1976: 25–52)

In the novel, the self-effacing attitude Ludlow Washington expresses in his "Interview" is supported by the action that precedes and follows it. That is, Kelley represents Washington as a musician who achieves originality by working hard, learning from his predecessors and peers, and having the courage never to cease searching for new sounds to express himself: "He had known too that he was tired of what music sounded like—heavy and loud—and so at sessions he had suggested to the other men how they might play a certain song. But he had never thought of this as a new style; he was simply trying to get a sound to the music that he liked" (1965: 131).

Above all else, then, Washington's gift for music is depicted as coming from, being developed by, and being intended for African American people. Washington's character evolves along a trajectory that emphasizes a network of African American musicians and is similar to the one followed by Charlie Parker: he starts as an "apprentice" in a band with a nurturing leader (Bud Rodney/Jay McShann); learns about innovation by listening carefully to the recorded sounds of an established player (Norman Spencer/Lester Young); develops a modern jazz language in cooperation with other contemporary players; and influences the subsequent generation of younger musicians. The cultural specificity of this trajectory is reinforced by a narrative that continually notes the fundamental differences between black and white musicians and black and white audiences. Although Washington himself is depicted as naive when it comes to racial difference (obviously because of his lack of eyesight), he is continually told and discovers that there are significant differences and conflicts between blacks and whites. Washington gains intimate knowledge of these differences and conflicts after he feels abused by a white woman with whom he has a relationship.

These themes are brought together at the end of the novel when Washington decides to leave New York to find work elsewhere. Washington leaves, specifically, because he becomes discouraged playing for mostly white audiences that do not appreciate his music: "But in New York they did not dance, they did not listen. The audience sat and talked, and in a corner, where their music would not bother the audience too much the musicians played" (1965: 230). These audiences are juxtaposed, in Washington's mind, to those he has been told existed in Harlem in earlier years: "He remembered what Norman Spencer had told him once about the old Harlem rent parties. 'We wasn't making no money then, but hell, man, you knew that the twenty or thirty or fifty folks in that one small, cabbage-smelling room was enjoying what you was doing. You'd lean into the keys, and behind you they was having the best old time ever. Shit, you ask me why I don't go downtown? That's another reason.' Ludlow smiled, remembering the pianist's bitter voice. Too bad there were no more rent parties" (1965: 231). However, unlike Charlie Parker or the Euro American constructed Charlie Parker character who self-destructs because of his lack of acceptance and recognition, Washington decides to leave "the jazz life" and return to the "folk": "There were other, better places to go. He might find that storefront church, or perhaps a church on a dirt road in the South, no more than a shack, with a congregation of twelve or so, without an organ to help their high, shaky voices carry tunes of their hymns. A place like that would need a good musician" (1965: 237).

The actual Charlie Parker's last days were only pathetically similar to Kelley's romantic account of Ludlow Washington. According to Gary Giddins, near the end of his life Parker, in fact, "sometimes played in joints that were little more than storefronts, usually with minor musicians" (1987: 115). However, these anonymous gigs were not part of a greater, more noble plan of Parker's to return to his roots and the people who loved him. Instead, they were the only, meager shards of self-respect that Parker could gather from his shattered life. According to Ross Russell, during Parker's last few months, "he roamed Washington Square, the lower Village and the East Side, visited bars and small night clubs and occasionally played, with young musicians he scarcely knew, with no other compensation than a few drinks grudgingly poured by the management" (1996: 342). Parker's final attempt at a comeback—the infamous, disastrous show at Birdland in early March 1955—ended in a wretched argument between Parker and Bud Powell. Parker died a few weeks later.

A sign of the instability of our knowledge of Parker's life at present is the fact that the most comprehensive biography of Bird—Ross Russell's *Bird Lives*—is famous for its blend of fact and fiction. Short though it was (he died at thirty-four), Parker's life was so full of contradictory impulses and actions that it provided material for a range of representations, none of which can claim the status of truth. The story of Parker's life and work became a touchstone for every kind of authenticity that was important in the postwar period: using it, hipsters and Beats validated their rejection of American society's middle-class values; jazz musicians measured their quest for pure, bluesy, musical solos; and African Americans verified the pain and joy of their condition in the United States.

4.

(Up)Staging Jazz

Representations of Jazz Performance

> I remember one day being in a music history class and a white woman was the teacher. She was up in front of the class saying that the reason black people played the blues was because they were poor and had to pick cotton. So they were sad and that's where the blues came from, their sadness. My hand went up in a flash and I stood up and said, "I'm from East St. Louis and my father is rich, he's a dentist, and I play the blues. My father didn't never pick no cotton and I didn't wake up this morning sad and start playing the blues. There's more to it than that." (Davis 1989: 59)

Like the figure of Charlie Parker, jazz performance is a significant site of conflict between African and Euro American literary representations. Because of its indisputable importance to jazz, "live performance"—that is, musicians working in front of an audience on the street, in a club or theater, at a celebration, or anywhere else—figures prominently in the literary uses and depictions of jazz and jazz musicians by both African and Euro Americans. A comparison of these uses and depictions, however, reveals significant differences between the two kinds of texts. This chapter will focus on differences in the representation of two aspects of jazz performance: the relationship between musicians and the audience, and relationships among the players themselves.

Before we look at the literature of the 1950s and 1960s, a few brief points should be made about the importance of live performance to jazz. Unlike some other kinds of music, performance is essential to jazz. Unlike European classical music, for example, jazz emphasizes improvisation—invention during the act of performance—over either composition or reproducing a written score. Jazz is part of a cultural tradition in which live performance is central to the creation of music. Historians agree that this tradition reaches back to West African culture in which music was "an integral part of everyday life" and was used in a wide variety of rituals and ceremonies (Southern 1983: 21–22). According to Eileen Southern, the importance of performance did not decrease following the diaspora and the experience of slavery in the United States: "The single most important element of the slave music was its performance as, indeed, is true of black folk music in the twentieth century" (1983: 200).

Furthermore, in both West Africa and the United States musical performance was vital to the establishment and development of a community of people. As James Lincoln Collier notes, the communal nature of musical performance can be traced back to West Africa: "Besides ritual, the African has another device for affirming his bond with group: music . . . [it] is a social glue; it is a way for him to act out many of his feelings for his tribe, his family, the people around him" (1978: 7–8). As Lawrence W. Levine makes clear, this same communal value in music—in the form of the call-and-response or antiphonal pattern—was equally important in the development of such African American genres as the work song and the spiritual (1977: 24, 33). "Communal participation" was so important to music during this time, in fact, that Eileen Southern goes so far as to say that "among blacks there was no audience, only performers and nonperformers" (1983: 202).

Jazz itself developed, according to Collier, out of such performance venues as "honky-tonks, the picnic grounds, the brothels, [and] the streets of New Orleans" (1978: 63). This lineage of public performance means that, from the beginning, jazz musicians learned to play first by listening to other players and imitating their sounds, and second by interacting with and responding to the audience. These methods of learning and of playing became part of the jazz tradition. Even among modern jazz musicians, many of whom have formal training, these methods are deemed essential. Pianist Cecil Taylor, for example, says, "I had found that you get more from the musicians if you teach them the tunes by ear, if they have to listen for changes instead of reading them off the page, which again has something to do with the whole jazz tradition, with how the cats in New Orleans at the turn of the century made their tunes. That's our thing, and not composition" (Spellman 1985: 70–71). On the importance of the audience to performance, Collier says that "Most jazz musicians like to work in front of a live audience, especially a dancing audience. They get something back from an audience that is reacting, that is involved with them in the music" (1978: 6). Thus, although jazz developed simultaneously with (and, according to Marshall Stearns, in large part because of) the spread of phonograph records, live public performance has remained an essential part of the vitality of jazz (Stearns 1958: 190). It is not surprising, then, that the live jazz performance has been invested with so much symbolic power by both African and Euro American texts.

The particular foci of these representations are the interaction between the performer and the audience, and the creative process of the performer himself. The first of these obviously reflects the communal value that has been constitutive of musical performance in the African and African American tradition. Both Euro and African American writers interested in jazz recognize the importance of performer/audience interaction to the creation of the music. As we will see, however, the particular communities constructed by Euro and African American authors are quite different. The second focal point of these representations also reflects an essential element of African American music: improvisation. In this literature, improvisation—or, more generally, the jazz musician's creative process while on the bandstand—is invested with a multiplicity of meanings, ranging from the strictly musical to the cultural, political, historical, and social.

James Baldwin's 1957 short story "Sonny's Blues" is, perhaps, jazz literature's most widely read piece. At least part of the reason for its popularity is its eloquent, evocative depiction of a specific dual energy in African American music: the expression of both individual and collective experience. As Albert Murray suggests in *Stomping the Blues*, the most significant contributions to the blues and jazz— "the music of Jelly Roll Morton, King Oliver, Bessie Smith, Louis Armstrong, Duke Ellington, Lester Young, and Charlie Parker"—are the result of the colliding forces of invention (that is, individual experience transformed by genius or talent) and convention (that is, inherited experience encoded in existing forms): "the revolutionary nature of their improvisations and syntheses was not nearly so much a matter of a quest for newness for the sake of change as of the modifications necessary in order to maintain the definitive essentials of the idiom" (Murray 1976: 252). As Murray implies, the colliding forces of invention and convention are equally responsible for the evolution of styles within African American music (as with all aesthetic productions). This point is significant with respect to jazz because the intense focus on improvisation in jazz very often misleads observers either to privilege invention and individuality over convention and collectivity or to ignore the latter altogether. This is, in fact, true of most of the Euro American texts from this period that include representations of jazz.

African American texts, on the other hand, are more often cognizant of the dual forces of invention and convention in jazz. This may have as much to do with their complex relationship with the United States itself as with their greater knowledge of the jazz and blues idioms. With his sure feel for the complexity, hypocrisy, irony and other conflicting conditions in American life, James Baldwin was well-suited to offer a representation of jazz that did not succumb to any of the simplifications that nag most attempts to render it in literature. In "Sonny's Blues," Baldwin's sensitivity to the complexity of jazz means that he takes seriously the musician's (Sonny's) individual experiences, talents, and aspirations as well as the collective forces—tradition, history, family—shaping the expression of his individuality. His story about a relationship between two brothers develops themes that reveal tensions in postwar African American communities.[1] In part, Baldwin does this by comparing the brothers' conflicts to those reported in the media between the older and younger generations of jazz musicians—Louis Armstrong and the beboppers. However, as with this well-reported (but, according to retrospective accounts by the participants, overblown) tension in the 1940s and 1950s between boppers, like Gillespie and Parker, and the one established jazz "star"—Louis Armstrong—Sonny and the narrator have much more in common than their superficial differences would suggest.

Baldwin reveals these commonalities in the story's concluding scene, in which the narrator ventures into a Greenwich Village nightclub to hear his brother perform. Following on the heels of an extended, passionate discussion between the brothers about human suffering and the various ways—socially acceptable and not—people express and alleviate it, the narrator's attendance at the nightclub is a mutual attempt by the brothers to set aside their differences and reestablish their lapsed bonds of kinship and support. The performance marks not only the first time the narrator has heard Sonny perform in public, but also the first time Sonny has performed since he was hospitalized to cure his heroin addiction. By creating tension around each of these narrative elements, Baldwin imbues Sonny's performance (and the narrator's experience of it) with the weight of the story's symbolic meaning.

A significant part of this symbolic meaning is attached to the interaction between Sonny, the performer, and his brother, an audience member. Although there is a personal or private dimension to this interaction (that is, a line of communication from brother to brother), Baldwin makes clear that the significance of this interaction has another, perhaps more important level. He does this in two ways. First, during Sonny's performance the narrator consistently shifts from singular to collective first person pronouns (that is, from "I" to "we" and "us") to guide the reader's attention from the personal level to a more general one that includes at least the empathic parts of the nightclub audience and, perhaps, even the African American community as a whole: "Freedom lurked around us and I understood, at last, that he [Sonny] could help us to be free if we would listen, that he would never be free until we did" (Baldwin 1990: 129). Baldwin's use of the trope "freedom" to express the possibilities inherent in the improvisational performance of jazz strongly connects the music and this depiction to African American history and tradition.

Baldwin provides an even clearer clue to the larger significance of jazz performance, however, in a passage in which the narrator *tells* the reader that the music, when it is successful, communicates truths that transcend the personal and form a bond between performer and audience: "All I know about music is that not many people ever really hear it. And even then, on the rare occasions when something opens within, and the music enters, what we mainly hear, or hear corroborated, are personal, private, vanishing evocations. But the man who creates the music is hearing something else, is dealing with the roar rising from the void and imposing order on it as it hits the air. What is evoked in him, then, is of another order, more terrible because it has no words, and triumphant, too, for that same reason. And his triumph, when he triumphs, is ours" (1990: 127). Baldwin's narrator suggests that, in the abstract, the performer and his audience are connected in two ways. First, this bond consists of their common recognition of some horrible, ineffable experience that is expressed in music during the performance. Second, the performer/audience nexus comprises a common present-tense experience of "triumphing" over "the roar rising from the void" by performing/listening to the music at the time it is performed.

The concepts expressed in this passage remain vague at this point in the story because the narrator has not yet heard Sonny perform. Not having had much experience with jazz or live performance (remember, his musical knowledge seems to have stopped with Louis Armstrong), the narrator offers his initial ideas about the connection between performer and audience as limited speculation: "All I know about music is. . . ." However, once he hears Sonny and his fellow musicians play, the narrator amplifies his ideas based on his own experience in the Greenwich Village nightclub. Listening to Sonny play intensifies the narrator's beliefs about the way jazz is created (from experiences that contain but also transcend the musician's own life) and the connection between the performer and audience (one that is tight and based on both the ugliness and the beauty of existence) but, more importantly, grounds his initial speculation in the specific tradition of African American experience. The vaguer wording of the narrator's initial comments on music are echoed during the performance scene, but embellished with more specific descriptors and referents that link his earlier, more universal description to the specific history of black people in the United States.

In the earlier passage the narrator noted that the musician creates music by "dealing with the roar rising from the void and imposing order on it as it hits the air." However, as he describes Sonny's playing, the narrator clarifies what the "void" and the "order" are. These two poles of the "terrible" and the "triumphant" are revealed on several different levels as the narrator witnesses Sonny put "himself" into his music. On the most basic level, the void is signified by the song the group plays: the popular composition "Am I Blue." A popular song of the sort that musicians during the bebop era loved to perversely and purposefully twist into all sorts of unconventional harmonic and rhythmic shapes, "Am I Blue" is given an "almost sardonic" treatment by the quartet. The musicians take this hollow standard (the "void") which has co-opted the basic element of African American music in its title—the blues—and transform it into, return it to, that very African American form (the "order"). Moreover, by reappropriating this song Sonny and the band make the music—both the whitened version of the blues and the blues itself—theirs: "Creole [the bassist] began to tell us what the blues were all about. They were not about anything very new. He and his boys up there were keeping it new, at the risk of ruin, destruction, madness, and death, in order to find new ways to make us listen. For, while the tale of how we suffer, and how we are delighted, and how we may triumph is never new, it always must be heard" (1990: 129). The musicians are able to make the music "theirs," while at the same time "keeping it new" by adding their experience to those experiences that have preceded them: "Sonny's fingers filled the air with life, his life. But that life contained so many others" (1990: 129).

Baldwin characterizes the link between the performer and the audience (as represented by the narrator's understanding of Sonny's music) in terms that lead the reader to associate the music with the African American experience. As he becomes increasingly immersed in the music via his brother's solo, the narrator returns to the idea that Sonny's performance is telling the story of many people's lives: "He had made it his; that long line, of which we knew only Mama and Daddy" (1990: 129). Although the connections he makes with his brother through the music begin with their common experiences as family members, the images themselves—involving three dead family members—and the experiences depicted in them transcend the particular and resonate with a more general African American history. According to Amiri and Amina Baraka, this connection between black music and African American history is fundamental: "But also its sound, its total art face, carries the lives, history, tradition, pain, and hope, in the main of the African-American people, not accidentally or as a form of sterile hat tipping but as a *result*, one significant result of all those categories. The music is one part of black life that identifies it as what it is, African-American" (Baraka and Baraka 1987: 320).

All three of the images remembered by the narrator in "Sonny's Blues" involve his grief over the suffering of someone he loved. First, the narrator "sees" the image of his mother, a woman who Baldwin has earlier, superficially, represented as having lived a life subordinated to her husband's anger and her own concern over the safety of her "men" (that is, her husband and two sons). Sonny's interpretation of the music, though, enables the narrator to focus on his mother's own suffering: "I saw my mother's face again, and felt, for the first time, how the stones of the road she had walked on must have bruised her feet." The narrator transcends the purely personal with this image first by using a metaphor for his mother's suffering. Then, by using a metaphor that connects his mother's life and suffering to a rural experience, the narrator subtly associates his mother's life with the historical experience of African American women.

The preceding metaphor also links the image of the mother with the next one, of "the moonlit road where my father's brother died." This image reminds the reader of an earlier story, told by the narrator's mother, about a black man (the brothers' uncle) who was run over by a car "full of white men" while he was walking on a country road. Telling her oldest son this story while he is on leave from the Army, the mother uses it to instruct the narrator about the need for him to look after and take care of his brother (she believes—correctly, it turns out—that *she* is dying). The narrator's recollection of the story during Sonny's solo is significant for a number of reasons. First, as with the preceding metaphor, the introduction of this piece of family history in the context of rural life—a "moonlit road"—ensures that it resonates back through African American history. Second, the image reminds the reader of another salient aspect of African American history—racist violence and its effect on African American people. The story of the uncle's death is one that is horrible in its simplicity, senselessness, and tragedy: the white men "aimed the car straight at" the uncle because they were "having fun, they just wanted to scare him, the way they do sometimes, you know." However, being drunk, the uncle could not get out of the way in time and he was hit and killed. Moreover, the boys' father is devastated by his brother's death. His wife says that he "never did really get right again. Till the day he died he weren't sure but that every white man he saw was the man that killed his brother" (1990: 107). Third, the image refers the reader to the mother's motivation for telling the narrator the story—worried about Sonny (and sensing she will not be around long enough to take care of him), she reminds the narrator that the dangers his father and uncle faced on those country roads still exist.

The final image in this sequence concerns the narrator's two-year-old daughter, Grace, who has recently died of polio. This image is explicitly connected to the preceding one and brings the rush of the narrator's emotion deriving from Sonny's music to an apotheosis: "And it ['the moonlit road' of the previous image] brought something else back to me, and carried me past it; I saw my little girl again and felt Isabel's tears again, and I felt my own tears begin to rise" (1990: 130). Once again, this image refers to an earlier passage in the story, in which the narrator describes how his daughter died: suddenly one day she collapsed on the living room floor without a sound. The narrator's wife, Isabel, ran into the room to find "little Grace on the floor, all twisted up, and the reason she hadn't screamed was that she couldn't get her breath. And when she did scream, it was the worst sound" (1990: 117). Their daughter's death, occurring in this terrible manner, haunts Isabel so much that she hears their daughter's scream in her sleep. When she does, the narrator says, "Isabel will sometimes wake me up with a low, moaning, strangled sound, and I have to be quick to awaken her and hold her to me, and where Isabel is weeping against me seems a mortal wound" (1990: 117). On the most obvious level, the memory of the narrator's daughter (and her tragic death) during Sonny's solo completes a circle of family suffering and tragedy—

from the distant past (the uncle the narrator did not know) through the more recent past (his mother) through the present and potential future (his daughter). The daughter's death, though, also represents the narrator's inability to look after his loved one, his ward. In this sense as well, her death is connected both to his uncle's death and his father's suffering (that is, his father's inability to protect his brother), and to his own commitment to take care of Sonny. In the earlier scene describing his daughter's death, the narrator says that he "may have written Sonny the very day that little Grace was buried. I was sitting in the living room in the dark, by myself, and I suddenly thought of Sonny. My trouble made his real" (1990: 117).

While the death of his daughter brought the narrator closer to an intellectual understanding of his brother's pain and suffering, it is not until Sonny's solo that the narrator experiences the emotions associated with his and his family's tragedies: "I felt my own tears begin to rise." Baldwin represents the music, then, as important in its ability to evoke not only common experiences among individuals and groups but also the emotions that create and secure experiential bonds among people. Even more importantly, though, Baldwin recognizes that music is powerful but greatly limited compared to the dangers posed by society: "And I was yet aware that this was only a moment, that the world waited outside, as hungry as a tiger, and that trouble stretched above us, longer than the sky" (1990: 130). Unlike most of the Euro Americans who are enamored of jazz and see it as capable of great, almost religious or magical transcendence, Baldwin and other African Americans temper their representations of jazz with the recognition that the transformative effect of music is only one weapon in the arsenal against hate, violence, and hardship. In the case of Sonny and the narrator, for example, Baldwin makes it clear that however much the music fortifies them or enables them to speak to each other, the real work—in the "world outside"—is up to them.

In his novels Jack Kerouac evinces an interest in both of these focal points of jazz performance, but especially in the interaction between performer and audience. In passages both related and unrelated to his idolization of Charlie Parker, Kerouac constructs this relationship in a unique, but unsurprising way: as a conduit of empathy and energy flowing from African American performers to particular Euro American audience members. In other words, the specific community Kerouac constructs with this relationship includes African and Euro Americans together but not in equal positions. The inequity of these positions is indicated by the typical form of these passages: most often they begin with the focus on the performer onstage, playing wildly with great emotion, and then shift to the sympathetic members of the audience—usually the Kerouac character, the Neal Cassady character, or both.

A good example of this strategy is the passage from *The Subterraneans* we looked at in connection with its portrayal of Charlie Parker: "and up on the stand Bird Parker with solemn eyes who'd been busted fairly recently and had now returned to a kind of bop dead Frisco but had just discovered or been told about the Red Drum, the great new generation gang wailing and gathering there, so here he was on the stand, examining them with his eyes as he blew his now-settled-down-into-regulated-design 'crazy' notes" (1971: 18–19). In this scene Kerouac's character—Leo Percepied—and his girlfriend are part of an avant-garde group of jazz aficionados who are listening to Charlie Parker in a jazz club in San Francisco. What is significant about this passage is Kerouac's portrayal of Parker as playing the Red Drum not simply because he has been booked into another jazz club where he can earn some money, but as being interested in this particular club because of the audience that would be seeing and hearing him: "that great new generation."[2] The connection between Parker and his bohemian audience is made personal and momentous in this way; Parker is transformed in this passage, as W. T. Lhamon suggests, into a sort of secular priest, and the bohemian crowd is his loyal flock: "Frequently the jazz club or scene is a surrogate mass in Kerouac's work. The blowing soloist stands in for the priest, his horn for the censer, his stimulants for the chalice" (Lhamon 1990: 152).

As Lhamon suggests, this kind of transformation is important in Kerouac's work because of his passionate, romantic interest in transcending the everyday world's triviality through spirituality and ecstasy—moving "*out of the place.*" However, the effect of this kind of characterization is to figuratively neuter the jazz performer by depicting him as the Beat generation's priest. The priest's role in this "surrogate mass" is brief and essentially passive: he delivers the sacrament to the congregation and then recedes into the background. Moreover, the sacrament he administers is a sign of his lack of agency, because it is linked to his victimization. In this scene, for example, the audience is linked to Parker through the image of his eyes, which have already been designated (not just by this passage but by tradition as well) as the locus of Parker's emotional response to his victimization as a black jazz musician. Parker's "emotional response," then, serves as the sacrament because it bestows the effect of his martyrdom upon the worthy in the audience. As soon as this occurs, however, Parker's role is fulfilled. In Kerouac's "surrogate mass," in other words, the focus is on the congregation; the priest is superfluous once he administers the sacrament.

The nexus Kerouac emphasizes between the jazz performer and his bohemian audience is one the novelist repeats often in this and other works. Throughout *The Subterraneans* and *On the Road* are tossed-off references to Kerouac and friends being the "bop generation" or "children of bop." Moreover, even when the quasi-religious sense is absent from the performance scenes, the movement of agency and emphasis from performer to privileged audience is the same. In a scene from *On the Road*, for example, Sal Paradise and Dean Moriarty sit in a club listening to an anonymous African American tenor saxophonist: "Dean was in a trance. The tenorman's eyes were fixed straight on him; he had a madman who not only understood but cared and wanted to understand more and much more than there was, and they began dueling for this; everything came out of the horn, no more phrases, just cries, cries, 'Baugh' and down to 'Beep!' and up to 'EEEEE!' and down to clinkers and over to sideways-echoing horn-sounds" (1957: 163). Through his emotional and intellectual empathy Dean becomes the tenorman's sideman, psychically "dueling" with the musician and propelling him to greater musical heights. Dean becomes the source of this performer's improvisation. As this scene is further developed it bears a remarkable resemblance to the one reproduced above from *The Subterraneans*: "he [the African American tenor saxophone player] looked at us, Dean and me; with an expression that seemed to say, Hey now, and what's this thing we're all doing in this sad brown world? . . . because here we were dealing with the pit and prunejuice of poor beat life itself in the god-awful streets of man, so he said it and sang it 'Close—your—' and blew it way up to the ceiling and through to the stars and on out" (1957: 164). Again, this personal, emotional link between performer and audience is based on their common condition—both their positional similarity as "outsiders" and the correspondence of their emotional response to their position—but the benefit of this connection (the "community" that develops) is one-sided: Dean and Sal's lives reach a sort of apotheosis through the "intervention" of the saxophonist, but how does he gain from this encounter?

Similarly, in the previous scene from *The Subterraneans* depicting his "encounter" with Charlie Parker, Kerouac delineates a close bond between the performer and himself (as the fictionalized narrator) that wholly serves *his*, not Parker's, needs:

> returning to the Red Drum for sets, to hear Bird, whom I saw distinctly digging Mardou several times also myself directly into my eye looking to search if really I was that great writer I thought myself to be as if he knew my thoughts and ambitions or remembered me from other night clubs and other coasts, other Chicagos—not a challenging look but the king and founder of the bop generation at least the sound of it in digging his audience digging his eyes, the secret eyes him-watching, as he just pursed his lips and let great lungs and immortal fingers work, his eyes separate and interested and humane, the kindest jazz musician there could be while being and therefore naturally the greatest— watching Mardou and me in the infancy of our love and probably wondering why, or knowing it wouldn't last, or seeing who it was would be hurt, as now, obviously, but not quite yet, it was Mardou whose eyes were shining in my direction, though I could not have known and now do not definitely know. (1971: 19–20)

In this passage, the personal link based on position and condition is again suggested—Parker connects with Kerouac because both are suffering artists—but the emphasis is almost completely transferred from performer to audience member. Not only is there no external (e.g., historical) or internal (e.g., performer and listeners) community created here, but there is not even a reciprocal relationship established between performer and listener. Though this particular scene is consistent with Kerouac's delineation of the character of Leo Percepied throughout the novel—as a rather arrogant, self-absorbed man—in the context of Kerouac's overall pattern of depicting performer/audience interaction this scene simply extends to an extreme the model I have already described.

In his novels *The Horn* and *Go*, Kerouac's Beat colleague John Clellon Holmes uses scenes involving himself and a thinly fictionalized Neal Cassady to develop ideas very similar to Kerouac's.[3] In *The Horn*, for example, the primary performer/audience nexus formed is between the slowly dissipating saxophone legend Edgar Pool, the "horn," and two white hipsters. Pool first notices the hipsters standing in the cold outside a record store listening intently, passionately to the sounds of a jazz recording:

> For there, in front of a record store that had an outside speaker through which a husky tenor sax poured its poignant wail out upon the deaf, thronged sidewalks, were two young white men, muffled to the chins in flapping raincoats, transfixed upon the curb by the very sound, heads bobbing, fingers snapping as they sang along all unaware that they were singing, catching hold of one another as they teetered toward the gutter, their laughing, exultant faces astream with rain and sweat, riffing and entranced, oblivious of everything but that wild, hot horn. (1988b: 150–51)

Interrupting his drunken discussion with a younger musician about the growing elitism and commercialization in modern jazz, the sight of these two white jazz fans illustrates the accuracy of what Pool argues: in the attempt to elevate its aesthetic status to that of American classical music, jazz has moved away from its true source of meaning, the inspiration of and communication with the people.

However, this pseudo-populist construction of jazz music's roots has a decidedly Euro American twist—it is focused exclusively, almost fetishistically, on individual expression. First, in his discussion with the younger musician, Edgar Pool states the theme:

> And all over arrangements, charts, scores, paper, *paper*! And every goddamn fool thinks *that's* what it is. . . . Well, kid, let me tell you something, you silly fool—I can read them notes as good as anybody, but it's *still* what a man gets up, all alone with only his goddamn horn on some fool's tune, and blows out of his own head that makes the difference, that changes it from what it was before he got up *nerve* enough to do it.

Yes! . . . I don't care how much music paper, or music school, or fancy suspenders, or funny Stravinsky you got, cause all them scores, all them significant tone poems, all that—man, it ain't no *fun* if you can't get free of it long enough to blow your own damn thing. (1988b: 150)

This theme is then picked up in the overheard conversation of the two white jazz fans who excitedly anticipate that "first, vast, really *great* solo tonight, just tonight" that will strike the audience so strongly that "everyone'll be destroyed by it, and amazed they could have gotten through their lives not knowing it, not realizing!" (1988b: 151). Conjuring up this image, the white fans also think about the saxophonist's "old bedroom down in Fayetteville or someplace, and his yellow Saturday shoes, and his hair straightener before he came up North, copying records all those years, all alone" (151). Leaving aside the cartoonish racism of the last quote, these characterizations of the process of jazz creation only credit the contributions of the individual—"blows out of his own head," "really great *solo*," "all alone" (twice).

This focus on individual expression, while extreme, only becomes a uniquely Euro American construction when Holmes makes it the primary, universalized power of jazz music. While he alludes to it here, he makes this construction explicit in a later scene depicting a final encounter between Pool and the same two jazz fans. In a scene that is strikingly similar to Kerouac's depiction of Charlie Parker in *The Subterraneans*, Pool (who is in the audience, not performing onstage) observes the two white jazz fans sitting at a table in a club "their faces full of ecstasy and music, and all at once, staring and shivering, he seemed to *know* them, their very souls" (231).

Like Kerouac's Parker, Holmes's Pool possesses an almost supernatural power to "know" them. What Pool knows is that they are "crippled young Americans whom jazz alone has reconciled to [their] country" (232). Pool, moreover, places them in a long line of alienated white youth who have turned to African American music for meaning. Despite Holmes's overly sanguine judgment of the music's power (I doubt that too many alienated, young, white people feel a greater attachment to their country, society, or culture because of the existence of great African American music), his characterization of white attraction to black music because of its greater vitality than dominant, mainstream American culture is accurate. It is also illuminating that Holmes portrays Pool, a black musician, as being aware of the subversive power of African American culture. However, in a uniquely Euro American move, Holmes deflates this subversive power by using Pool to conflate the different experiences of African Americans and Euro Americans: " 'It's all the same,' he thought, staring at them. 'It's just the same for them as me,' black or white—no matter how they shouted at him now, no matter what they said; in spite of bitterness and irony and scars. They loved the thing he loved, and it had spoken to all of them alike, and that generous, eager, joyful softness of anticipation in their faces had been in his face, too" (232). Although uttered by an African American character, this is the construction of a Euro American who is unaware of or unwilling to accept the privilege that is his by virtue of his skin color; it is a construction that ignores the real effects of racism and the unequal social, cultural, economic, and political power in the United States.

Holmes mines a similar vein in *Go*, his fictionalized chronicle of the Beat generation. In one scene, for example, two young white men travel to an illegal Harlem "after-hours joint" with friends to meet a drug connection. At the club the men, Paul Hobbes (Holmes) and Hart Kennedy (Neal Cassady), listen to an African American jazz singer and her accompanists and become involved in the music: "Hobbes, leaning toward him [the African American pianist], was, through his giddiness, suddenly possessed by the illusion of emotional eloquence and started to chant softly, improvising broken phrases. The Negro glanced up for an instant, nodding abstractly, long gone, and with no resentment at the intrusion" (1988: 138). While the Holmes character merely sits chanting, self-consciously, to himself, the Cassady character gets slightly more immersed:

> The singer was moving across the open space toward the bar and Hart, his head bobbing up and down and his eyes narrowed, was shuffling to meet her, stooped over and clapping his hands like an euphoric savage who erupts into a magic rite at the moment of his seizure. She watched him coming toward her, with dark experienced eyes, and for an instant sang just for him, her shoulders swinging on the deep strums of the guitarist who tarried behind, watchful and yet also appreciative. Hart stopped before her, bobbing, ecstatic, and then, falling down on his knees he cried: "Y-e-s! Blow! Blow! . . . You know who you are!" for this was his offering, all he could give. And, as if she accepted it in lieu of money, with a wave of her hand, a bright wink at the crowd, and a great display of heaving bosom, she strutted on. (139)

The resemblance of the Kerouac and Holmes scenes suggests that they accurately portray Cassady's behavior in jazz clubs and bars. Beyond this, however, Holmes's scene is interesting because it offers a reading of Cassady's behavior related to the one in *On the Road*, but a revealingly different take on the African American performer's reaction to this "possessed" audience member. As in Kerouac's scene from *On the Road*, Cassady is portrayed as becoming so involved in the music being performed that he interacts with the performer. Moreover, both Holmes and Kerouac present this scene as one in which the African American performer recognizes and is interested in the ecstatic behavior of the white bohemian audience member. However, whereas Kerouac represents

the saxophonist as being unreservedly sympathetic, even bonded, with Cassady—
"he had a madman who not only understood but cared and wanted to understand
more and much more than there was"—Holmes portrays the singer as reserving,
somewhat, her emotional involvement with Cassady—"watchful and yet also ap-
preciative." Furthermore, Kerouac depicts the communication between performer
and audience member as being mostly silent; that is, Cassady does not actually say
anything to the tenor saxophonist; instead their connection happens on some sort
of emotional or "psychic" level.

The result of this narrative strategy is that Kerouac completely gives himself,
as author/narrator, over to this romantic construct (that is, the affinity between
jazz performer and bohemian listener). Holmes, on the other hand, portrays the
communication between Cassady and the African American singer as being explicit
and thus achieves a different effect. Holmes depicts Cassady as saying something
to the singer—"Y-e-s! Blow! Blow! . . . You know who you are!"—which can be
interpreted (especially given the vivid portrait of Cassady that precedes it) as being
slightly comic because it is so vague and ineffectual. Moreover, the narrator's
comment—"for this was his offering, all he could give"—following Cassady's
exclamation underscores the imprecision and impotence of his words.

Although it is possible that Holmes meant this entire passage to be pregnant with poignancy and pathos (by emphasizing the imaginative and, especially,
economic poverty of Cassady's response to a form of expression he worships),
instead it diverts the narrative and emotional attention away from the singer's
expressiveness to Cassady. In this way, the passage puts Cassady's inarticulate,
ineloquent expression on a level with the singer's by replacing the singer's emotion
with his "suffering." Furthermore, Holmes legitimizes this narrative sleight-of-
hand by having the singer "accept" Cassady's expression as payment for her
artistic/entertaining expression (1988a: 138).

The transference of attention to Cassady also accomplishes the connection
between jazz musicians and the bohemian audience we find in Kerouac's work. By
having the singer "accept" Cassady's payment, Holmes is forging a sort of alliance
between the performer and Cassady. This micro-alliance mirrors the larger unity
of outsiders that Holmes asserts exists in American society among those—black
and white—in whom "the modern world (by starving our intuitive faculties) has
aroused a hunger in us for the spontaneities of the spirit" (Holmes 1967: 131).
Moreover, Holmes claims that jazz, for these outsiders, is the common expression
of their dissatisfaction with contemporary society as well as of their "tribal" unity:
"In this modern jazz, they heard something rebel and nameless that spoke for
them, and their lives knew a gospel for the first time. It was more than a music; it
became an attitude toward life, a way of walking, a language and a costume; and
these introverted kids (emotional outcasts of a war they had been too young to

join, or in which they had lost their innocence), who had never belonged anywhere before, now felt somewhere at last" (1988a: 161).

The exchange between Cassady and the African American singer at the end of the previous passage is especially interesting, given Holmes's claim to jazz for white outsiders such as Cassady. While Holmes suggests that there is some actual connection between jazz/jazz musicians and their bohemian audience—"they [the bohemians] became willingly transported when cued by the musicians, who played only to them and remained bitterly indifferent to the noisy parties at the tables in between"—the exchange between the singer and Cassady suggests something quite different from Holmes's use of it. Rather than declaring the singer's acceptance of Cassady's involvement in her music "in lieu of money," the singer's expression— "with a wave of her hand, a bright wink at the crowd, and a great display of heaving bosom, she strutted on"—was probably meant to "signify" on Cassady's silly, pitiful performance (1988a: 161). Unless Holmes's language completely distorts Cassady's behavior—"his head bobbing up and down and his eyes narrowed . . . shuffling to meet her, stooped over and clapping his hands like an euphoric savage who erupts into a magic rite at the moment of seizure"—it seems reasonable to assume that the singer's response recognized Cassady's unconscious racism and communicated (to that segment of the audience that would understand) her contempt for it.

A story such as Richard Yates's 1958 "A Really Good Jazz Piano" presents a parallel to the novels by Beat writers. Ostensibly portraying the emptiness of the lives of two well-educated, upper-class, male college students, the story also uses jazz in a way that is not fundamentally different from that in Kerouac's and Holmes's novels. In part this similarity is due to the very fact that this story's focus, as in Kerouac and Holmes, is on the needs and problems of young, privileged *white* people. Moreover, as in the work of the Beat writers, the story's primary purpose— to reveal the hollowness and meanness in middle-class, mainstream American society—is accomplished by presenting "the African American experience" as either the means of American society's salvation (in the case of the Beats), or simply evidence of American society's degeneration (as in Yates's story). In either instance, however, the African American characters (and, by extension, African American experience and culture) in these works are only represented as being important because of what they tell the reader about white people in American society. Thus, despite the fact that one way of reading his story is as a critique of the very kind of white racism that exists in the writings of Beat authors, Yates's representations of African American characters, experience, and culture do not differ substantially from those in Kerouac's and Holmes's work.

Although the performance scenes in "A Really Good Jazz Piano" are few and brief, taken together they constitute a fertile locus for examining Yates's depiction of African American characters, experience, and culture. The jazz performer in the story is an African American jazz pianist named Sid who has been "discovered" in "an expensive bar" in Cannes, France, by an American college student named Ken Platt who is traveling the continent with a classmate. Sid is the feather in Platt's cap: "discovering" him is the one thing he has done in his otherwise undistinguished life that elevates him in his own eyes and in those of his revered friend and traveling companion, Carson Wyler. At first, Sid appears to be a fabulous "find": "it was no small thing to have turned up an incorruptible jazz talent in the back streets of a foreign city, all alone" (Yates 1990: 170). Both Platt and Wyler (but especially Platt) admire Sid initially because he has apparently chosen to leave the United States rather than compromise himself by playing for money there. Yates develops the two college students, then, as characters who have constructed a certain type of jazz musician—the suffering, destitute, and principled artist. This image, furthermore, does not necessarily have anything to do with Sid himself. About Sid, Platt says, "People accept him here. As an artist, I mean, as well as a man. Nobody condescends to him, nobody tries to interfere with his music, and that's all he wants out of life. Oh, I mean he doesn't tell you all this—probably be a bore if he did—it's just a thing you sense about him" (1990: 169). Moreover, it is clear from this quote that Platt and Wyler link Sid's position as an exiled American musician with his race—"As an artist, I mean, *as well as a man.*" This connection is reinforced by Platt's previous comment about Sid's girlfriend: "One thing, of course, he's got a girl here, this really lovely French girl, and I guess he couldn't very well take her back with him" (169).

As the story develops, however, Sid makes it clear that he wants to go back to the United States with his French girlfriend and wants to make as good a living as he can playing his music. Sid tells the American college duo when they come to see him perform that very night that an "owner of nightclubs in Las Vegas," Murray Diamond, is scheduled to hear him play, and Sid hopes this informal audition might be his "big break." The performance, then, becomes a test not only of Sid's musical abilities, but also of Platt's and Wyler's attitudes toward professional (rather than artistic) musicians and, specifically, *African American* jazz players. The scene's primary focus, in fact, is Platt's and Wyler's reaction to Sid's behavior during his performance. This focus makes it necessary for Yates to exaggerate his portrayal of Sid's performance to emphasize his contrast to their image of the African American jazz musician as a principled, rebellious artist.

From the moment they enter the bar Platt and Wyler realize that something different is going on: they hear Sid singing a composition they had heard him perform earlier as an instrumental—"Sweet Lorraine." Subsequent to this obvious indication that Sid has commercialized or "sold out" whatever musical integrity he had, the pair sees that amid the capacity crowd Sid is clearly performing for two members of the audience: "Settled there, they could see now that Sid wasn't looking into the crowd at large. He was singing directly to a bored-looking couple in evening clothes who sat a few tables away, a silver-blonde girl who could have been a movie starlet and a small, chubby bald man with a deep tan, a man so obviously Murray Diamond that a casting director might have sent him here to play the part" (1990: 179). It is perhaps not incidental to the overall effect of this passage that Yates not only begins to differentiate Sid and the college boys racially but also stigmatizes the Jewish nightclub owner, Murray Diamond, as exploitive Jewish intermediary, an almost-white man (or is he almost-black—"with a deep tan"?) who, through his money-grubbing, corrupts the white man's pure object of desire. During his performance Sid seems to concentrate on only one task—impressing the nightclub owner and his date and checking for their reaction: "Sometimes Sid's large eyes would stray to other parts of the room or to the smoke-hung ceiling, but they seemed to come into focus only when he looked at these two people. Even when the song ended and the piano took off alone on a long, intricate variation, even when he kept glancing up to see if they were watching" (179).

Yates's representation of performer/audience interaction during jazz performance in "A Really Good Jazz Piano" resembles those in Kerouac's and Holmes's work because it is used merely as a vehicle to develop some aspect of whiteness. To put the white characters in the audience at the center of this representation, these authors must subordinate their portrayals of the African American performer to the needs (whatever they may be) of their Euro American characters. Therefore the reader learns nothing at all about the performers—their needs, motives, conflicts; instead they remain static, usually exaggerated, projections of the white audience members. Also, the performer/audience interaction developed in these representations is purely exploitative: not only are the African American performers decentered in these scenes, but they are romantically caricatured, exaggerated, and juxtaposed to white characters who are made to benefit from the African American performers' romanticized characteristics while they are also permitted to retain their positions as *white* characters. In Kerouac and Holmes the fictionalized Neal Cassady characters occupy an elevated status (compared not only to the African American performers in the scenes, but also to the other Euro American characters) because they are not only alienated white social outsiders, but are connected with the deeper, seemingly more organic and creative suffering embodied by the African American singer and musician. Furthermore, in the context of these stories the Cassady characters wander from scene to similar scene profiting from these juxtapositions without ever becoming involved with the characters in any personal way.

In Yates's story the exploitation is only slightly different. Because Yates's perspective is critical of the white characters at the center of the narrative they are not positively enhanced by their confrontation with the jazz performer the way the

Cassady characters are in the Holmes and Kerouac scenes. Rather, Platt and Wyler are diminished as characters by their horrendously insensitive, racist treatment of Sid, the jazz piano player. Nevertheless, by privileging their emotional turmoil in the aftermath of the confrontation with Sid during his performance Yates exploits Sid's suffering to gain the reader's sympathy for his white characters. Though Sid is in fact the one who is wronged in this specific scene, and also represents a specific historical victimization (that is, the exploitation of African American jazz musicians), Yates's narrative positions Platt and Wyler as suffering victimizers. Whereas Sid's reaction to his conflict with Wyler is described in sparse, unaffecting imagery—"Sid sat down and began to play, looking at nothing"—Wyler's response is empathetically detailed by the third-person voice of his buddy Platt: "it was that his face was stricken with the uncannily familiar look of his own heart, the very face he himself, Lard-Ass Platt, had shown all his life to others: haunted and vulnerable and terribly dependent, trying to smile, a look that said Please don't leave me alone" (1990: 183–84). Thus, Platt and Wyler seem even more pathetic and pitiable because their suffering is depicted as being deeper and more profound than is Sid's. This reading is further reinforced by the end of the scene in which Platt and Wyler symbolically crush Sid's creative claim to victimhood when the sound of their retreat drowns out Sid's piano: "the piano only came up loud for a second or two before it diminished and died behind them under the rhythm of their heels" (184).

As revealing as the depictions of performer/audience interaction are the representations of the performers' behavior and interaction on the bandstand. As we shall see, the Euro Americans' limited use of performance (mostly in terms of technical virtuosity or as a metaphor for anomalous, idiosyncratic, individual genius) contrasts with African Americans' interest in jazz performance as a powerful metaphor for larger issues such as the historical experience of racism, group solidarity, the expression of intensely felt emotions, and the development of African American culture. While African Americans also recognize the musical achievements of jazz improvisation they tend to underplay this aspect in favor of the metaphorical possibilities of improvisational music. Moreover, African Americans often set the individualistic elements of jazz performance in a context that leads the reader to focus on the importance of the music to such larger groups of people as the band members, the immediate social or cultural community, or African Americans as a whole. This emphasis may derive from their understanding of modern jazz itself as a collective, rather than individual, achievement. Their representations echo jazz critic Andre Hodeir's insightful comment that "modern jazz was a collective creation. Every man in this group was responsible for a certain number of innovations that were synthesized only by a joint effort" (Hodeir 1979: 101).

Kid Jones's emotional performance in Ann Petry's "Solo on Drums," for example, is the expression of his despair over the experience of being left by his wife for the band's piano player. However, during the course of this brief narrative Petry transforms the personal, emotional basis of his masterful drumming into a variety of performative positions that result in Kid Jones's loss of ego as he fuses with the music. As the performance begins, Kid Jones plays the role of the accompanist for the trumpet and piano players: "He hits the drums lightly. Regularly. A soft, barely discernible rhythm. A background. A repeated emphasis for the horns and the piano" (1990: 54). As the trumpet player solos Jones hears in it the story of his early morning tragedy: "It was that whispering voice, making him shiver. Hating it and not being able to do anything about it. 'I'm leaving it's the guy who plays the piano I'm in love with him and I'm leaving now today'" (55). This is significant because it indicates that Jones draws inspiration from the music played by the other band members.

Jones's creative energy is bumped to the next level of intensity by a rhythmic duel he has with his nemesis, the piano-playing Marquis of Brund. Occurring in the performance immediately before Jones takes his first solo, this duet also serves to suggest the symbiotic effect contributed by even the most competitive, hostile interaction between band members: "The Marquis of Brund, pianist with the band, turned to the piano. The drums and the piano talked the same rhythm. The piano high. A little more insistent than the drums. . . . The drummer and pianist were silhouetted in two separate brilliant shafts of light. The drums slowly dominated the piano" (55–56).

When he begins his solo, Jones is intent upon his wife's early morning hurtful statement of betrayal: "The one who said, 'I'm leaving'" (56). However, as he continues to play his solo, Jones performs a series of ritualistic scenarios that gradually take him away from himself. First, Jones engages in an imaginary battle with his wife's new suitor: "When he hit the drums again it was with the thought that he was fighting with the piano player. He was choking the Marquis of Brund. He was putting a knife in clean between his ribs. He was slitting his throat with a long straight blade. Take my woman. Take your life. The drums leaped with the fury that was in him" (56). Venting his immediate, personal anger through the beating of his drums, Jones follows as the music leads him further away from his suffering: "The drums took him away from them, took him back, and back, and back, in time and space. He built up an illusion. He was sending out the news" (57). But as his solo ends, Jones is brought back to the present moment and the fact of his wife's betrayal. "He couldn't help himself. He stopped hitting the drums and stared at the Marquis of Brund—a long malevolent look, filled with hate" (57).

Jones then engages in some interplay with the horn player before it becomes time for him to solo for the final time. Unsure that he can summon up the courage to confront his emotions again, Jones begins tentatively: "He touched the drums lightly. They quivered and answered him." Once he starts this solo, however, Jones plays the drums with an intensity that he has never approached before. Fueled by his memories of women (including, but not limited to, his wife) who have hated him, Jones solos madly, wildly. He and the drums merge as the music reaches an angry crescendo: "He forgot the theater, forgot everything but the drums. He was welded to the drums, sucked inside them. All of him. His pulse beat. His heart beat. He had become part of the drums. They had become part of him" (58).

Significantly, however, as Petry describes Jones's increasingly intense solo she becomes less specific about Jones and the details of his life. For example, she uses the more general pronoun "he" to refer to Jones (rather than his name or even "the drummer") and characterizes his wife's betrayal with less specificity (she stops referring to his mantric memory of his wife's "I'm leaving"). Petry describes the crescendo of Jones's solo as a cataclysmic collision of emotion and music:

> He made the big drum rumble and reverberate. He went a little mad on the big drum. Again and again he filled the theater with a sound like thunder. The sound seemed to come not from the drums but from deep inside himself; it was a sound that was being wrenched out of him—a violent, raging, roaring sound. As it issued from him he thought, This is the story of my love, this is the story of my hate, this is all there is left of me. And the sound echoed and reechoed far up under the roof of the theater. (58)

Petry's representation of jazz performance subtly combines the individual and the group. While the emotional energy in Kid Jones's solo starts from his private experience, it soon becomes fused with the music itself—a music with a heritage that stretches back to African talking drums—and the music the rest of the band is making. In other words, even though Kid Jones is the featured performer in the band (his name is in lights on the marquee below that of the band), his solos are part of the band's complete performance. Petry signals this idea by her frequent references to Jones's musical interplay with the rest of the band (especially the Marquis of Brund and the trumpet player), to the contributions the other band members make to Jones's extraordinary performance, and to the "spotlight" which shifts from soloist to soloist. Most importantly, Petry depicts a communally developed performance by individuals through her skillful narrative development of the performance so that the story begins slowly and quietly with Jones accompanying the trumpet and piano and then gathers momentum as it builds toward Kid Jones's emotional finale. Petry's skillful depiction of the seemingly paradoxical relationship between individuals and the collective in jazz performances is reinforced by jazz critic Andre Hodeir: "It would seem that jazz can expect to speak a perfect collective language only if it is worked out by individuals (this paradox is more apparent than real)" (1979: 180).

James Baldwin, in "Sonny's Blues," also skillfully negotiates the terrain of the jazz performer's individual and collective expression. Returning to the story's concluding scene in a Greenwich Village nightclub, we discover that Baldwin clearly characterizes Sonny's climactic performance as the accomplishment of an individual in a collective setting. From the moment Sonny and the narrator enter the nightclub, the reader is given information that establishes the absolutely vital significance of the people with whom and for whom Sonny plays. Baldwin introduces the musicians as surrogate relatives: Creole, the band's leader and bassist, is the father figure. "[A]n enormous black man, much older than Sonny or [the narrator]," Creole addresses the narrator as "boy" and "son," "put[s] his arm around Sonny's shoulder" and also "slap[s] him, lightly, affectionately, with the back of his hand." The drummer—"a coal-black, cheerful looking man, built close to the ground"— is a brother who, upon meeting the narrator, "immediately began confiding to me, at the top of his lungs, the most terrible things about Sonny." Finally, the audience members are also all people who know and believe in Sonny: "everyone at the bar knew Sonny, or almost everyone; some were musicians, working there, or nearby, or not working, some were simply hangers-on, and some were there to hear Sonny play" (1990: 125). Although the narrator somewhat jealously characterizes the total environment of the nightclub as Sonny's "kingdom," Baldwin's narrative establishes it more generously as a secular (perhaps a family reunion) or religious ceremony in which a member who has fallen away is welcomed back, reinstated into the group's good graces, and personally renewed and absolved.

Within this ceremonial setting Baldwin depicts an interdependent relationship between Sonny—the band's main attraction—and the rest of the players (especially Creole). Played out on a stage bathed in an "indigo" light, this relationship is portrayed as unusually reciprocal because the performance is Sonny's first since recovering from his drug addiction. Sonny is clearly the center of attention and the focus of the band's concentration. At the start of the performance, however, the narrator notices that Sonny's playing (as well as that by the other band members) is entirely dependent on Creole's direction: "And I had the feeling that, in a way, everyone on the bandstand was waiting for him [Sonny], both waiting for him and pushing him along. But as I began to watch Creole, I realized that it was Creole who held them all back. He had them on a short rein" (127). As the narrator describes it, Sonny needs Creole's help to regain not only his "chops," his jazz form, but his ability to express himself. Moreover, it is significant that Sonny's renewal occurs not in a practice session—not, that is, while the musicians are woodshedding—but on the bandstand in front of a live audience:

Up there, keeping the beat with his [Creole's] whole body, wailing on the fiddle, with his eyes half closed, he was listening to everything, but he was listening to Sonny. He was having a dialogue with Sonny. He wanted Sonny to leave the shoreline and strike out for the deep water. He was Sonny's witness that deep water and drowning were not the same thing—he had been there, and he knew. And he wanted Sonny to know. He was waiting for Sonny to do the things on the keys which would let Creole know that Sonny was in the water.

And, while Creole listened, Sonny moved deep within, exactly like someone in torment. (127)

Mixing three different metaphors, Baldwin forcefully communicates three ideas: first, that communication during a jazz performance is vital ("listening," "having a dialogue"); second, that older musicians (perhaps, even, older African American men in general) provide guidance and leadership for younger musicians ("he had been there, and he knew"); and third, that individual expression is fundamentally linked to the generative environment of the jazz collective (this is supported by the whole passage).

This essential interaction between Sonny and the group members continues as Sonny finds his voice on the piano. Baldwin makes it clear that Sonny's playing needs help from his fellow musicians on the level of both music and creativity or expression: "And Sonny hadn't been near a piano for over a year. And he wasn't on much better terms with his life, not the life that stretched before him now" (128). The other players encourage Sonny to express himself, to take chances, as they trade musical phrases: "And Creole let out the reins. The dry, low, black man said something awful on the drums; Creole answered, and the drums talked back. Then the horn insisted, sweet and high, slightly detached perhaps, and Creole listened commenting now and then, dry, and driving, beautiful and calm and old. Then they all came together again, and Sonny was part of the family again" (128). The musical interaction between Sonny, Creole, and the other players helps prepare Sonny to tell the musical "tale of how we suffer, and how we are delighted, and how we may triumph" (129). Thus, Baldwin depicts Sonny's expressive individualism (in his solo) as the direct outgrowth of the group's interactive, communally derived expression. This depiction concurs with Portia Maultsby's description of the process of creation in the performance of African American music: "The fundamental concept that governs music performance in African and African-derived cultures is that music-making is a participatory group activity that serves to unite black people into a cohesive group for a common purpose" (Maultsby 1990: 187).

As the story and performance wind their way toward Sonny's tale/solo, Creole remains the man in firm control of Sonny's fate. Playing the multiple roles of bandleader, father-figure, preacher, teacher, and guardian of group knowledge, Creole is essential to Sonny's success in his return performance.[4] Baldwin makes

Creole's significance clear in the passages immediately preceding Sonny's solo. Preparing the way for Sonny, "Creole step[s] forward to remind them that what they were playing was the blues" (128) More plainly than ever, Baldwin connects the performance of jazz to the African American tradition by invoking the blues in this context. The notion that modern jazz (especially bebop) was intimately connected to the African American folk tradition was hotly contested at the time Baldwin wrote "Sonny's Blues." Baldwin's construction here puts him squarely in the camp of those who narrate jazz history as a tradition in which the innovators continuously reinvent, reinterpret folk elements.

Writing about the bebop era, for example, Albert Murray claims that "[Charlie] Parker, unlike so many of his so-called progressive but often only pretentious followers, was not looking for ways to stop blues from swinging; he was looking for ways to make it swing even more" (Murray 1976: 252). Many of the most innovative musicians from the 1950s and 1960s also dispel the notion that they were trying to transcend the blues in their music. In his autobiography Dizzy Gillespie says, "Beboppers couldn't destroy the blues without seriously injuring themselves. The modern jazz musicians always remained very close to the blues musician. That was a characteristic of the bopper . . . we knew where our music came from. Ain't no need of denying your father. That's a fool, and there were few fools in this movement. Technical differences existed between modern jazz and blues musicians. However, modern jazz musicians would have to know the blues" (Gillespie 1979: 294).

Baldwin, moreover, characterizes the blues and Creole's role in the band's performance in ways that put the reader in touch with a living African American tradition. Creole, Baldwin says, reminds the musicians and listeners that the blues tell "the tale of how we suffer, and how we are delighted, and how we may triumph" (Baldwin 1990: 129). This accurately represents the spirit of a music that is not simply about personal or collective suffering but, as Albert Murray says, about "mak[ing] people feel good" (1976: 45). Baldwin also takes seriously the mentoring—including both technical and emotional support—that older jazz musicians provide for younger players. Creole not only guards the blues tradition; he also prepares the way for Sonny to build, to improvise, on that tradition: "Listen, Creole seemed to be saying, listen. Now these are Sonny's blues. He made the little black man on the drums know it, and the bright, brown man on the horn, Creole wasn't trying any longer to get Sonny in the water. He was wishing him Godspeed. Then he stepped back, very slowly, filling the air with the immense suggestion that Sonny speak for himself" (129). Creole's function of simultaneously grounding and opening the tradition echoes the view encountered often in the recollections of jazz musicians that the tradition and canon of jazz is built upon the successive innovations of individual musicians. A quote from pianist Cecil Taylor is representative: "I have a tradition, and my tradition informs me the way that theirs [Euro American musicians'] informs them, perhaps. I don't have the academies to forward my tradition, but I do have that small department that Bud Powell was teaching" (Spellman 1985: 41). In a similar way, Creole, as an older musician, carries the tradition forward to Sonny.

In his description of Sonny's solo, Baldwin continues to illuminate, and enlarge upon, the idea that the jazz soloist's expressive individualism is intricately linked to group identity. Baldwin makes this connection immediately: "Sonny's fingers filled the air with life, his life. But that life contained so many others" (129). The clear implication here is that the jazz soloist expresses not only his own personal experiences but also those that connect him to some larger entity. While Sonny solos, the narrator listens to the music and hears the order, the cultural logic, it expresses. He characterizes the music Sonny plays in terms that resonate for anyone familiar with the African American historical condition: what starts as a blues, a "lament," becomes "very beautiful because it wasn't hurried and it was no longer a lament. I seemed to hear with what burning he had made it his, with what burning we had yet to make it ours, how we could cease lamenting. Freedom lurked around us and I understood, at last, that he could help us to be free if we would listen, that he would never be free until we did" (129). Suggesting the history of African American oppression and resistance, Baldwin's narrator reinforces this connection in his subsequent observation: "I heard what he had gone through, and would continue to go through until he came to rest in earth. He had made it his; that long line, of which we knew only Mama and Daddy" (129). Oblique as it is, this narration brings together Baldwin's earlier references to the tradition of succession in jazz with Sonny's personal experiences, and the historical experiences of African American people in general.

The narrator's construction here of a link between the jazz performer's transcendence of his personal suffering and the possibility of transcendence for his people beautifully illustrates the relatedness of individual and group expression that many have identified in African American music. Lawrence Levine's comments about black music from an earlier era, for example, echo Baldwin's depiction:

> This is, perhaps, the final thing to be said about the music: it gave a sense of power, of control. If it did not affect the material being of its creator, it certainly did have an impact upon their psychic state and emotional health. It allowed them to assert themselves and their feelings and their values, to communicate continuously with themselves and their peers and their oppressors as well. . . . Black secular song, along with other forms of the oral tradition, allowed them to express themselves communally and individually, to derive great aesthetic pleasure, to perpetuate traditions, to keep values from eroding, and to begin to create new expressive modes. (Levine 1977: 297)

Levine's description of the function of African American music also fits Amiri Baraka's short story "The Screamers," which offers a slightly different angle from Baldwin's on the links between jazz, community, and power. Written a decade after Baldwin's story, Baraka's work in "The Screamers" indicates that the black cultural nationalism of the mid- to late 1960s changed the emphasis but not the basic values prevalent in African American culture. Like Baldwin, Baraka uses jazz to explore relationships among African Americans and between African Americans and Euro Americans.

In contrast to Baldwin's setting in "Sonny's Blues"—a bourgeois/bohemian, integrated nightclub in Greenwich Village—Baraka sets "The Screamers" in a funky, almost all-black nightclub in Newark, a place that attracts "only the wild or the very poor" (1990: 262). As with "Sonny's Blues," however, Baraka's story begins by developing differences among African Americans themselves. As narrated by Baraka's anonymous audience member, the story constructs differences among African Americans on the basis of color, style, gender, and particularly class. However, these differences mark African Americans as diverse rather than separate. Transcending the boundaries constructed for them by the dominant society, the African American nightclubbers come together in their passion for the music and the physicality and emotion that accompany its performance. Dancing, shouting, and moving, these children of "social-worker mothers and postman fathers" and those "laundromat workers, beauticians, [and] pregnant short-haired jail bait" subordinate their differences in the nightclub.

Significantly, Baraka portrays the audience's leader as a member of that class of African Americans who embody "a greasy hip-ness, down-ness, nobody in our camp believed" (260). A member of the "folk," in other words, the leader—the sax-playing Lynn Hope—is a man who "could be a common hero, from whatever side we saw him" (261). As he plays the music he leads the audience but also responds to them: "Lynn would oblige [the narrator's need for a partner]. He would make the most perverted hopes sensual and possible. Chanting at that dark crowd" (261). Together, the leader and his audience form a select group of African Americans; they are only those who "could be roused by Lynn's histories and rhythms. America had choked the rest, who could sit still for hours under popular songs, or be readied for citizenship by slightly bohemian social workers" (262).

The music itself and the process of creation are presented as integral aspects of the African American community's unity and power. Baraka focuses, for example, on the development of a particular saxophone style he calls "the honk." Baraka chooses the honk to anchor "The Screamers" because of its metaphorical possibilities. More closely adhering to a blues aesthetic than other sax styles of the 1950s and 1960s because of its imitation of the human voice, the honk invites a link to human experience via the emotions: "The repeated rhythmic figure, a screamed riff, pushed in its insistence past music. It was hatred and frustration, secrecy and despair. It spurted out of the diphthong culture, and reinforced the black cults of emotion" (264). Baraka, of course, also constructs the honk as the expression of emotions—hatred, frustration, secrecy, and despair—that derive directly from African American experience with slavery, segregation, and other racist structures. Moreover, by constructing the honk as an expression of these emotions Baraka can fashion it into a weapon to be used against those who erect racist structures: "There was no compromise, no dreary sophistication, only the elegance of something that is too ugly to be described and is diluted only at the agent's peril . . . [it] spread like fire thru the cabarets and joints of the black cities, so that the sound itself became a basis for thought, and the innovators searched for uglier modes" (264).

The honk is also significant for Baraka because as a close relative of the blues aesthetic it represents a "folk" expression. It is, in other words, the expression most appropriate for a "common hero" like Lynn Hope: "All the saxophonists of that world were honkers, Illinois, Gator, Big Jay, Jug, the great sounds of our day. Ethnic historians, actors, priests of the unconscious" (264). Lynn Hope is able to achieve the status of "common hero," in other words, because his adoption and development of this particular saxophone style links him with the history and the unconscious of the people for whom he plays and of whom he is part. As in *Blues People*, his 1963 history of African American music, Baraka uses "The Screamers" to assert a logical, unified link between the experience of the African American folk avant garde and African American expression. This link encompasses not only music, but dance and other forms of expression: "All extremes were popular with that crowd. The singers shouted, the musicians stomped and howled. The dancers ground each other past passion or moved so fast it blurred intelligence" (264).

The connection between jazz performance and the African American folk reaches an apotheosis in Baraka's story through Lynn Hope's playing of the honk. Inspired by the crowd and his own sense of outdueling the reputation of another player, Hope sounds this "repeated rhythmic figure" to a greater and greater intensity: "Then Lynn got his riff, that rhythmic figure we knew he would repeat, the honked note that would be his personal evaluation of the world. And he screamed it so the veins in his face stood out like neon. 'Uhh, yeh, Uhh, yeh, Uhh, yeh,' we all screamed to push him further" (266). "March[ing] in time with his riff," Hope, his fellow musicians, and members of the audience "strut" around the hall and out the door into the street where the musicians continue to honk their horns and the audience members yell along with them. Lynn Hope "marched right in the center of the street," stopping traffic, while they all "made to destroy the ghetto." Called out, in other words, by the magic of the honk, the folk assert their collective power: "We screamed and screamed at the clear image of ourselves as we should always be. Ecstatic, completed, involved in a secret communal expression. It would be the form of the sweetest revolution, to hucklebuck into the fallen capital, and let the oppressors lindy hop out" (267). In this metaphorical apotheosis, identity, ecstasy, liberation, and community are harmoniously united in the desire embodied in the sound of a honking saxophone (and echoed, of course, by the name of the saxophone player).

As in "Sonny's Blues," however, this transcendence cannot and does not last: the outside world—"the real"—intrudes. In "The Screamers," the carnival-like, wishfully revolutionary behavior of the crowd in the streets is interrupted by the police and transformed into a bloody racial struggle between white ethnic police officers and African Americans: "The paddy wagons and cruisers pulled in from both sides, and sticks and billies started flying, heavy streams of water splattering the marchers up and down the street. America's responsible immigrants were doing her light work again" (267). In another similarity with Baldwin's story, Baraka's narrator notes the ironic relationship peculiar to African Americans between the terror of "the real" and the beauty of their expression: "But for a while, before the war had reached its peak, Lynn and his musicians, a few other fools, and I, still marched, screaming thru the maddened crowd. Onto the sidewalk, into the lobby, halfway up the stairs, then we all broke our different ways, to save whatever it was each of us thought we loved" (268). True to the pattern of African American history, the beauty of expression and the terror of "the real" exist together for a moment because of the foolish courage of a few individuals.

Even in African American portrayals of Euro American jazz performers the significance of tradition and of the "lived relations" between blacks and whites in the United States is emphasized. In the short story "McDougal," for example, Frank London Brown offers a depiction of a white musician, the title character, whose musical prowess is assessed, by African American musicians and audience members, according to his ability "to blow the real thing" (Brown 1968: 203). The "real thing," in McDougal's case, is based both on his understanding of the jazz and blues lineage and on his life experience. Written during an era of heightened racial rhetoric by an author who had read short stories to the accompaniment of such jazz musicians as Thelonious Monk, the story illustrates a point Ben Sidran has made about white musicians during the bop era: "it [bop] developed the notion of 'blackness' as a cultural, rather than genetic, condition. Thus the white musician whose life style, and then whose music, fitted the revolution was accepted" (Sidran 1971: 96).

McDougal jams in a nightclub with a black musician named Pro, a musician so hot, so steeped in the tradition, that he "had blown choruses that dripped with the smell of cornbread and cabbage and had roared like a late 'L' and had cried like a blues singer on the last night of a good gig" (Brown 1968: 202). Moreover, Brown implies, Pro's solo tells the "truth" about the African American condition and tells it "so plainly, so passionately that it had scared everybody in the place, even Pro" (202). This is the circumstance that McDougal encounters as he begins his solo: Pro and the predominantly African American audience are waiting, skeptically, to "hear what the white man had to say." Before he begins to play McDougal is already marked as a unique "white man" by his appearance on the stage: although he is a young man he "had many wrinkles and his young body slouched and his shoulders hung round and loose. He was listening to Little Jug's bass yet he also seemed to be listening to something else, almost as if he were still listening to the truth Pro had told" (203).

Soon it becomes clear to the reader just why McDougal's face is wrinkled, his body is misshapen, and his attention is so tightly focused on Pro's frightening truth. Between notes, beats, and chords, the musicians swap what they know of McDougal's life: "'Man, that cat has suffered for that brownskin woman,' Little Jug added. 'And those . . . three little brownskin crumb-crushers.' Percy R. Brookings, hit another chord and then 'Do you know none of the white folks'll rent to him now?' Little Jug laughed. 'Why hell yes . . . will they rent to me?'" (203). These experiences, so common to the African American musicians that they laugh at them, are what enable McDougal, unlike most Euro Americans ("Like he's no Harry James") to "blow the real thing." Jazz in Brown's representation is clearly connected to a specific kind of experience, an African American experience McDougal is privy to because of his marriage to an African American woman. The other musicians know about his life but they can also hear the effect of his life in his playing: "'he knows the happenings. . . . I mean about where we get it, you dig? I mean like with Leola and those kids and Forty Seventh Street and those jive landlords, you dig? The man's been burnt, Percy. Listen to that somitch—listen to him!'" (204).

Predictably, Euro American writers describing the process of improvisational creation focus almost exclusively on what is happening on the stage—that is, the *appearance* of the performers and performance. This focus takes different forms— the technical virtuosity of the performers, the apparent "competition" between players, or the personal connections among the musicians. Perhaps this emphasis comes from the Euro American writer's greater need to prove his connection with and mastery of this subcultural idiom. That is, claiming a musical expertise substitutes for being able (or, at least, *feeling* able) to link oneself with the experience of racism or the development of African American culture.

Ross Russell's novel *The Sound* provides the clearest example of the Euro American writer who positions himself as a jazz authority through his narrative interest in the technical virtuosity of bebop performers on the bandstand. Russell's focus on the musical dexterity of jazz performers is not surprising given his primary occupations as both a jazz producer and author of two well-respected nonfiction books on jazz. In fact, as critic Richard N. Albert notes, the primary value of *The Sound* is in Russell's "first-hand knowledge of the jazz scene during the bop period . . . [his] veritable catalog of jazz musicians and styles and [his] lexicon of jazz jargon" (Albert 1990: 4). While Russell's descriptions of jazz performance are indeed impressive because of the amount of information they offer about jazz technique, they never extend beyond the very knowledgeable listener's catalogue of chord changes, rhythmic patterns, tempos, physical skills, and note runs. Russell never takes the reader behind the gauze of craft to glimpse the driving force of artistry. Nor does he infuse the moment of performance with the metaphorical power it seems to invite.

In a typical performance scene from early in *The Sound*, for example, Russell presents his virtuoso, Charlie Parker-like trumpet-player, Red Travers, in a live nightclub show with several less accomplished musicians. Depicting the first time his main white character, Bernie Rich, plays with the notorious Red Travers, Russell has designed this scene to communicate to the reader both Travers's incredible improvisational talent and the difficulty and thrill of playing (especially for a traditionally schooled white player) with such an exacting, innovative musician. Russell builds the tension and drama of the scene, however, by focusing almost completely on the *musical* interaction among the players on the bandstand. Documenting his *own* comprehensive knowledge of jazz music and the jazz milieu, Russell offers a portrayal of jazz performance in this scene that consists, simply, of four musicians struggling for fifteen minutes to keep up with the demanding tempo, complex rhythms, and creative changes required to accompany Red Travers.

Each musician in the quintet (even such members as Bernie and Hassan, the drummer, who are important to the developing story) is characterized in only the most cursory manner so that Russell can focus his narrative attention on his elaborate descriptions of the sound of the music and the musicians' techniques. Near the opening of this section Russell introduces Bernie Rich as a "new music" neophyte whose inclusion in this quintet seems to set the stage for some sort of confrontation between him and Travers: "Bernie Rich was conditioned to a more orderly type of performance. Of course, practically everybody knew the chords to 'I Got Rhythm.' Bernie Rich knew them. Bleakly, they flashed through his mind's eye—B-flat, C-minor seventh, F seventh, B-flat, C-minor seventh, so on. Except that he had not the faintest notion of the new riff based on these chords. It had not been among any of the Red Travers' records to which he had listened again and again at Zaida's apartment. Nor had he the faintest idea of how a trumpet could be tongued at the insane tempo Hass was now setting up" (1961: 49). Even this passage, which introduces some information about Bernie Rich, gets slightly lost in technical information with the list of chord changes for "I Got Rhythm."

More significantly, however, Russell does nothing much with this potential for the development of Bernie Rich's character during this performance: the group plays on, Bernie feels dragged along by the music (as though he's on a roller coaster again for the first time), his wrist muscles get tired, and the tune ends.

Similarly, the drummer Hassan is not developed in his own right in this nightclub scene; he is used simply to reflect Red Travers's virtuosity and as the passive vehicle for Russell's own skillful display of knowledge:

> Hassan's ride cymbal began to vibrate, pumping its shimmering sound across the bandstand. He was playing six notes to the bar, And-One-TWO, And-Three-FOUR, but the notes seemed to run together so that the big cymbal, with light splashing off its gentle coolie-hat curves, had a musical pulse of its own. The stick flew in the drummer's wiry wrist and fell against the alloyed metal, hammered to paper thinness by the craftsman who had forged it. Hassan's fingers maintained the stick in a suspended motion, like a juggler with a stream of balls flying. . . . Hassan began to add little percussive figures, muffled thuds on the bass, pistol shots on the snares, jungly throbs on the tom-tom, puffs of air lightly caught between the surfaces of the high hat and charged with a bubbly froth of sound, truncated press rolls that were like thunder heard briefly and at a distance—his mosaic of skilled, subtle sounds. (1961: 49)

Offering a stunning example of Russell's ability to put life into the depiction of jazz playing itself, this passage is also significant because it shows just how completely Russell's narrative emphasis on the technical aspect of music obscures the musician/character himself. In this passage, Hassan is simply another object, like the cymbal or snare drum, except he is described with much less care and in much less detail than they are. The description of Hassan's playing stays strictly on the surface of the scene, describing (admittedly with evocative figures and language) the sound of the music and the appearance of the drummer's instruments and motions, but the musician remains a cipher and the music and performance rouse nothing more than the noisy, smoky nightclub scene itself.

Russell's apparent lack of interest in developing Hassan and even Bernie Rich as characters in performance scenes might be attributed to their secondary roles in the novel. However, Russell does not even use the opportunity of these scenes to develop trumpeter Red Travers much beyond his status as a demanding, innovative jazz musician. In this scene, for example, Travers performs an incendiary solo during " 'Seein' Red', a grim parody on the old Gershwin tune." However, as with Russell's portrayals of Bernie Rich and Hassan, nothing more than style and technique is revealed about the man: "Red played an entire chorus with only the three notes of the triad. But he varied them infinitely; altered their intonation and attack, bent and fitted them into various positions of the bar structure, creating a whole series of rhythmic patterns and levels, each more complex than the other" (51). As the scene builds with the "excitement" of Travers's remarkable solo, the reader expects that Russell's narrative will stretch for an epiphany or some other daring metaphorical moment. Instead Russell settles for a clichéd image that never even reaches the point of metaphor: "Man and instrument moved in a solid block. In one piece. He blew with his cheeks hard packed from compressed air, a glazed look on his face, his throat distended like a bellows" (51). Even at this climactic moment in Travers's performance— the apex of this supremely talented musician's creative, innovative solo—Russell develops nothing beyond the platitude of "the man and his instrument were as one" (unlike Ann Petry in "Solo on Drums") followed by more description of Travers's perfectly placed notes and "longest melodic line that Bernie had ever heard." Unfortunately Russell's description of Travers's solo does not apply to Russell's own narrative: "The technique itself was prodigious, yet always sub-jected to a greater creativity. Never in the long solo did he suffer it to exist for itself. Not once did he embellish with a mechanical device or easy trumpet figuration."

Russell not only fails to use the entire performance scene described in detail here (or other performance scenes like it) to develop any of the larger social issues presented in the book as a whole; he also fails to use it to develop any fundamental characteristic about the musicians or the relationships between the musicians. Like Red Travers's supporting cast during the fifteen-minute performance of "Seein' Red," the characters in the scene remain static figures thoroughly dominated by Russell's own display of his exceptional knowledge, skill, and authority.

As we can see in the work of Jack Kerouac, even when a Euro American author tries to endow jazz performance with a significance beyond what is "happening" on the bandstand, his efforts degenerate into a vagueness that universalizes jazz and jazz performance and, worse, weakens the specific power of this potentially significant metaphorical moment. Representing himself to the world as a jazz-influenced writer, Kerouac was especially interested in the spontaneous, asso-ciational creativity he identified with the jazz solo during performance. In his programmatic statements on writing—"Essentials of Spontaneous Prose" and "Belief and Technique for Modern Prose"—in fact, Kerouac, valorizes the notion that the writer should compose in the manner of a "jazz musician." He advocates, for example, that the writer compose in the moment by focusing one's attention on what he calls the "jewel center of interest in subject of image," and, essentially, transcribing the words as they occur in the writer's mind: "sketching language in undisturbed flow from the mind of personal secret idea-words, *blowing* (as per jazz musician) on subject of image" (1961b: 65–67). Using this method, Kerouac believed, the writer could and would achieve "art" rather than "craft" because he or she would tap into what is most unique about him or herself unencumbered by existing patterns of expression: "tap from yourself the song of yourself, *blow!*—*now!*—*your* way is your only way—'good'—or 'bad'—always honest, ('ludicrous'), spontaneous, 'confessional' interesting, because not 'crafted'" (1961b: 65–67).

Setting aside until chapter 5 questions about the validity, originality, and viability of Kerouac's method, we can nevertheless see that Kerouac's understanding of the process of creativity in jazz influenced his own professed novelistic strategy. Significantly, Kerouac's understanding of the creative process in jazz (as presented in these programmatic statements) emphasizes the personal and even the private: "Blow as deep as you want—write as deeply, fish as far down as you want, satisfy yourself first" (1961b: 65–67). No mention is made anywhere in Kerouac's pronouncements of study being necessary prior to the undertaking of "spontaneous prose." Kerouac's instructions and "List of Essentials" for this creative activity suggest that the writer's improvisations (like the jazz musician's, he implies) require nothing more than consciousness, emotions, and life experience. Included on Kerouac's "List of Essentials" in the document "Belief and Technique for Modern Prose" are: "Be in love with yr life"; "Something that you feel will find its own form"; "No fear or shame in the dignity of yr experience, language & knowledge"; "Composing wild, undisciplined, pure, coming in from under, crazier the better"; "You're a Genius all the time" (1961a: 64).

Kerouac takes possession of and represents jazz improvisation as a process that is individualistic, ahistorical, and "naive." Thus, when Kerouac portrays a climactic, meaningful moment in jazz improvisation—a moment, for example, when the musician reaches some sort of apex of intensity while soloing—he does so in descriptive and explanatory terms that are mysterious, vague, and at best only suggestive. Of course, descriptions of music in literature are notoriously vague and suggestive because of the difficulty of "capturing" in language the sound of music and the effect of it on the individual. However, in Kerouac's case, the representational vagueness occurs not in his depiction of the sound of jazz music itself (in fact, he uses a variety of onomatopoeic words that clearly simulate jazz sounds—"beep," "honk," "ee-yah," for example), but in his attempt to attribute greater meaning to the playing of the music. Despite his attempts, Kerouac is never able to place the creative process in jazz in a precise and meaningful metaphorical or analogical context.

In *On the Road* there are several passages that contain vividly descriptive scenes of formal and informal jazz performances that rely, for their greater meaning, on Kerouac's rather vague concept of "IT." According to Regina Weinreich, Kerouac's use of "IT" in *On the Road* is part of a larger pattern in his work that posits "heightened moments of 'meaning-excitement'" as the object of his heroic quest (Weinreich 1990: 52). These "epiphanies," Weinreich asserts, are "thrill[s] for a moment" or moments of "instant gratification" that derive their significance in contrast to both the nobility of the historical heroic quest (the quest for the Holy Grail in the Arthurian legend, for example) and the ordinariness of American life of the 1940s and 1950s. With these epiphanic moments Kerouac dramatizes his belief that heroism is necessary but, ultimately, futile in modern America—the best one can do is achieve momentary enlightenment or, even, satisfaction.

In *On the Road*, these "heightened moments of 'meaning-excitement'" are communicated in the word "IT" and are, as Weinreich says, "explicitly" analogized "with the action of the jazzman" (1990: 53). Kerouac locates the jazz musician's significance as an artist in mysterious moments of musical meaning that can only be hinted at by such vague metaphors as "IT":

> The behatted tenorman was blowing at the peak of a wonderfully satisfactory free idea, a rising and falling riff that went from "EE-yah!" to a crazier "EE-de-lee-yah!" and blasted along to the rolling crash of butt-scarred drums hammered by a big brutal Negro with a bullneck who didn't give a damn about anything but punishing his busted tubs, crash, rattle-ti-boom, crash. Uproars of music and the tenorman *had it* and everybody knew he had it. Dean was clutching his head in the crowd, and it was a mad crowd. They were all urging that tenorman to hold it and keep it with cries and wild eyes, and he was raising himself from a crouch and going down again with his horn, looping it up in a clear cry above the furor. (1957: 162)

Although Kerouac's sense of "IT" as a metaphor for meaning in jazz performance is unexplained in this passage, one does get an indication of its significance for Kerouac's construction of aesthetic creation and communication. This moment of epiphany or transcendence is depicted as being important not only for the musician ("the tenorman *had it*") but also for the connection between the musician and audience ("it was a mad crowd. They were all urging that tenorman to hold it and keep it with cries and wild eyes"). Kerouac reaches for some sign that can contain the transcendence, community, and emotion suggested by this scene and settles for one that can possibly mean everything and nothing—"IT." The sense of this scene suggests that this sign was suggested by the actual comments shouted by audience members during the many jazz club performances Kerouac witnessed in New York City during the 1940s and 1950s: " 'Stay with it, man!' roared a man with a foghorn voice, and let out a big groan that must have been heard clear out in Sacramento, ah-haa!" (163). This scene, then, exemplifies the limitations of Kerouac's (and that of many of the white writers I have studied) representation of jazz performance: despite his familiarity and identification with jazz and jazz musicians (to the extent of having been one of a select group of Euro Americans that ventured up to Harlem to hear it in person), Kerouac's use of it in literature does not transcend the simple, if vivid, mimetic depiction of the jazz milieu. Furthermore, this weakness in his use of jazz illustrates Kerouac's failure to concretize jazz performance in a way that could generate the kind of value and meaning that would sustain his readers.

The extent of this inability (or unwillingness) to connect jazz with any notion other than a universalized spirituality can be found several pages following the above scene in a passage in which Kerouac tries to clarify the meaning of "IT." Significantly, Kerouac puts the words of this attempted explanation into the mouth of Dean Moriarty. Dean, the object of Sal's (Kerouac's surrogate) worship and the catalyst of his self-understanding and freedom, educates Sal about experiences that are beyond the scope of people, like Sal, who are relative "tourists" to social outsiderism (Weinreich 1990: 38):

> "Now, man, that alto man last night had IT—he held it once he found it; I've never seen a guy who could hold so long." I wanted to know what "IT" meant. "Ah well"— Dean laughed—"now you're asking me impon-de-rables—ahem! Here's a guy and everybody's there, right? Up to him to put down what's on everybody's mind. He starts the first chorus, then lines up his ideas, people, yeah, yeah, but get it, and then he rises to his fate and has to blow equal to it. All of a sudden somewhere in the middle of the chorus he *gets* it—everybody looks up and knows; they listen; he picks it up and carries. Time stops. He's filling empty space with the substance of our lives, confessions of his bellybottom strain, remembrance of ideas, rehashes of old blowing. He has to blow across bridges and come back and do it with such infinite feeling soul-exploratory for the tune of the moment that everybody knows it's not the tune that counts but IT—" Dean could go no further; he was sweating telling about it. (1957: 170)

Dean's attempt to explicate this nebulous concept follows a rambling, circuitous path of the kind that an alto sax solo might seem to take (he even sweats during his "performance"). Beginning and ending with declarations suggesting the importance of "IT" in jazz solos, Dean's explanation reveals his inability to describe the substance of jazz performance in anything beyond the vaguest intimations of meaningfulness ("filling empty space with the substance of our lives, confessions of his bellybottom strain, remembrance of ideas, rehashes of old blowing"). Despite his firsthand knowledge of jazz performance, his status as subterranean-mentor, and his seemingly unpracticed (and thus authentic) jazz-like oral performance Dean cannot enlighten Sal or us about the function of live jazz performance for either the performer or the audience; this function remains one of the "impon-de-rables."

Perhaps Kerouac's intention in this scene is to use Dean's exuberant but incoherent description to mock his/our inability to explain aesthetic and spiritual experiences. One could, for example, cite James Joyce's work as a model for Kerouac's use of a punning, word-playing, spontaneous voice to signify a kind of worldly transcendence that is, in itself, the closest human beings can come to any universal spirituality.[5] However, it is more likely that Dean's explanation of jazz performance represents Kerouac's genuine ideas about the spiritual effect jazz can have on listeners. According to biographer Gerald Nicosia, Kerouac and other social and cultural outsiders were attracted to "the jazz milieu" because it "wasn't in the least political," but instead "was a way of crossing . . . boundaries into new worlds, where the magic of the unexpected converted you like a miracle" (1983: 366). Kerouac genuinely believed, in other words, that listening to jazz was a window into some sort of universal spirituality. Nicosia quotes surrealist poet Philip Lamantia to indicate Kerouac's own understanding of the spiritual power of jazz: "There were ways in which, as one sat listening to Bird in 1948 or to completely unknown people in Little Harlem [in San Francisco], one actually was elevated to the stars!" (1983: 366).

Although Kerouac's and Lamantia's hyperbolic characterizations are obviously attempts to magnify the significance of jazz, they actually diminish or erode its meaning. First, the significance attributed to jazz by their characterizations is so grand and so extensive that it cannot possibly be fulfilled by the music. Second, disconnecting it from any political, historical, or social context in favor of a universalized one makes a fetish out of jazz and thus prepares it to be recuperated by the Euro American mainstream.

We can glimpse this recuperation in television and film productions of the early 1960s. Rod Serling's series *The Twilight Zone*, noted for its intelligent 30-minute teleplays, offered a production with a jazz theme and score during its first season (1959–60). Written by Serling, this episode, titled "A Passage for Trumpet," adapts Frank Capra's plot in *It's a Wonderful Life* to depict the redemption of a hip white jazz trumpeter named Joey Crown who is so alienated from life that he has become an alcoholic, lost his friends, destroyed his relationships with club owners, and, finally, thrown himself into the street in front of an oncoming truck. The musician is saved by an angel ("Call me Gabe. . . . Short for Gabriel") who convinces Crown that his life actually is not as joyless as he thought. The angel persuades Joey Crown that his music is the central element in his past and future happiness: if Joey has faith in the music it will reward him with unexpected joy and beauty. In the show's closing scene Joey "performs" his redemption: after he is saved by Gabriel, Joey sits alone on the roof of a Manhattan skyscraper playing a romantic trumpet solo to an uncaring city below when, suddenly, a young woman ascends to the rooftop. A fresh-faced newcomer to the big city, she is attracted to Joey's beautiful music and asks him if he will introduce New York to her; he agrees.

Clearly the depiction of jazz as a redemptive force in this television program resonates with the spiritual emphasis in Kerouac's work. Although "A Passage for Trumpet" is focused on the performer rather than the listener, Serling's approach to the significance of jazz, like Kerouac's, foregrounds a romantic, universal spiritual transformation rather than locating jazz in any kind of historical, social, or cultural context. Moreover, the two uses share a focus on *individual* transformation rather than any group connection. Of course, Serling's popular expression extends these depictions to an even greater degree of romanticism, universality, and individualism than did Kerouac or any of the other Euro American writers. In "A Passage for Trumpet" the musician's music is vital only to himself, is "literally" redemptive, and is performed for either no audience or an audience of one.

Whether or not Serling had read Kerouac's work or had any direct contact with the other work of this era that was influenced by jazz, this *Twilight Zone* episode demonstrates the propinquity of the wholly recuperated image of jazz in the mainstream to the one constructed by the Euro American outsider. Moreover, the mainstream acceptability of Serling's representation is indicated by Serling's experiences first as a writer of live television drama and then as a creator and writer for filmed episodic programs. Initially the highly-regarded writer of such live television dramas as "Requiem for a Heavyweight," Serling was one of the few writers to make the transition to the more rigidly controlled filmed programs. Criticized by contemporary critics as being "formulaic" and driven by the needs and desires of sponsors, these filmed programs were, according to William Boddy, subjected to the approval of network and advertising executives. Discussing this external control in a 1958 interview Serling stated: "I have pre-censored myself in the sense that I know that I'm not going to write those things that are socially sticky and unacceptable in terms of the mass medium. . . . It's best I write those things that can be shown. The only alternative is to try another medium—theatre or novel-writing—where you can say what you please" (Boddy 1990: 193–94, 203). Not surprisingly, Serling's use of jazz as a redemptive force capable of transforming the life of a white, solitary, alienated, alcoholic musician was not one that the network, sponsors, or audience would have objected to seeing in their living rooms.

Similarly, John Cassavetes' 1961 film *Too Late Blues* offers a recuperated version of the Euro American outsider's use of jazz. The first Hollywood production by a film director who was himself a lifelong industry outsider, *Too Late Blues* offers a construction of the significance of jazz performance different from, but related to, that presented in *The Twilight Zone*. Shunning the spiritual transformation Kerouac and Serling attribute to jazz, Cassavetes' film constructs jazz performance as the primary sign of a nebulous artistic integrity. By opening and closing with performance scenes that signify essential characteristics of the film's white musicians, the film specifically connects the white outsider's concept of artistic integrity with blues-based jazz performance. Moreover, the film's construction of this white concept of artistic integrity is contrasted with a black musician's ethic that is debased because it is presented as being commercialized and cynical.[6]

There are three significant performance scenes in *Too Late Blues* involving the white musicians: the opening scene in an orphanage for African American children, a gig in a public park, and the closing scene in a club. Played out under the credits, the opening scene offers viewers the sight of an all-white jazz band playing to a captive audience of African American children in an orphanage. Lined up along the walls, up the staircase, and surrounding the group, the children snap their fingers and swing their feet to the sound of the group's soulless music. As the group winds toward the end of their composition, the saxophonist puts down his instrument, which is then snatched by a young boy who has been sullenly watching the group play. The boy takes the saxophone, runs up the stairs, and begins to play the sax wildly and out-of-tune. As the children and the other musicians laugh and scream madly, the saxophonist follows the boy up the stairs and asks, "May I have my sax back please?" Played humorously, the scene is intended to show (as we discover later in the film) that the musicians are good-natured, well-intentioned guys who would rather play nonpaying gigs in orphanages and "old-lady homes" where they can play the music they like and believe in than play "commercial" music in paying venues. However, one of only a few scenes involving African American characters, the orphanage gig also states a theme that will be developed, implicitly, in the rest of the film: these white musicians—cultural and social outsiders—are the guardians of the true blues/jazz tradition (the band's "best" original composition is simply titled "The Blues"), and African Americans need to learn from them in order to return to their roots.

This theme is developed in a couple of ways. First, in the film's other two major performance scenes the group is again presented as being willing to suffer indignities in order not to compromise their integrity. One performance is in a public park where nobody shows up. The musicians play a melancholy tune that the leader, Ghost Wakefield, says they usually play better. The only audience around, as the following quote illustrates, are the park regulars (including the playground director and a practicing baseball team):

Charlie [the sax player]: Oh man, this is for the birds.
Red [the bass player]: C'mon Charlie, stop talking to the customers!
Charlie: Man, you reach for a high one and for what? For nobody.

Through this and several other scenes it is made clear that the major obstacle to the group's commercialization is their leader and composer, Wakefield. However, even though the other band members complain a lot about these horrible gigs, the lack of an audience, and their meager pay, the film suggests that there is a core of integrity to these white musicians as well. After all, according to the film's prehistory they gave up more lucrative work to stay with Wakefield. Moreover, in the film's final scene, the band (who has previously split with Wakefield because of his erratic behavior) returns to his fold by playing his most acclaimed composition.

Finally, the film implicitly switches the traditional values of white and black by linking white with the blues and black with commercialism. Soon after the orphanage scene, the film offers two scenes at a party that help confirm this pattern. First, the party's host is an African American musician (the only one named in the film), Baby Jackson, who has sold out. When he sees Wakefield and his group at the party he tells them in a patronizing voice, "I really dig what you guys are playing." With this, he goes off to "schmooze" the various club owners attending the party. He returns a few minutes later to fetch his agent (who is also Wakefield's agent) to clear up a "problem" concerning where and for how much he is playing next summer. As he leaves he tells the women Wakefield is talking to, "He's got wonderful stories, like Mother Goose and Peter Pan"—a clearly sarcastic reference to Wakefield's uncompromising, innocent integrity. This scene is supported by another at the party where a young white female singer (Wakefield's future girlfriend) is practically destroyed by a group of cynical African American musicians who are testing her vocal ability. It is clear from these two scenes where the heart and soul of the blues resides.

Given some of Cassavetes' other work (especially the earlier *Shadows*), it may be true, as Ray Carney argues, that many of the filmic and ideological problems in *Too Late Blues* are the result of Cassavetes' uneasy marriage with the Hollywood bureaucracy (Carney 1984: 63–77). However, *Too Late Blues* perfectly marks the reversal of the values that were pioneered (innocently enough) by white outsiders like Kerouac and Holmes and incorporated by the Hollywood media machine: white on top, black underneath.

5.

Improvising the Text

Euro American and African American Approaches to Jazz Narrative

Perhaps the discomfort about protest in books by Negro authors comes because since the nineteenth century American literature has avoided profound moral searching. It was too painful, and besides, there were specific problems of language and form to which the writers could address themselves. They did wonderful things, but perhaps they left the real problems untouched. There are exceptions, of course, like Faulkner, who has been working the great moral theme all along, taking it up where Mark Twain put it down. (Ellison 1964: 182–83)

To examine the use of jazz as a model for literary narrative during the immediate postwar period is to understand clearly and vividly the differences in ideas and experiences that were building at the time among black and white people of good will struggling to achieve justice and equality for African Americans. Even more so than a scrutiny of social experience in Greenwich Village or of the use of predominating jazz symbols in American culture, an analysis of the mediated influence of jazz on literary narrative reveals the possibilities of and obstacles to genuine racial understanding at the time and in the present. In their various translations of jazz into literary narrative, African American and Euro American writers demonstrate significant differences in terms of their understanding of the jazz tradition, the function of the jazz musician, the connections between music and literature and between literature and social reality, and the nature of improvisation. More than simply disagreements over aesthetic matters, these differences suggest that the serious ideological and experiential conflicts that existed between African and Euro Americans were opening a wide chasm between the two groups that has since only deepened and widened.[1]

As suggested by the above quotation from Ralph Ellison, the fundamental conflicts between African and Euro Americans derive from moral questions:

What is equality? How do we achieve it? What is freedom? Who has it? Can we all achieve it? While the political and social answers to these questions (in the form of equal accommodations and schooling, voting rights, etc.) have always occupied center stage in American racial discourse, the cultural answers—that is, the meaning of equality and freedom themselves—have been neglected. Should we, for example, continue to define equality and freedom simply as the opportunity for African Americans (and those in other racial, ethnic, gender, or sexual groups who have been historically discriminated against) to gain access to the institutions and material goods that Euro Americans have had? Or should/can we redefine equality and freedom so that their new meanings change the way we construct basic American values and beliefs? In a sense, then, we can see the political and social answers to these moral questions as the "problems of language and form" Ellison discusses, and the cultural answers as the "real problems" he says have been evaded. In this perspective, public policy measures like affirmative action are doomed to fail unless and until Americans change the way they understand equality and freedom.

Taken from a 1955 *Paris Review* interview, Ellison's quote specifically addresses twentieth-century literary politics, but also exposes the structure of feeling of the postwar era's racial politics, particularly among people enmeshed in the struggle for African Americans' civil rights. Most of the focus of "sensitive" Euro Americans (inside and outside the movement and the government) during this period centered on the "language and form" of equality and freedom while their essential meanings remained unchallenged. This is not to suggest, of course, that African Americans (especially during the earliest periods of the civil rights movement—that is, before the 1964 Democratic National Convention fiasco) were not also invested in the struggle to change the "language and form" of American racial politics; certainly, they fervently wanted an end to legal segregation and discrimination. However, from the beginning of this period, and increasingly from the mid-1960s, many African Americans also sought to change the very terms of the struggle by contesting the meaning of key American concepts like justice, freedom, and equality. Thus, the end of the decade witnessed the development of social, political, and cultural nationalism on a scale never seen before. Largely, this shift from a pragmatic to an ideological effort to attack racism was an African American response not only to slow and inadequate governmental reforms but also to the diminishing national interest in and commitment to abolishing racial inequality.

The period under study here (roughly from 1945 to 1967), then, encompasses a rift between African Americans and so-called progressive Euro Americans (those sensitive to and involved in the struggle for African American civil rights) that develops from a submerged fissure to an obvious and gaping chasm. Identifying and analyzing this rift in some detail yields further insight into the continuing racial conflict in the United States because it highlights the enduring differences between African and Euro American perspectives. While the late-1960s split between the traditional civil rights movement (including both African Americans and Euro Americans) and the emerging Black Power movement is well documented, my perspective differs in its emphasis on the nascent ideological divisions between progressive whites and blacks. I am suggesting that even before the most public signs of African and Euro American disunion—Stokely Carmichael's break with the Student Non-violent Coordinating Committee (SNCC) in 1966 and the formation of the Black Panther Party in 1967—the ideological divisions between whites and blacks were profound and distinct.

This division becomes apparent when we compare approaches to the jazz narrative from works written during the 1950s and early 1960s. To make the connection between literary narrative and a more general experiential or "affective" social content typical of this period I am using Raymond Williams's formulation of the structure of feeling (1977: 128–35). Williams characterizes structure of feeling as a "cultural hypothesis" used to describe social changes that occur in a historical period before they are formalized in a world-view or ideology (132). Williams indicates that these changes are manifested in the way people think and feel—in the way people *live*. Moreover, Williams theorizes, these changes are very often represented in art and literature "where the true social content is in a significant number of cases of this present and affective kind, which cannot without loss be reduced to belief-systems, institutions, or explicit general relationships" (133). In Williams's view, then, literature can be used as an index of the emerging changes in social experience: "The idea of a structure of feeling can be specifically related to the evidence of forms and conventions—semantic figures—which, in art and literature, are often among the very first indications that such a new structure is forming" (133).

Postwar jazz narrative, a site at which different cultural and literary traditions crossed, offers insight into the specific tensions, contradictions, and ironies that characterize American racial interaction between 1945 and 1966. Euro American writers who were disenchanted with what they perceived as the emptiness of both American society and American literature looked toward African American culture (and particularly jazz music and culture) for more vital forms and subjects. In this sense, these Euro American artists were, in Renato Poggioli's terms, consummately "modern" artists: "We must never forget that, in fact, his [the modern artist's] social protest shows itself principally on the level of form, and thus alienation from society also becomes *alienation from tradition*" (1968: 127; emphasis in original).

Influenced directly and indirectly by European avant-garde experiments with techniques such as automatic writing, which were thought to help gain access to the unconscious, some Euro American literary iconoclasts adopted methods and created forms that sought to transcend the extreme rationality and conformity of postwar American society by producing works that were spontaneous and random. Translated through the work of Americans like William Carlos Williams, however, the European avant-garde experiments became much more directed and structured in the work of Euro American postwar writers like Allen Ginsberg and Jack Kerouac. Williams's 1920 "improvisational" work *Kora in Hell* uses automatic writing not only to "descend deeper than ever into his poetic unconsciousness," but to bring his everyday life into the realm of literature (Mariani 1981: 148). Comprising entries written every day for a year before he went to bed and retrospective "interpretations" of these entries, *Kora in Hell* was designed, as Williams makes clear in the "Prologue," as an American antidote to the more traditional, formal innovations of T. S. Eliot (Williams 1967: 26–31). Williams's innovations prefigured (if not influenced) Kerouac's work with "spontaneous prose," and it is significant that *Kora in Hell* was reprinted in 1957 by Beat publisher Lawrence Ferlinghetti's City Lights Books. Whatever the specific route of transmission from Williams to Kerouac and others, Williams's work established the importance of improvisation and, according to poet and scholar Charles O. Hartman, "the logic of poetic authority" in the postwar era. Hartman diagrams this logic in the following manner (1991: 4):

   improvisation_
     spontaneity_
         genuineness_
           authenticity_
           authority

Hartman's diagramming reveals the ahistorical, even imperialistic logic behind the authority that derives from the Euro Americans' understanding of improvisation. For Euro American writers of this period, improvisation was a universal experimental technique—not tied to any particular cultural tradition—that they could adopt and modify for their own purposes. In this scheme, then, jazz improvisation was simply another model, although a uniquely American one, that offered these avant-gardists a way to express their desire for writing that was more free and more grounded in American lives.

Most of the African American writers of this period who incorporated elements of jazz into the structure of their work, on the other hand, saw improvisation as part of a specific cultural lineage. Most of these African American writers had relationships different from those of their Euro American counterparts with both the cultural tradition out of which jazz developed and the dominant literary tradition. First, African American writers using jazz resources had a deep, intimate knowledge of the African American musical and cultural heritage, and a perceived stake in maintaining the integrity of this tradition. Thus, LeRoi Jones, who was continually queried early in his career about the differences between his work and that of Beat writers he admired, notes that even for an avowed American avant-gardist like himself race is a significant distinguishing factor in his writing: "There are certain influences on me, as a Negro person, that certainly wouldn't apply to a poet like Allen Ginsberg. I couldn't have written that poem 'Kaddish,' for instance. And I'm sure he couldn't write certain things that have to deal with, say, Southern Baptist church rhythms. Everything applies—everything in your life. Sociologically, there are different influences, different things that I've seen, that I know, that Allen or no one knows" (Baraka 1994: 6). As we shall see, this difference in positioning toward the African American tradition contributes to the distinct uses of jazz structure by African and Euro American writers.

Another important element in this mix is the necessarily different positioning of African Americans (especially during the 1950s and early 1960s) vis-a-vis the literary and publishing establishment. Whereas most of the Euro American writers using jazz resources styled themselves as rebels against the literary establishment and made this rebellion central to their identity as artists and social/cultural outsiders, their African American counterparts (except, perhaps, for Amiri Baraka, Bob Kaufman, and Ted Joans) saw themselves essentially as writers struggling to gain a foothold in the very establishment that the Euro American avant-gardists disdained. Before he published his first novel in 1960, John A. Williams (author of the Charlie Parker–inspired novel *Night Song*), for example, honed his skills as a writer working as a journalist for African American magazines and as a self-published poet, and learned about the publishing business working as an editor for an independent press and an agent for a vanity press (Muller 1984: 1–21). Using these conventional avenues, Williams's development as a writer more closely resembles that of "establishment" writers than of 1950s rebels like Kerouac or Ginsberg, except for the very important difference that, as a "black" writer, he had to contend with additional obstacles that neither establishment writers nor literary rebels faced.[2] This latter point is significant because it suggests another distinction between these two groups of writers: for all their rebelliousness and anti-establishment identification, many of the Euro American writers had more access to what passes for power in the publishing industry than did the African American writers. The exception among African American writers is Amiri Baraka, who benefited to a certain extent from important relationships with white women. Hettie Jones, for example, helped Baraka make his initial mark with the New York intellectual crowd by getting William Barrett to publish his rebuttal to Norman Podhoretz's critical reveiw of *On the Road* in *Partisan Review* (Jones 1990: 56–57). Jack Kerouac, on the other hand, was able to publish novels at two critical junctures in his career because of his contacts with such influential literary figures as Mark Van Doren, Brom Weber, Alfred Kazin, and Malcolm Cowley. Kerouac's first novel, *The Town and the City*, was published with the help of Weber, Van Doren, and Kazin, while his milestone work, *On the Road*, was published by dint of Cowley's intervention. This is not to diminish, of course, the fact that Kerouac struggled for many years to get his more adventurous work published: in the seven years between the publication of *The Town and the City* and *On the Road* Kerouac wrote part or all of fourteen different works that he had great difficulty placing with publishers. Nevertheless, one possible reading of these different, racialized scenarios is that their connections to at least the progressive wing of the publishing industry gave Euro American writers a certain degree of freedom or license to experiment that most of the African American writers, like Williams, did not have.[3]

John Williams's experience, and that of other African American writers of the time, suggests that their attitude toward their resources (including jazz) was not that of the literary rebel who self-consciously searched for material to substitute for lifeless form and content, like Kerouac or Ginsberg, or who purposely outraged the establishment, like Burroughs, but of the traditional artist who responded to the substance of his emotional, intellectual, and cultural experience. Thus, their work takes up jazz music and the jazz subculture as only one among many subjects and, more importantly, does not make a fetish out of any formal or structural notion of improvisation or spontaneity. This is not to say, certainly, that these African American writers do not attribute powerful values and functions to jazz or to the improvisational method (as we shall see). As Kimberly Benston notes in his excellent study of Amiri Baraka's work, African American poets—especially since Langston Hughes and others during the Harlem Renaissance era—have made continual, if different, use of black music as a source for cultural meaning (Benston 1976: 70–71). However, even an African American artist like Amiri Baraka, for whom jazz has revolutionary potential, does not formulate a programmatic aesthetic theory that valorizes an *imitation* of jazz; instead he incorporates jazz sounds, methods, and history into a holistic theory of African American culture.[4] Thus, for example, when Baraka is asked in a recent interview whether he believes in and follows Ginsberg's partly jazz-influenced dictum, "First thought, best thought," he answers disdainfully, "No. (Laughs.) Obviously." When further pressed about whether he revises, Baraka says, "Yes, sure. So does he [Ginsberg]—so what? (Laughs.)" (Baraka 1994: 210).[5]

The key to understanding the different uses of jazz by African and Euro Americans in structuring their narratives lies specifically in recognizing their distinct interpretation of the concept of improvisation and their application of it in fiction. As indicated by Ginsberg's dictum, "First thought, best thought," Euro Americans generally adopted a simplistic, ahistorical understanding of improvisation and applied this understanding to their narrative structure in an imitative or mimetic manner. As we shall see, Jack Kerouac takes this approach to its logical extreme in his fiction and his aesthetic statement, "Essentials of Spontaneous Prose." African American writers, on the other hand, interpreted improvisation much more deeply and broadly, seeing it as controlling not just (or even primarily) the form and structure of their narrative but the content and meaning as well. For these writers, improvisation is not only a process of creation that emphasizes freedom and spontaneity, but also a culturally specific concept that is ineluctably connected to historical and contemporary social contexts. Poet Michael S. Harper has described the significance of jazz in these terms:

> I think the most important thing here to remember is that jazz and blues are open-ended forms, not programmatic and not abstract. They're modal. And by modality I mean some very complicated perceptual and moral things. Modality assumes many things which society really has not fully understood, although there are singular members of the society who do accept them. Number one is that man is basically spiritual. Second is that one has a "wholistic" concept of the universe. This means that the universe is not fragmented, that man has a place in it, that man is a reflection of the environment, and that the environment is a reflection of man. John Coltrane was a modal musician. One of the things that is important about Coltrane's music is the energy and passion with which he approached his instrument and music. Such energy was perhaps akin to the nature of oppression generally and the kind of energy it takes to break oppressive conditions, oppressive musical strictures, and oppressive societal situations. (in O'Brien 1973: 97–98)

Although Harper's explanation goes somewhat far afield from what I am arguing here, it demonstrates the sense shared by many African American writers that improvisation in jazz and blues is connected to more than simply a single person's unconscious, emotional life or creative genius.

The differences between Euro American and African American interpretations and applications of improvisation derive, as I have already suggested, from a cluster of elements that includes the writer's social experience, position in relation to the dominant literary and publishing establishments, and understanding of and respect for African American musical and cultural traditions. While the first two parts of this cluster are easily understood, the last is controversial enough to warrant further explanation. Characterizing the relationship between writer and traditions this way does not imply that there are correct and incorrect understandings of and/or proper and improper respect for this particular tradition, nor that the tradition is a static entity whose meaning and significance needs to be policed. As with every tradition, the African American cultural and literary traditions have been and continue to be constructed by their interpreters. However, because it is common for emergent or nondominant traditions to be denied even the status of a fully developed tradition with canonical works, progressive or cumulative patterns of development, tropes, themes, and conventions, it is important to determine whether interpreters of the tradition have an awareness of it as such. Albert Murray, for example, notes that many Americans do not "consider the blues idiom a major cultural achievement. Not even those writers who have referred to it as being perhaps the only truly American innovation in contemporary artistic expression seem able to concede it any more significance than of some vague minor potential not unlike that of some exotic spice" (Murray 1983: 56). As we shall see, the Euro American writers who use jazz as a resource for their experimentation with form and content demonstrate less awareness of and respect for these traditions, which they admire, than they do the dominant tradition they perceive as incapacitated. The use of jazz resources by African American writers of this period, on the other hand, illustrates different ironies. Encased in narrative forms that are conventionally composed and structured—that is, written and rewritten over a long period of time and linearly plotted—fiction by African American writers nonetheless contains narrative elements that strongly evoke the cultural aesthetic of jazz improvisation.

A brief explanation of improvisation in jazz is necessary to introduce these jazz-like narrative elements in African American fiction. Contrary to commonly held beliefs about jazz, improvisation is not simply a matter of creating music freely, from the unconscious, at the moment it is performed. As music scholar Paul F. Berliner makes clear in his recent, comprehensive study, *Thinking in Jazz*, improvisation requires a specific kind of knowledge, training, and skills, and thus is inseparable from the tradition within which it is embedded: "Overall, the jazz community's educational system sets the students on paths of development directly related to their goal: the creation of a unique improvisational voice within the jazz tradition" (Berliner 1994: 59). Unlike the romantic notion of naive, folk-like, spontaneous creation, true jazz improvisation occurs only at the end of a long process of learning and performing. This is not to say, of course, that real-time, spontaneous composition does not occur in jazz (it is, in fact, the most commonly used measure of jazz creativity)—only that it is the end product of a process of learning.

According to Berliner, in fact, not all jazz players reach the point at which they can truly be called improvisers. Adopting a notion developed by saxophonist Lee Konitz, Berliner presents "a continuum from interpretation to improvisation" that indicates the varying levels of compositional "intensity" jazz musicians may achieve in their soloing: many musicians, he says, never progress beyond "embellishing" existing forms (1994: 221). Another important point to recognize, according to Berliner, is that even among musicians who reach the level of "improvisation," there is a scale of originality that progresses from "imitation" through "assimilation" to "innovation" (273).

The different levels of compositional intensity and improvisational originality are themselves evidence of the variety of existing material the jazz player has to know and select from to create his music. Referred to by Berliner as the musician's "vocabulary," this material constitutes the jazz tradition and comprises such diverse forms as blues songs, variations on pop melodies, chord progressions, intervals, scales, rhythmic patterns, and other performers' improvised solos. By putting these elements together in different ways, the jazz musician takes his place within the jazz tradition and begins to establish his unique voice. In this sense, jazz playing is as much a traditional approach as it is an individual one.

Even in terms of the most creative, original jazz players, improvising cannot be characterized accurately without referring to the kinds of modifications of existing material that reflect dedication and rumination rather than pure spontaneous inspiration. Charlie Parker, for example, who is often credited with leading a revolution in jazz, described the genesis of that radical change this way: "Now I'd been getting bored with the stereotyped changes that were being used all the time at the time, and I kept thinking there's bound to be something else. I could hear it sometimes but I couldn't play it. Well, that night I was working over *Cherokee*, and as I did, I found that by using the higher intervals of a chord as a melody line and backing them with appropriately related changes, I could play the thing I'd been hearing. I came alive" (Shapiro and Hentoff 1966: 354). The evolution of jazz music encompasses inventions like Parker's, which in a sense was really only a slight modification, but one that significantly altered the sound of the music being played.

Jazz improvisation also has other essential elements that have significant implications for narratives modeled upon it. First, as Paul Berliner characterizes it, improvisation at its most creative is the stringing together of musical ideas not for their own sake but for the expression of something larger. The form of an improvised solo should not be, as one performer says, "disconnected demonstrations of technique"; rather, it should refer to something outside of itself. Among the most common referents for improvised solos are tributes to other jazz performers' work, personal experience, collective experience, or emotions. Whether this something larger is a "personal story" or an emotion, however, the successful improvised solo, according to Berliner, is carefully shaped to build drama, suspense, and tension before its resolution. In fact, an important metaphor used by jazz musicians to evaluate a solo is "storytelling." Berliner notes that "[Roy] Eldridge himself found a comparable model for performance in the playing of Louis Armstrong, who 'built his solos like a book—first, an introduction, then chapters, each one coming out of the one before and building to a climax.'" Even more modern, experimental performers like John Coltrane build their solos linearly; Wynton Marsalis recalls being overwhelmed by a Coltrane solo that "formed a beautiful melodic curve, 'and the key points in the phrases he was playing all went in a line'" (Berliner 1994: 262–63).

Improvised jazz solos, in other words, are to a great extent both linear and referential. At least as they are conceived by musicians themselves, improvised solos, even those composed in "real time," are less modernist (or postmodernist) pastiches of sound for sound's sake than they are structured stories with "meaning" for their composers and empathic listeners. As Albert Murray says, "The most elementary and hence the least dispensable objective of all serious artistic expression, whether aboriginal or sophisticated, is to make human existence *meaningful.* Man's primary concern with life is to make it as significant as possible, and the blues are part of this effort" (Murray 1983: 58; emphasis in original). Murray further explains that meaning in the blues idiom, which grows out of spirituals and work songs and is linked to jazz, connects to the specific historical experiences of African Americans and their responses to those experiences. Thus, inhering in blues tropes like signifyin(g) and call-and-response are those social and economic experiences—slavery, urban migration, Jim Crow, and so on—that are unique to African Americans.

This is the understanding of African American culture generally and jazz music specifically that we find in the writing of African Americans during this period. That is to say, rather than celebrating jazz as a creative process and aesthetic structure built on one person's present-moment, real-time, spontaneous associations (as we shall see that Euro American writers do), African American writers mediate it as a blues-based form that foregrounds an improvisation of themes, characters, and ideas connected to the social and economic experience of African Americans. Asked in a recent interview whether he distinguishes between himself as a "blues poet" and a "jazz poet," Amiri Baraka replied, "I don't think you can really deal with jazz unless you have some feeling for the blues. Without the blues, jazz is a music without memory—it has no national identity. . . . The blues is definitely the connection [drawling] 'to the way we been and the way we'z now'" (Baraka 1994: 263). Given this perspective on jazz, I use improvisation here to follow what Albert Murray has written about the nature of the blues artist's creative process: "Extemporizing in response to the exigencies of the situation in which he finds himself, he is confronting, acknowledging, and contending with the infernal absurdities and ever-impending frustrations inherent in the nature of all existence *by playing with the possibilities that are also there*" (Murray 1983: 58).[6] Improvising (or "extemporizing") in the blues idiom, in Murray's reading, depends upon both the "situation" in which the artist finds him or herself and the artist's imaginative response to that situation. Resonating with the historical experiences of African Americans, Murray's characterization of the idiom is further localized (even though he tries to universalize it) by his description of the blues artist's situation as rife with "infernal absurdities and ever-impending frustrations."

John A. Williams's 1961 novel *Night Song* provides an example of this use of jazz resources. With a story developed realistically and linearly, Williams's novel displays little obvious jazz influence other than such superficial elements as its setting in the Greenwich Village jazz/bohemian milieu, a primary character explicitly modeled after Charlie Parker, and some use of jazz argot. However, when *Night Song* is analyzed through Murray's lens an improvisational structure emerges. As earlier commentators have noted, the key to understanding this structure is the interplay between the novel's four main characters.[7] Against the field of its jazz setting, the novel works out several of the most salient racial issues of the time through four main characters: Keel Robinson, an African American man—former Harvard-trained minister, former Muslim—who owns a Greenwich Village coffeehouse; Della Madison, Robinson's Euro American girlfriend; Richie "Eagle" Stokes— great, neglected bebop saxophonist with a heroin addiction; and David Hillary, a Euro American college professor whose life has been destroyed by his guilt over a car accident that killed his wife. Eschewing a single central character, Williams uses these four characters as variations on the theme of racial identity to give the novel its improvisational structure. This notion of thematic improvisation is suggested by Williams's analysis of his own writing: "What I try to do with the novels is to deal in forms that are not standard, to improvise as jazz musicians do with their music, so that a standard theme comes out looking brand new. This is all I try to do with a novel and, like those musicians, I am trying to do things with form that are not always immediately perceptible to most people" (O'Brien 1973: 230).

Concerned with many of the same themes—the superficiality of middle-class values, the bohemian response to that emptiness, interracial sexual relationships between men and women, artistic suffering—that preoccupy Jack Kerouac in *The Subterraneans*, Williams's novel works them out in a narrative structure that emphasizes the social, cultural, and economic predicaments and their effects on diverse groups and individuals rather than foregrounding a single position (as Kerouac does). Moreover, *Night Song* specifically connects each character's situation to his or her racial position: Keel Robinson's primary dilemmas are those of an educated black man in a relationship with a white woman; Della's are those of a white woman crossing the racial boundary line; Eagle's are those typical of the African American artist; and David Hillary's are those of the Euro American outsider. None of these positions is excessively valorized or romanticized; each is accorded positive and negative values (which is not to say that all are presented as being equal) that help defamiliarize these identities and the relationships among them. In this sense, Williams's novel approaches a kind of blues-based center of consciousness by "playing with the possibilities" of racial being and offering no solutions.

Although some African American critics have diminished the thematic and formal adventurousness of *Night Song* by emphasizing its "integrationism" and "neo-realism," an understanding of its improvisational structure reveals that these criticisms are off the mark. Similarly, Euro American interpretations of the novel that underemphasize the importance of race, especially racial identity, to lend greater significance to the universal implications miss a very important aspect of the novel. Williams's greatest achievements in *Night Song* arise from his deviation from the requirements of protest, integrationist, and assimilationist novels. The field on which Williams manipulates these characters' racial identities is not one that can be reduced to colony, utopia, or even pluralist refuge. The Greenwich Village depicted in *Night Song*, for example, offers some surcease for interracial couples like Keel and Della and some measure of sanctuary for suffering artists and social outsiders, but it also harbors racist jazz critics and bohemians masquerading as racial progressives. Most importantly, Williams's narrative structure combats the period's pervasive racial essentialism without denying (or even diminishing) the centrality of race to the formation of individual identity in the United States. Improvisational freedom for Williams, then, manifests itself in this extemporaneous fashioning of contemporary racial solutions, historical models and obstacles, and future possibilities.

Even in African American fiction of this period in which the narrative primarily revolves around a single central jazz musician, that character is tied to his or her historical and contemporary community as a center of consciousness through a series of improvisations on the theme of racial identity. Two novels published in the early 1960s provide examples of this narrative structure. Published in 1962, Herbert Simmons's *Man Walking on Eggshells* chronicles the formation of a jazz trumpeter named Raymond Douglas. In this novel, Simmons uses a variety of devices to link Douglas's development as a jazz musician to the social history and contemporary social situation of African Americans. The young boy is introduced to the musical tradition by his grandfather, who plays Raymond jazz on his windup record player, tells him stories about Storyville, and plays the music on an old trumpet that he polishes with great care before each session. The grandfather's "lessons" are even more significant because Raymond's mother has forbidden her father to play the music and tell the stories to her son. The mother associates jazz with the death of her mother, who was killed in the famous East St. Louis, Illinois, riot during a time when her father was in Chicago playing music. However, even though his mother tries her hardest to dissuade young Raymond from pursuing his interest in jazz, even forbidding her father and uncle to play for young Raymond, he hounds his grandfather and uncle to teach him everything they know.

Simmons also clearly connects jazz music to African American history in general terms. During an argument with his daughter over the value of jazz music,

Raymond's grandfather argues passionately that "that's your history coming out of them horns!"(Simmons 1965: 62). There can be no doubt about whether this history is personal, national, or racial; Raymond's grandfather and grandmother continually tell Raymond stories (also against the wishes of Raymond's mother) on topics including slavery, Nat Turner, Joe Louis, and Bessie Smith. These stories describe not only the horrors of social and economic racism, but the responses of African Americans to these injustices.

A final device Simmons uses to achieve the novel's improvisational effect is Raymond's metamorphosis through a variety of stages of racial identity. Encompassing a timespan that stretches from the early twentieth century to the 1960s, the novel follows Raymond through a number of identity changes that embody many of the most significant struggles African Americans encountered during this period. During the course of his young-adult musical career, Raymond sees himself and is seen by others as a "race hero," an integrationist, a nationalist, a revolutionary, and a professional man. Although Simmons provides readers with few historical milestones to use as a chronological guide, it is clear that Raymond assumes these different identities in response to specific historical circumstances. For example, Raymond's transformation into a black nationalist occurs around the time white "beatniks" begin to usurp jazz music. Because of the clear relationship between these identity changes and obvious parallels in the social and cultural history of African Americans, the novel's structural effect is different, perhaps more profound, than the typical *bildungsroman*.

Another African American novel from the end of this period, William Melvin Kelley's *A Drop of Patience* (1965), achieves a similar improvisational effect by repeatedly linking the trials and triumphs of its main character—a jazz innovator—with those of African American people generally and in response to the actions of Euro American people. Resembling the Euro American writers' work that uses jazz resources, Kelley's narrative explores the romantic myth of the alienated artist: blind bebop legend Ludlow Washington wanders the novel searching for and never really finding the acceptance and understanding his artistic achievements warrant. However, unlike the development of this plot in the novels by John Clellon Holmes and Jack Kerouac, *A Drop of Patience* uses opposing constructs of "black" and "white" to denote social forces that are more or less sustaining and/or hostile to the alienated African American artist. While Ludlow's idiosyncrasies (due, perhaps, to his musical genius, or to his unstable early childhood, or to his disability) prevent him from forming long-lasting, nurturing relationships with any groups or individuals, Kelley is clear that Ludlow's best chance for finding a receptive working and living environment is in the African American community. Barely given agency in the novel, whiteness is a sign of fear that manifests itself in jealous jazz musicians, condescending and exploitative lovers, dangerous agents and club owners, and indifferent audiences. As one character says to Ludlow, "don't never depend on no white man for nothing. He ain't strong enough to keep his promises" (1965: 140). Thus, as the novel closes, Washington rejects the city (even the downtown bohemian "utopia") and continues his search for more generative places to perform—a "storefront church," for example, or a rural church "on a dirt road in the South" (237). Although there is only a scant possibility at this point in the novel that Washington will find one of these places, Kelley indicates that the location of hope is at the racial source, not the interracial blossoming.

Even in African American writing that self-consciously adopts a more experimental narrative form to imitate the structure or sound of jazz music, there appears the same kind of blues-based thematic improvisation that one finds in "neo-realistic" African American fiction. Amiri Baraka's 1966 short story "The Screamers," for example, unfolds like an extended jazz solo with its energetic first person narrative, accentuated rhythm, vivid images, colloquial language, and alternating high- and pop-culture references. Although there are also significant differences, Baraka's story resembles Jack Kerouac's jazz-influenced, first-person writings in these formal elements. However, the story also displays very strong ties to the blues-based tradition in the themes included and connections made in its storytelling. While the story uses a first-person narrator to describe the action that takes place at the Newark nightclub where Lynn Hope and the other musicians play, the narrator is not individualized much: he has no name, little personal history, and ideas and desires that are described as being common to people in his social and economic position. In short, the narrator is presented as being part of the crowd, the "us," that hangs out at jazz clubs, dancing, socializing, and following "heroes" like musician Lynn Hope. While it is clear that Baraka distinguishes in this story between cultural and economic classes in African American society—for example, between the Baptists in church on this Sunday evening and those in the club—he nevertheless insists on the connection between jazz and African American people.

Baraka also insists on the blues-based notion that African American music (in this case, jazz) is a potentially emancipating response to oppression. As the story begins the people forming the audience, "the crowd," are united in their similarities—they are "only the wild or the very poor"—but are disorganized in their behavior and their desires—many are dancing, some are hanging out and listening to the music, some are drinking alcohol, some are trying to make romantic connections (Baraka 1990: 262). As the story progresses, however, and we learn more about who these people are as a collectivity, what they have experienced, and what they desire, the audience and musicians are both galvanized by the music to become a single, unified entity. As the intensity of the music and story reaches its peak, the audience and musicians form a strutting, screaming line that snakes around the club and, finally, outside into the street. For a brief span of time, the people from the club constitute a single revolutionary force, capable "of the sweetest revolution, to hucklebuck into the fallen capital, and let the oppressors lindy hop out" (267). When the police arrive, however, the violence begins and the formerly unified crowd becomes disorganized again, dispersing in all directions "to save whatever it was each of us thought we loved" (268).

Baraka's narrative clearly illustrates the connection among the African American writers who use jazz in their fiction: the music and the process of improvisation are seen as being inextricably linked with African American social and economic experience. Thus, the freedom embodied in jazz improvisation manifests itself in fiction that improvises on the *theme* of freedom. As we shall see with the Euro American writers using jazz, no such connection exists; these Euro American writers, in fact, make few connections between their work and any kind of collective social or economic experience. Perhaps this is because, as John A. Williams has noted, "white writers have [n]ever had to consciously or subconsciously concern themselves about real problems of life and survival" (O'Brien 1973: 229). Following a European and Euro American avant-garde tradition of literary experimentation, experiencing little resistance to their movement in and out of mainstream society, and occupying a position relative to the literary and publishing establishments that allowed them simultaneously to participate and to call for their destruction, the Euro American writers interpret and apply improvisational techniques more literally as freedom from any and all formal constraints than their African American counterparts. Ranging from John Clellon Holmes's artificial "Theme-Riff-Chorus" structure in *The Horn* to Jack Kerouac's more credible attempt to reproduce what he understands of the very conditions of jazz improvisation during performance, these Euro American writers use jazz forms to "liberate," or at least revitalize the structure of American fiction. On the other hand, because the African American writers incorporate elements from the "blues" narrative tradition, have experienced racism in their lives, and have struggled to be accepted into the established literary and publishing establishments, their fiction displays the influence of jazz less in terms of structural innovation and more in terms of the interlocking elements of structure and content.

The Euro American translation of jazz to fiction can be seen most clearly in works by John Clellon Holmes and Jack Kerouac. Friends and co-chroniclers of the Beat generation, Kerouac and Holmes shared a passion for jazz music, especially the innovations of bebop. According to Holmes, bebop not only provided the background music for what he and others of his generation did as young people; it defined who they were as young *white* men and how they were different from everyone else: "No one who was not involved in the Bop revolt can know all that it meant to us. If a person dug Bop, we knew something about his sex life, his

individualism
captured

kick in literature and the arts, his attitudes toward joy, violence, Negroes and the very processes of awareness" (Holmes 1967: 124). It is not surprising, then, that Holmes and Kerouac, being both passionate jazz fans and ambitious writers, tried to combine one with the other in the form of a narrative that would itself imitate the structure of jazz and would allow them, as authors, to simulate the role of the improvising jazz musician. While their solutions to the problem of creating a jazz-like narrative are different in substantial ways, they both worked from the understanding that the enormous power of jazz derived from its compatibility, as an aesthetic form, with the greatness and unpredictability of individual creativity. John Clellon Holmes has said: "Jazz is primarily the music of inner freedom, of improvisation, of the creative individual rather than the interpretive group. It is the music of a submerged people, who *feel* free, and this is precisely how young people feel today" (1967: 1224). Influenced by what they were witnessing at that moment in jazz history—bebop's full flowering of the jazz soloist—Holmes and Kerouac conflated the latest innovation in the tradition with the essence of improvisation itself.

In *The Horn*, Holmes structures his narrative to emphasize the uniqueness of individual creative genius by focusing on a single character, the soon-to-be-martyred saxophonist Edgar Pool ("the Horn"). To give the novel the overall appearance of a musical composition, Holmes adapts a simple musical form. The novel's present-tense narrative follows Pool on the last day of his life; Holmes calls these sections "Riffs," a jazz term he defines as "a melodic device, insistently repeated, the primary function of which is rhythmic."[8] Interspersed between the "Riff" sections are "Chorus" segments in which significant events in Pool's life are narrated by musicians/friends who have known and been affected by him. Longer and more fully developed than the "Riffs," the "Chorus" segments are intended as the novel's "melody" against which the rhythmic "Riffs" are counterpointed. The novel closes with a "Coda" chapter narrated by Cleo, a pianist who has accompanied Pool on his final day. Within this slightly idiosyncratic structure, the narrative is developed conventionally: third-person narration is used throughout, the plotting is logical if not exactly linear, dialogue is clearly indicated, flashbacks are distinguished from present-tense action, and so on. Unlike Kerouac's experimentation, Holmes's narrative seems only minimally, although obviously, influenced by the form of jazz: although he imitates a kind of musical structure, there seems to be little attempt to mimic, much less use, improvisational techniques.

One of the effects of Holmes's execution of this quasi-musical structure is to reinforce the novel's primary theme of the *individual* American artist's triumphs, struggles, and failures. Even though the novel uses a circle of secondary characters to narrate Pool's life, the sense of community and even the "collective improvisation" of jazz that Holmes obviously intends to develop is undermined to a great extent by the novel's unyielding insistence on Pool's life and work as the narrative's unifying elements.[9] The secondary characters' narratives respond too much to the story of Edgar Pool and too little to each other to evoke a sense of a multilayered communal organization. Moreover, Holmes's attempt to elevate the significance of his story by giving each character an analogue from the history of American literature (each "Chorus" is headed by a quote from the narrating character's literary "twin") emphasizes the uniqueness, the hermetic quality, of each character's identity rather than the way they interact—that is, the process of giving to and taking from each other. Although it is possible that Holmes intended this pantheon—Thoreau, Melville, Hawthorne, Dickinson, Twain, Whitman, and Poe—to stand as his own improvised tradition of American literature, the analogies detract from our understanding of the novel's characters—the jazz musicians— as a group of collective improvisers. Being encouraged by Holmes to think of these characters as great American artists, we have a hard time imagining such grand figures asserting and subordinating themselves in the development of a single theme, as they would have to do during a collective improvisation. Added together, then, Holmes's structural devices emphasize the generalized "American theme" of his novel more than either the specific characteristics of jazz musicians or the value of jazz's "collective improvisation."

In fact, given the perspectives and relationships of these characters, the jazz musicians in Holmes's novel more closely embody the qualities of a typical group of Euro American bohemians—like the Beats—than they do a collection of professional African American musicians. Holmes's description of the values held by his generation of hipsters and bohemians applies to the characters in his novel but not to the jazz musicians, who thought of themselves, above all else, as professionals: "A return to an older, more personal, but no less rigorous code of ethics, which includes the inviolability of comradeship, the respect for confidences, and an almost mystical regard for courage—all of which are the ethics of the tribe, rather than the community" (Holmes 1967: 123).

As this quotation suggests, Holmes's romantic notion of the ideal human collective involves an aggressive return to an older form of organization—the voluntary association of outsiders exemplified by bohemians, for example—rather than the less tight-knit association of professionals—including teachers, students, friends, competitors, mentors, and so on—found in the community of jazz musicians during the bebop era. Even more significantly, *The Horn* almost completely ignores the notion that these characters are interdependent because of the challenges they shared being marginalized African American artists/professionals in a Euro American society.

In the final analysis, Holmes's narrative structure narrowly interprets improvisation to mean the Euro American tradition of individual artistic creativity. The notion of freedom that is inherent in improvisational activity finds its illustration only in the tension between the needs of the artist and the constraints put upon him/her by society. Strangely enough, although Holmes's novel is populated almost totally by African American characters, the historical trope of freedom found in African American culture (with its allusions to overcoming racism and the struggle for justice and equal rights) is neglected. Holmes himself notes in a Preface to the 1988 edition of *The Horn* that while writing the novel he was aware of his "own limited adequacies to deal with black experience and black music," yet decided to pursue the subject anyway, hoping that "the flaws [would] justify themselves by my passion and sincerity."[10] Because it is hard to believe that Holmes was unaware of the special significance freedom has in African American culture, it seems likely that he chose to omit this significant dimension of the social reality of jazz in order to make his novel more universal. His omission greatly weakens the power and resonance his experimentation with a jazz-like narrative form might have created.

Critic Paul Garon's judgment of "white blues" could stand as a comment on Holmes's achievement in *The Horn*: "Removed from the unique historical configurations that produced the blues, that is, the socio-economic and cultural conditions through which blues came into being, the melodic similarities produced by the white imitators appear weak, trivial, spineless and without substance" (Garon 1975: 61). For all of the aspects of the novel that Holmes gets right—his familiarity with some of the musical elements of jazz, with some of the subcultural elements of the postwar jazz scene in New York City, and with the history of the bebop revolution—*The Horn*'s omissions, universalisms, and romanticisms reveal the mediation of African American culture that, in the end, helps define Holmes's generation's relation to the object of their desire.[11]

Jack Kerouac also uses jazz resources to celebrate the greatness of the individual artist's creativity, but he does so unabashedly as the artist whose creative artistry is being celebrated. Unlike Holmes's jazz-like narrative in *The Horn*, which ostensibly obscures the Euro American author behind a veneer of African American experience and culture (however incompletely represented), Kerouac's narrative in a novel such as *The Subterraneans* presents the author in the role of the jazz musician, using language to improvise themes, rhythms, and sounds in a storytelling performance.

The differences between their composing and writing styles was apparently one of the reasons Holmes and Kerouac could mine the same cultural vein without an excess of animosity toward each other. Another reason was their distinct approaches to jazz history—Holmes's interests ran to more conventional information about jazz, while Kerouac's attention focused on the grander implications of the jazz tradition. According to Kerouac biographer Gerald Nicosia, "Jack thought it was possible for both of them to do jazz novels, as long as Holmes dealt chiefly with jazz as a social phenomenon, leaving Jack the spiritual aspects: the 'mystery' of jazz characters' interacting, and the evolution from joyous to cool" (1983: 412).

While *The Subterraneans* is not, strictly speaking, a jazz novel (not having jazz musicians or jazz culture as its primary subject), it is the novel that inspired the jazz-influenced aesthetic principles Kerouac outlined in "Essentials of Spontaneous Prose." According to Nicosia, Kerouac produced this statement after writing *The Subterraneans* in response to requests by William Burroughs and Allen Ginsberg (Nicosia 1983: 453–54). Thus it is the most appropriate of his works to use to examine his approach to adapting jazz-like improvisation techniques to literature. Nevertheless, it is difficult to discuss jazz as the organizing principle of *The Subterraneans*, as the basis for the novel's narrative structure. There is no question that Kerouac designed his prose style, in part, to imitate not only the creative process of jazz—specifically, the spontaneity that comes from improvising—but also the sound of jazz or, more specifically, the sound of bebop. However, the question of how successful he is in being as spontaneous as a jazz musician or (even more difficult to determine) imitating the sound of bebop is, it seems to me, a thorny one. How does one, finally, determine whether or how much Kerouac's prose sounds like or patterns itself after the alto sax lines created by Charlie Parker?

Although it is well accepted that Kerouac identified himself with jazz musicians and modeled his *stated* methodology on the jazz process and jazz structures, a short discussion of the evidence for this notion is necessary. In "Essentials of Spontaneous Prose," the one major statement of his writing method, Kerouac relies heavily on jazz metaphors to characterize his process.[12] Specifically, under "Procedure," Kerouac emphasizes spontaneity and improvisation. Mixing jazz and visual art metaphors, he states that "sketching language is undisturbed flow from the mind of personal secret idea-words blowing (as per the jazz musician) on the subject of image." Under "Method," Kerouac advises using a different kind of punctuation to inject more vitality into writing: rather than using periods, colons, or commas to separate sentences, one should use "the space dash separating rhetorical breathing (as jazz musician drawing breath between outblown phrases)." Finally, discussing what should be the subject of one's writing, Kerouac exhorts writers to "Blow as deep as you want . . . tap from yourself the song of yourself, *blow!*— *now!*" (1961b: 65–67). Similarly, in his 1968 *Paris Review* interview, Kerouac focuses on the same jazz metaphors—breath and blowing—to talk about the connection between his writing and jazz. In response to a question about the influence of jazz and bop on his writing, Kerouac says, "Yes jazz and bop, in the sense of a, say, a tenor man drawing a breath and blowing a phrase on his saxophone, till he runs out of breath, and when he does, his sentence, his statement's been made . . . that's how I therefore separate my sentences, as breath separations of the mind" (1968: 83).

Leaving aside for now the question of whether his understanding of the creative process in jazz is accurate, one can say that Kerouac's own sense of the connection between jazz and his writing revolves around two major activities: (1) recreating the improvisational nature of the creative process in jazz, and (2) representing or simulating the spontaneity of this improvisation in words. By his own account, then, it seems that Kerouac did not intend (as many critics have contended) anything as literally imitative of jazz as to mimic the rhythmic or harmonic content of bop, but that he was more interested simply in the concept of improvisation and the representation of that process in language.

One significant aspect of jazz creation Kerouac completely neglects is the importance of tradition. As noted earlier, much of what jazz musicians themselves say about their creative process involves the importance to them of an inheritance of specific conventions and themes, which they use or transmute to contribute to the development of this tradition. Much of the improvising and innovation in jazz, apparently, involves (as with almost any other art form) reconfiguring the existing elements in a *specific* tradition. The writer A. B. Spellman identifies "the definitive substance of jazz" as being "all those blues chords and chord changes, rhythms and melodies" (1985: 36). Far from being, as Kerouac represents it, simply a process of tapping into one's emotional life and blowing, jazz improvisation involves a thorough knowledge of those performers and performances that have come before. The pianist Cecil Taylor, for example, says, "The notes that we play are old music, man. It's old in the sense that there's nothing new there" (Spellman 1985: 20). In this sense, then, Kerouac distorts or borrows *very* selectively part of the jazz tradition in order to romanticize his own creative process.

The passages from *The Subterraneans* analyzed in chapter 2 offer a useful example to consider the success of Kerouac's approximation of jazz improvisation because they are part of a scene—occurring in a jazz club featuring the great Charlie Parker—one would expect to transport the reader to Kerouac's jazzy milieu. Moreover, this scene is used by at least two Kerouac critics (John Tytell and Regina Weinreich) to exemplify Kerouac's musicality. Both of these critics point to the same formal device—the building of "associations" or the "spontaneous flow" of images—as the technique that convinces them that Kerouac's goal of approximating the spontaneity of the jazz musician has been reached. Really, though, this is only to call what has been practiced by previous writers—Joyce or Faulkner, for example—by another name. "Stream-of-consciousness," for example, becomes "spontaneous prose"; or, put another way, a practice based on a psychoanalytical model becomes one based on a musical model. Granting Kerouac's facility for imitating sound generally, it still seems to me that there is nothing *inherently* musical or jazz-like in Kerouac's writing. Composing without editing (if indeed he did do this), replacing standard punctuation with dashes, and tapping into some sort of essential part of oneself do not necessarily make Kerouac's prose sound more like jazz.

This scene from *The Subterraneans* is also a suggestive one for consideration because there is a recording of Kerouac reading it. Recorded in 1959 on the jazz label Verve and recently re-released on *The Jack Kerouac Collection*, this recording is touted (in the booklet accompanying the recent compilation) by Kerouac biographer Gerald Nicosia as being "so immediate, intense, and full of subtle emotional changes that it rivals any piece Bird himself ever recorded" (1983: 10). Nicosia, moreover, says that "As with the greatest jazz musicians, Kerouac is not just blowing a tune, he is blowing his own life, up on the bandstand for all the world to witness" (11). Setting aside the likelihood that Nicosia's hyperbole is calculated to magnify the significance of this "product," these are substantial claims for Kerouac's writing and performing (this latter is supposed to be believable despite the fact that both Nicosia and Ann Charters report that Kerouac's late-1950s Village Vanguard performances were not successful). And yet my repeated listenings to this recording followed by listenings to Charlie Parker convince me that only a very sympathetic listener (to put it kindly) would agree that Kerouac's sound "rivals" Charlie Parker, or even that Kerouac's performance is like the performance of a jazz musician. Perhaps my bemused, skeptical reaction at this late and distanced date to Kerouac's reading has as much to do with the fact that the type of Beat literary reading Kerouac exemplifies has become an American pop cultural cliche (even parodied in Gap commercials) as it does with Kerouac's achievements as a literary performer. This is not to say, moreover, that there are not any similarities between Kerouac's prose and jazz. He does move from association to association, modulate his tone, and underpin his prose with a quick, quirky rhythm that is clearly linked to the jazz musician's use of long lines of breath. However, if, in jazz historian James Lincoln Collier's words, "Bop was, in the exact sense of the word, a musical revolution," then Kerouac's prose—following Joyce, Faulkner, and others—did not "rival" Charlie Parker's music because it was not, in any sense of the word, a literary revolution (Collier 1978: 361).

Furthermore, Nicosia claims that this and other recordings of Kerouac reading his work reveal "that the essence of Kerouac's artistry lies in a spontaneity that is totally faithful to his own impulses at the moment of creation or utterance" (1983: 9). If true, this claim would greatly bolster Kerouac's assertion that his creative process reproduces the spontaneity of the jazz process. It seems clear that Kerouac's readings (judging by what is on these recordings made relatively late—1959—in Kerouac's career) were inflected by a kind of emotional spontaneity that gives them a limited but certain immediate power. However, to evaluate Kerouac's improvisational skills solely on the basis of their emotional intensity is to simplify and diminish the skills a jazz musician brings to his work. Moreover,

Kerouac's own demands for spontaneity in writing exceed the mere modulation of emotion to encompass in-the-moment changes in words and ideas. In "Essentials," for example, he emphasizes as "procedure" composing in an "undisturbed flow from the mind of personal idea-words." However, comparing his reading of this passage from *The Subterraneans* with the published passage reveals only a few minor differences—adding the real name of the bar, changing a "get" to a "go" and a "myself" to "me"—of the kind that would be labeled retrospective editing or could even be called random. The only substantial change is the one that Nicosia (of course) mentions: Kerouac changes "Bird . . . into my eye looking to search if really I was that great writer I thought myself to be" to "if really I was that great *nut*. . . ." This is a funny, evocative, and self-deprecating change to make, but being the only substantial one hardly supports Nicosia's claim of spontaneity for Kerouac. Neither is Nicosia's claim supported by the passage from *Desolation Angels* Kerouac reads on *The Jack Kerouac Collection*. Once again, the difference between the printed and spoken versions are few and mostly minor: real names substituted for pseudonyms, synonyms used occasionally (such as "holy" for "beat" or "times" for "generation"), and a word or two dropped or added. Even granting Nicosia's assertion that Kerouac's intention with these changes was to "get the sound flowing faster" or "balance the rhythm better," the changes do not add up to a jazz-like spontaneous improvisation. Instead, they seem like the kind of changes that would be made by any writer reading his or her work and recognizing that small changes will slightly improve its sound. On the basis of these readings, then, it seems that Kerouac is no less faithful to his written word than any other typical writer.

And yet almost all of Kerouac's biographers and sympathetic critics agree with Warren Tallman that Kerouac's writing is the literary equivalent of bop. To support this evaluation, however, these writers only point to the most general of similarities. Tallman, for example, the earliest and most influential of commentators on the influence of jazz on Kerouac's formal achievements, talks vaguely about "a principle of spontaneous creative freedom which has been taken over by the Beat writers" and about Bop being "the shaping spirit of his imagination" (1961: 219, 229). John Tytell, Regina Weinreich, and W. T. Lhamon, the most recent and thorough scholars of Kerouac's structural innovations, discuss his spontaneous method and practice more specifically but are still fuzzy when it comes to explaining *how* his prose imitates jazz. Like Warren Tallman, these critics settle for emphasizing that Kerouac's design for his prose invokes jazz method and sound, and for using words popularly associated with jazz to describe his effects. Tytell notes that the music of the beboppers "formed the basis of a new sense of rhythm which he adapted to his own prose line" (1986: 144). Lhamon identifies "Kerouac's improvisations, repetitions, stuttering starts and stops" as coming "directly from the jazz worlds he entered on both coasts and both banks of the Mississippi River" (1990: 70).

After discussing the ways Kerouac *claimed* his language imitated jazz structures, Weinreich (whose study is the most comprehensive examination of Kerouac's spontaneous prose method) concedes that "as yet no critical methodology has emerged from the musical analogy for the discussion of Kerouac's work" (1990: 10). Given that almost all of Kerouac's admirers have tried to develop this connection, Weinreich's concession seems, finally, to lead to the conclusion that the connection between jazz and Kerouac's writing remains more of an influence or motivation than a successfully executed narrative methodology. Amiri Baraka's retrospective comment, in fact, may be closest to the truth: he says Kerouac's spontaneous bop prosody "is a hyped-up version of Joyce with a nod in the direction of black improvisational music" (1984: 158).[13]

Nevertheless, what is more crucial for our purposes than Kerouac's success or failure in imitating jazz is the *way* Kerouac *characterizes* the jazz structures he tries to imitate in his prose. Just as he primitivizes the image of Charlie Parker in *The Subterraneans*, so Kerouac primitivizes the process a jazz musician uses to create the music he plays. This can be seen most clearly if we look again at the parts of Kerouac's "Essentials of Spontaneous Prose" I have already quoted. In the jazz metaphors Kerouac uses to characterize his writing process the emphasis is on the notion of spontaneity and improvisation—"sketching language is undisturbed flow from the mind of personal secret idea-words blowing (as per the jazz musician) on the subject of image"—as well as one's intuitive sense of oneself: "Blow as deep as you want . . . tap from yourself the song of yourself, *blow!—now!*" (1961b: 65–67). In his *Paris Review* interview, too, Kerouac's statements on his jazz-influenced method privilege the intuitive over acquired or developed skills: "FEELING, Goddamn it, FEELING is what I like in art, not CRAFTINESS and the hiding of feelings" (1968: 65).

Taken by themselves, Kerouac's statements of method might not add up to a primitivized depiction of the *jazz* process. However, combined with the portrayals of African American jazz musicians (such as the one of Charlie Parker in *The Subterraneans*) in his fiction that obliterate their offstage lives and dehistoricize them, Kerouac's overarching depiction of the process of creation in jazz is one that requires almost no training, skill, or education: just pick up a horn, tap into your emotions, and "blow." Jazz is, of course, a music that expresses great emotion, but as with visual artists or authors of literature this emotional expression is the product of dedicated training and enormous skill. Nevertheless, Kerouac repeatedly distills the creative process in jazz to this essence even though, according to Gerald Nicosia, Kerouac himself had to learn to hear and appreciate the technical innovations of bop (Nicosia 1983: 125). In Kerouac's work, the jazz process remains one that is not the result of a cultural development on the group level and disciplined practice on the individual level, but one that is fundamental to any "primal" human existence.

By using jazz as a metaphor for his revolt against the literary establishment (that is, by comparing his rebellion of "*feeling*" and improvisation against the establishment's reason and craft to the implied *similar* differences between jazz and European classical music), Kerouac misuses the jazz tradition. The "feeling" and improvisation Kerouac admires in jazz are not the extent of the tradition of jazz, but a part of that whole. Furthermore, these characteristics developed not out of a revolt against European classical music but as part of jazz's slow, deliberate process of development as a syncretic music (that is, a music that continually fuses elements from different traditions, including the European). Although Kerouac's intention is to elevate the status of jazz by praising characteristics that he believes are more valuable and useful than those in the European tradition, he actually diminishes the authority of its particular musical heritage. This implied comparison suggests that the improvisation in jazz is merely a response to classical composition, rather than as much a constitutive element of its heritage as written composition is of the classical music tradition. Cecil Taylor, for example, indicates the importance of improvisation to the jazz tradition in the following quotation: "you get more from the musicians if you teach them the tunes by ear, if they have to listen for changes instead of reading them off the page, which again has something to do with the whole jazz tradition, with how the cats in New Orleans at the turn of the century made their tunes. That's our thing, and not composition" (Spellman 1985: 70–71). To indicate that improvisation is simply a revolt against composition rather than an integral part of the musical structure of jazz is to imply that jazz is a derivative, second-class musical tradition.

In their pursuit of a new, energized form of American writing, Euro Americans like Kerouac and Holmes constructed a meaning for jazz improvisation that differed from that of their African American counterparts. Requiring little (if any) historical knowledge and relieving the burden of racism, this Euro American construction of improvisation proved popular and enduring with white outsiders and audiences generally. Throughout Greenwich Village and other bohemian outposts during the late 1950s and early 1960s, extemporaneously created poetry was recited with and without the accompaniment of bongo drums and other jazz instrumentation. Even today, in the mid-1990s, the revival of coffeehouses that has swept the country includes numerous places in which young and old climb onto the stage to read lines of prose and poetry that were composed without revision or editing. In addition, the popular image of improvisation in jazz remains the one promulgated by Euro American admirers: "Blow as deep as you want . . . tap from yourself the song of yourself, *blow!*—*now!*" (Kerouac 1961b: 65–67).

Epilogue

While writing this book, I have been concerned that my distinctions between white and black uses of jazz have been too rigid and my criticism of white Americans too harsh. After all, many have said and will say, the racist discourse I identify in these representations is not, for the most part, the most invidious and malicious kind that we are used to seeing condemned in public. Instead, this racism on the margins of American culture—in the work of the Beats and other oppositional white groups of the era—seems to have been the product of enormous energy, attraction, and imagination; in other words, it is a relation of white to black that is in some sense "positive," a romanticization. Many of those white people who listened to, wrote about, and mythologized jazz, including Jack Kerouac and Ross Russell, had enormous admiration for African American culture and people. I have tried to be careful not to condemn these individuals because their expression of interest and admiration could not transcend the limitations imposed on them by the dominant culture of their time.

However, I think it is fair and necessary to ask whether this ostensibly positive form of racial relation is an obstacle or an opening to racial understanding and solidarity. It seems clear to me that although many bohemians of the immediate postwar period had good intentions in their personal relationships with African American people and genuine interest in and attraction to African American culture, any potential for better interracial relations, personal or cultural, was hindered by structural inequality. Not only were material relations corrupted by the almost total white ownership of dominant and emergent cultural resources; the discourse on race and racial difference was monopolized by the dominant white idea of color-blindness and by white challenges that could never really break from this idea. In the discursive as well as the material sphere white people were too invested in the status quo to want or be able to mount radical challenges. Moreover, the most promising challenge to the established racial discourse, that of the black civil rights movement, was framed in language—collectivism—that was anathema to white people who were determined not to follow earlier white radicals into that abyss. Thus, even white people who were dissatisfied with the dominant racial discourse could only offer romantic fantasies of individualistic African American geniuses and wan Euro American imitations of these models.

The answer to the question of the efficacy of white attraction to black culture is particularly pertinent now because of recent developments regarding race in both academic and popular culture. These developments have helped to change the context in which this white attraction has its specific meaning. Social and cultural context, as Ian Haney Lopez says in *White by Law*, is the "setting in which races are recognized, constructed, and contested" (1996: 191). Though racism and racial inequality have not disappeared from American society over the past thirty years, they have changed their shapes. So, too, has racial discourse changed. Though color-blindness still holds sway as the dominant American racial discourse, its hold is much less sure than it was during the period under study in this book. As Ruth Frankenberg explains, the many social movements of the 1960s and 1970s legitimized and popularized challenges to color-blindness that redefined race-consciousness as a positive, non-hierarchical discourse (1993: 14–15). These challenges have helped to bring various forms of "blackness" from margin to center of American popular culture, to move white American cultures slightly off-center, and to stigmatize unabashed white appropriation of black culture.

Recently, cultural studies scholars have been writing and talking a lot about "cultural hybridity" as the most accurate and generative way to construct racial and ethnic traditions. This quasi-Darwinian emphasis on cultural blending, scholars say, has the twin virtues of debunking the myth of a pure white American culture and properly recognizing the influence of African American and other minority cultures. Other academics have been promoting the notion of the "race traitor," a white person who renounces his or her white privilege by actively transgressing society's still-strict racial boundaries, either as an individual or with other race traitors in groups. At the same time that academics have been theorizing hybridized American culture and race treason, popular culture has been showing signs of producing a blended product and race traitors all by itself (and, in fact, the question of which occurred first is yet another of the chicken-and-egg variety). This hybridizing in the popular realm has occurred especially in the reception by young Americans of Hollywood movies and music.

Though it has received more attention recently than ever before, the theoretical notion of hybridization is not new. Most prominently, Ralph Ellison and Albert Murray have long been writing about the profound African American influence on dominant American culture. While recognizing the aesthetic entities—the blues, for example—that are specific to African American culture, they see these entities as hybridized, the particular product of the black-white *American* experience; moreover, they see these entities as profoundly affecting the formation of dominant

American culture. However, unlike white writers and academics who have deployed these ideas, Ellison and Murray have done so from a position of respecting the integrity of the various cultural traditions that have developed in the United States, and without wanting to *replace* these traditions with a synthesized alternative. This is to say that neither Murray nor Ellison allow their desire to forge common ground—links—between white and black Americans to erase or obscure the reality of American racial politics. Thus, in his recent book, *The Blue Devils of Nada*, Murray persuasively and elaborately presents the case for using the "blues aesthetic" to understand expressive products of American culture and *still* feels the need to use his Epilogue to lobby his white readers (presumably) for a renegotiated American cultural pantheon Ralph Waldo Emerson and Louis Armstrong, Jack Johnson and Henry James, Jelly Roll Morton and Mark Twain, Count Basie and Walt Whitman, Duke Ellington and Herman Melville can proudly occupy together.

My belief that white Americans on the whole still do not respect the integrity of African American culture (and thus would not be inclined to accept Murray's pantheon) is part of what motivated my interest in disentangling the myths of racial interconnectedness in the culture of the postwar era. As the history I describe here indicates, even those white Americans who were strongly attracted to African American culture were mostly unable or unwilling to recognize the subtle and profound ways in which that culture spun off different angles of vision on such cherished American ideals as individualism, freedom, and equality. Equally important, most white Americans were unable or unwilling even to put themselves in the position of subordinating themselves to black people and black culture. As Hettie Jones has written (with unintended accuracy) about the white Beats' use of jazz, "they weren't content to leave it where it had always been left—in its 'place'" (1990: 47). Because of the inequality of racial categories in the United States (especially during this period), it was a different (and perhaps inescapably dominating) activity altogether for white men to forge a synthesis of white and black cultures than it would have been for black men or women to do so.

Unlike cultural hybridity, the "race traitor" concept has been developed recently as a radical attempt to destabilize racial difference and fight racial inequality. Like hybridity, however, the race traitor idea is not new. It has links to the activity of radical nineteenth-century abolitionists like John Brown who gave up everything to throw their lot in with black people. However, in its current meaning, a race traitor is anyone who acts in such a way (individually or collectively) that he or she disrupts the racial status quo: from white suburban kids who listen to hip-hop music and wear "gang" clothes to white people who marry outside their race to teachers who refuse to implement laws that discriminate against (mostly nonwhite) immigrants to groups of white Americans who monitor police departments (Ignatiev and Garvey 1996: 1–5). An activist application of social construction theory, the race traitor concept is interesting, subversive, and generative. However, a couple of its aspects are bothersome to me. First, race traitor theorists always seem to end up valorizing, privileging, and reasserting the "superiority" of white people. The white people they celebrate, of course, are those doing valuable antiracist work. Very often, however, honoring these white people, either in the past or the present, results in more romanticizations similar to those I have discussed in many white Americans' celebration of jazz musicians—except this time, white people are romanticizing other white people (e.g., John Brown, Jack Kerouac, even the Blues Brothers). More important, though, the race traitor concept almost completely erases cultural difference to emphasize the greater "truth" (or maybe it is "necessity") of social construction. Thus, the highest form of antiracist work is simply "going over to the other side" rather than doing the longer, more painstaking (notice I do not say "more difficult") work of understanding the complexity of African American culture and of the relationship between it and Euro American culture.

At the level of American cultural production, hybridity and race treason are occurring at a steady rate. As David Roediger writes, "The process goes on, superficially and at times deeply" (1995: 662). Almost anywhere we look these days we see cultural changes that reach back to the nationalist and feminist social movements of the 1960s and 1970s and have slowly been gaining momentum since then: the greater influence of racial minorities and women in culture and, to a much lesser extent, over the means of cultural production. Hip-hop culture, for example, has had a significant effect not only in music but also in movies, television, and fashion; female artists are more visible and influential in all areas of popular culture; multiculturalism has affected what art is funded, what plays are produced, and what books are published and read, especially in colleges and universities. These changes signal not only an increasing diversity in the cultural marketplace—more kinds of products available for consumption—but also an increasing visibility for cultural products that retain some cultural integrity.

However, in an echo of the 1950s, the popular media, still predominantly controlled by white Americans, has focused their attention on the influence minority cultures have exercised on the style of cultural productions by white males. Quentin Tarantino, for example, has garnered an enormous amount of attention for his use in *Pulp Fiction* of images and conventions from African American movies as well as for his company's desire to provide the financing to revive neglected 1970s "blaxploitation" movies. In popular music, such groups as the Beastie Boys, the Red Hot Chili Peppers, and The Jon Spencer Blues Explosion, and such solo artists as Beck have attracted popular support and critical acclaim among white audiences by imitating and incorporating rap, hip-hop, and blues into their work. Even more significant than its manifestation in the work of these popular artists, the hip-hop influence is obvious in corporate advertising associated with everything from athletics to fast food. Unlike in previous eras (like the one covered in this work), African American cultural style is not limited to a small, hip subculture—it suffuses popular culture generally.

More important for my purposes, these cultural changes have been accompanied by a sizeable increase in the number of white people (especially youth) who are interested in and follow African American culture. By now it is commonly known that rap albums are as popular among white suburban kids as among black urban kids. White youth in general are now more conversant with contemporary African American culture and style than ever before. Of course, whether this cultural competency is superficial or profound is debatable. The steady stream of vitriolic attacks on rap music and "multiculturalism" by conservative critics over the past ten years indicates that those with an interest in preserving the cultural status quo believe these cultural challenges are catching the imagination of white youth in a substantial way.

My own interaction with white college students suggests that the transgression of racial boundaries they experience in popular culture has an extremely limited effect on their ideas about race and racial difference. Though they come to my classes wearing baggy clothes and backward baseball caps and as fans of such pop culture icons as Michael Jordan and Shaquille O'Neal, Whitney Houston and Denzel Washington, John Singleton and Spike Lee, and Dr. Dre and the Fugees, their familiarity with African American culture does not extend much beyond a superficial familiarity with this contemporary lexicon. While their gaps in historical knowledge do not bother me, I am disturbed that their familiarity with contemporary African American culture has done nothing to change their ideas about African American people, whom they still see stereotypically, or about African American culture, which they do not recognize as existing apart from, in conflict with, or even in conjunction with dominant American culture. The problem is that most of these white students are still so indoctrinated in the individualistic ethic of color-blindness that they do not see African American culture "stars" or their products as anything other than manifestations of singular human talent: Spike Lee or Quentin Tarantino, Eddie Vedder or Snoop Doggy Dogg, Whoopi Goldberg or Billy Crystal, all are products and purveyors of an amorphously blended dominant American culture. Moreover, even when white students recognize that a particular film, television show, or song is the product of an African American sensibility (again, amorphously defined), they mostly explain away, as a convention of that "genre," any part of the content of the product that expresses cultural opposition or political discontent.

The diverse cultural marketplace and the high visibility of black artists, athletes, and performers in popular culture promotes the illusion that American society is integrated and color-blind. More than in any previous historical era, the media possess the technology to make this virtual reality seem real. As George Lipsitz notes, to judge the status of race relations by looking through the lens of popular culture one would be misled: "Many of the key institutions of our society seem open to black culture, but not black people. They want the music, but not the musicians; they want the art, but not the artists; they want the literature, but they ignore the context that gives the literature its determinate contours" (1995b: 703). I would extend Lipsitz's argument to state that American society is not truly open to black culture either, only to the "exceptional" black artist. To a certain extent, this indicates a larger problem with the popular media: they generally do not do a good job of providing history and context for consumers, dominated as they are by speeding images. However, because Euro American culture is dominant and African American culture is still subordinated, this gap in the popular media is more critical for African American than for Euro American culture: white people do not learn about it anywhere else.

The common link among all of the problems I have written about is whiteness; in the mainstream and on the margins white people have been unable to fashion a historical narrative or a contemporary identity that frees them from the dominance and privilege of racism. To do this, to make a white identity that is nondominanting, is the formidable task facing antiracist white people at the end of the twentieth century. While I have no prescription for it, I think the starting point is in one's relation to self, others, and culture; it is a relation that demands that white people voluntarily subordinate themselves, renounce their power, and listen.

Notes

Introduction

1. See, for example, recent work on the Beats and other white cultural outsiders in Lhamon 1990 and Leonard 1987.

2. Although this process began during the New Deal era before World War II, it became firmly established after 1945. See Lipsitz 1995a: 372–75; and Quadrano 1994: 22–24.

3. This is not to suggest, of course, that all of the work mentioned achieves, or even wishes to achieve, these five goals. Without question, there are significant differences in the perspectives and conclusions reached by these scholars. However, from my vantage point as a student of this emerging field of whiteness, these five goals are within reach because of the research and theorizing that has already been done.

4. A recent Whitney Museum exhibition of Beat movement art and culture periodized its subject only slightly differently: 1950–1965 (see Phillips 1995). Also, in *Making Movies Black*, Thomas Cripps identifies a concurrent era—one he says contains movies offering a "liberalism of conscience"—in the depiction of African Americans in movies. Bracketing the era between 1951 and 1967, Cripps describes the movies African Americans appeared in as "marked by [their] preference for the virtues of consensus and restraint," and the African American characters in these movies as "normative" and "doomed to be the eternal subjects of a tale of an already attained goal—one black figure per group" (Cripps 1993: 250–261).

5. In *Black Talk*, for example, Ben Sidran provides evidence of ideological and actual links between those young people who listened to jazz and those who were politically active during the 1960s (1971: 130–45).

6. Such is skeptical of any posited causal link between sociopolitical condition and musical structure because of such unquantifiable factors as individual taste and will and specific criteria for establishing links between experience and musical elements (1993: 27–28).

Chapter 1. The Hidden History of Postwar Racial Politics

1. Michael Omi and Howard Winant define "racialization" as the "extension of racial meaning to a previously unclassified relationship" (1986: 64).

2. As Quadrano notes, the Social Security Act also "perpetuated gender inequality" by excluding from coverage many occupations that were "heavily dominated by women" (1994: 157).

3. The Social Security Act was amended in 1954 and 1956 to extend coverage to farm workers, domestic servants, and many other occupations. The racist practices by American labor unions, aided by the National Labor Relations Act, diminished during the period between its passage and 1955 due to the more progressive policies of the Committee for Industrial Organization (CIO) (Quadrano 1994: 22–23, 158).

4. This desire to romanticize the 1950s is, not surprisingly, due to the fact that many of those who have written the more recent histories were members of the generation that came of age then.

5. The concept of "cultural hegemony" comes from Gramsci by way of Jackson Lears (1989: 50).

6. Although Jack Kerouac, for example, is commonly recognized as apolitical (at best), Tom Hayden has stated that he was an avid reader of Kerouac's novels and that, in fact, Kerouac's work influenced him to travel across the country (from Michigan) in 1960 to visit San Francisco's North Beach and the Democratic National Convention in Los Angeles. The unexpected result of this trip was that Hayden ended up being transformed in Berkeley from a vaguely rebellious existentialist to a political organizer. See either Gitlin (1987: 54) or James Miller (1987: 45).

Chapter 2. Euro and African American Interaction in Greenwich Village

1. Especially during the earlier part of the period being described here, Euro Americans' interest in racial freedom or rebellion was less important than their interest in sexual, artistic, or economic freedom or rebellion.

2. Polsky lists three acceptable roles: the entertainer, the victim, and the primitive. Polsky's classifications are supported by the roles African Americans fulfill in Jack Kerouac's fiction.

Chapter 3. Charlie Parker Meets the Postwar Construction of the Jazz Musician

1. Although Charlie Christian died at an even younger age—22 years old—than Parker, his career was too short for as intense a legend to develop around his image or career. As James Lincoln Collier says, "From the time he joined Goodman until the time he entered the hospital, there had passed hardly more than twenty months, and his entire professional career was barely seven years long. Yet in those twenty months with Goodman he left an indelible mark on jazz" (1978: 346).

2. As Dana D. Nelson reports, even Thomas Morton—one of American history's most famous and earliest "primitivists"—was interested not in subordinating himself to the Indians, but in adopting those of their modes of living that replicated the earliest stages of British civilization (Nelson 1992: 10).

3. This needs qualification because, according to James Collier, Mezzrow's jazz playing contradicted this asserted belief: "Despite his interest in black consciousness, his principal model [of playing the clarinet] was [white musician] Frank Teschemacher" (Collier 1978: 333). Of course, as far as Mezzrow's discursive influence is concerned, it doesn't matter if his playing contradicts his ideology—his book was widely read by later white bohemians while his playing was not widely heard.

4. It is interesting to compare Kerouac's fictional intimacy with Parker with one that is reported as having actually happened to Chicago author and Charlie Parker fan Frank Sanderford:

> Soon I noticed Bird watching me. I told myself that it was just my imagination. Then he touched Miles' sleeve slightly, and they both stared at me. I began to feel conspicuous and had to remind myself many times that others in the audience looked and dressed in more unconventional ways than I. But it was small solace, for their stares became more noticeable, and they were smiling and whispering together. Before the number they were playing was over, Bird left the stand and walked uncertainly to the back, down the aisle between the stand and the bar, circled the bar, and came slowly toward me and stopped next to me. He didn't look at me, and he said nothing. Finally, in a sort of desperation, I said hello. . . . Bird demanded that I go out and bring him back a hamburger. . . . "Stay here," he ordered. . . . Well, I had met the fabulous Bird. (Reisner 1977: 205–6)

As in Kerouac's fiction, Parker fixes Sanderford with his eyes; unlike in Kerouac's fantasy, Parker only wants to demonstrate his power over the worshipful fan.

5. As W. T. Lhamon notes, even Cody—the fictionalized Neal Cassady in *Visions of Cody*—takes Kerouac to task for this. Lhamon says that Cody "wants to listen for the central voices of black culture—or whatever else he is attending to—for their own sake: 'listen to the man play the horn, that's all.'" Kerouac, Lhamon says, cannot heed Cassady's advice "because it would inhibit his writing" (1990: 162).

6. Many of Parker's contemporaries describe him as a man of such enormous appetites that anyone who tried to follow his example was doomed to failure and, even, death. See, for example, Howard McGhee's description of Parker (Gitler 1985: 174).

7. The idea that Kid Jones's drumming "has functioned as a kind of catharsis, a purgation ritual," comes from Jones (1991: 97).

Chapter 4. Representations of Jazz Performance

1. See chapter 3 for plot summary.

2. Kerouac's romanticization here is at odds with what Gary Giddins says about Bird's relationship to his fans: "he did not seek followers and tended to be contemptuous of idolizers" (1987: 10). More recently, jazz pianist Cecil Taylor told A. B. Spellman that the main reason jazz musicians started playing in Greenwich Village during the 1950s was "because that's where the money was" (Spellman 1985: 18).

3. In his Foreword to the 1988 edition of *Go* James Atlas says that "Holmes' claim that *Go* is 'almost literal truth' can be verified" (in Holmes 1988a: xiii).

4. Some critics (see, for example, Richard N. Albert) infer from Baldwin's use of the name "Creole" for this character as well as the importance of the character to the story an approving reference to the integrated history of jazz. This attempt to "whiten" the character (and the meaning of Baldwin's story) seems wrongheaded to me. On the contrary, it seems pretty clear to me that Baldwin intends this character to be read as "black." From his description of Creole as "an enormous black man" to his suggestion that Creole had experienced some of the same problems as Sonny to his characterization of Creole's "sardonic" playing of the white pop standard "Am I Blue" to his use of Creole in the role of caretaker of the blues, Baldwin maintains the African American identification of the character. Moreover, as James Lincoln Collier makes clear, the confluence of European and African musical traditions in the meeting of blacks and black Creoles is not the result of harmonious interaction between the races. That is, even though it is probably true that "the Creole musician was entirely European in tradition" and that jazz formed out of the association of black Creoles and blacks, this interaction is peculiarly the product of the American racial structure. Black Creoles and blacks came together, in other words, because of the inane and insidious character of a racial classification that designated individuals in groups such as the Creoles, despite their historical voluntary association with a white, European identity, as "black"—especially after the institution of Jim Crow laws (Collier 1978: 60–65). This history makes an interpretation of Creole as "white" in any meaningful way (especially with all of Baldwin's other characterizations) wishful thinking. As Albert Murray says, although the blues "is a synthesis of African and European elements, [it] is the product of an *Afro-American sensibility* in an American mainland situation" (Murray 1976: 63; italics mine).

5. Both Ann Charters and Gerald Nicosia mention that Kerouac often compared himself and his work to Joyce, and particularly to *Ulysses* and *Finnegans Wake*. Charters says, for example, that Kerouac thought *On the Road* compared favorably with *Ulysses* and so should be "accorded the same seriousness" (Charters 1987: 155; Nicosia 1983: 365).

6. I argue this point knowing that the influential Cassavetes scholar Ray Carney has written that Cassavetes "is among the most color-blind of filmmakers" (Carney 1994: 286 n. 5). While it is interesting that Carney (and, apparently, Cassavetes himself) insists on this point, it is clear to me from watching both *Too Late Blues* and the earlier *Shadows* that Cassavetes does indeed have a hipster-like attraction/repulsion relationship with black people and culture.

Chapter 5. Euro American and African American Approaches to Jazz Narrative

1. What was previously thought to be the "declining significance of race" has recently revealed itself—in such social and cultural "pressure points" as the Rodney King beating and the debate over affirmative action—to be increasing not only in significance, but in misunderstanding and conflict as well.

2. See, for example, Williams's 1963 essay "The Literary Ghetto" (Williams 1970: 229–30).

3. Of course, the example of Bob Kaufman proves the tenuousness of such a generalization. A "Black Beat" poet who lived mostly in San Francisco, Kaufman lived his entire life according to the "nonconformist," "poetic" values at the heart of the Beat subculture. His poetry reflects this adventurous spirit in its thematic and formal experimentation. Kaufman remained committed to a life and work of nonconformist integrity and, as a result, was published irregularly and remained on the margins of the American literary establishment throughout his life (Damon 1988: 701–6).

4. An interesting discussion of Baraka's "jazz aesthetic" can be found in William J. Harris's study of Amiri Baraka's work (Harris 1985: 13–33). Stephen Henderson's *Understanding the New Black Poetry* (1973) is the best general introduction to the influence of jazz on African American poetry.

5. With Ginsberg and, to a lesser extent, Kerouac it is hard to separate how much of their interest in spontaneity comes from jazz and how much from their understanding of Buddhism. My sense is that Ginsberg's major influence in this regard is Buddhism and Kerouac's is jazz but that there is some of both in each one's work. In a *Paris Review* interview, Ginsberg says that the structure of "Howl" was, to some extent, informed by Kerouac's description of Lester Young's solos and Ginsberg's own listening to Illinois Jacquet (Ginsberg 1967: 284).

6. My understanding of the unique African American approach to jazz resources was greatly informed by William J. Harris's discussion of the "jazz aesthetic" (1985: 13–33).

7. My reading of *Night Song* was suggested by two sources: Bernard Bell's brief analysis of the novel in *The Afro-American Novel and Its Tradition* (1987: 254–56); and C. Lynn Munro's interpretation in the article "Culture and Quest in the Fiction of John A. Williams" (1978: 71–100). Bell identifies an "antiphonal" structure that

emphasizes the "call-and-response" relationship between the two main African American characters, Keel Robinson and Richie "Eagle" Stokes, counterpointed by the main male, Euro American character, David Hillary. Although he does not characterize its structure in musical terms, Munro also calls attention to the multicharacter plot of *Night Song*, calling it a "refinement of [Williams's] craft." Additionally, although I came upon it after I had already formed my ideas about the novel, Gilbert H. Muller's analysis of *Night Song* is sensitive and perceptive, and buttressed my interpretation (see Muller 1984: 53–60).

8. John Clellon Holmes, *The Horn* (1988b), unnumbered page containing the "Contents." My understanding of *The Horn*'s structure was informed by the insightful analyses in Gregory Stephenson's *The Daybreak Boys* (1990: 95–98) and Richard N. Albert's "Jazz and the Beat Generation: John Clellon Holmes' *The Horn*" (1989: 16–19).

9. In a prefatory note to *The Horn* Holmes writes, "The book, like the music that it celebrates, is a collective improvisation on an American theme; and if there are truths here, they are poetic truths."

10. Holmes, *The Horn*, unnumbered first page of the Preface.

11. In this regard it is interesting that the 1988 edition of *The Horn* contains a Foreword by jazz saxophonist Archie Shepp. A friend and 1960s-era colleague of Amiri Baraka, Shepp is often referred to (especially by white jazz critics) as the most militant of this era's black nationalist musicians. A kind of "authenticating document," Shepp's Foreword is very complimentary of Holmes's work but seems very cold: it praises his knowledge but not his understanding.

12. While not denying Kerouac's affinity for jazz, George Dardess claims that "the most vigorous metaphors" in this manifesto derive not from jazz or pictorial art but from "nature" (Dardess 1975: 733–34). Although "most vigorous" is a bit too vague to be very meaningful, the argument is reasonable and allows Dardess to make interesting connections between Kerouac's method and Emerson's and Thoreau's methods.

13. It is interesting to me, moreover, that in his contemporary defenses of Kerouac's method—for example, his 1957 letter to *Partisan Review* responding to Norman Podhoretz's criticism of the Beat generation, or his 1959 letter to *The Evergreen Review* defending spontaneous writing—Baraka does not once discuss the connection between Kerouac's writing and jazz. This from a critic vitally interested in the African American jazz tradition.

Works Cited

Albert, Richard N. 1989. Jazz and the Beat generation: John Clellon Holmes' *The Horn*. *Moody Street Irregulars* (spring): 16–19.

———, ed. 1990. *From Blues to Bop: A Collection of Jazz Fiction*. Baton Rouge: Louisiana State University Press.

Amram, David. 1968. *Vibrations: The Adventures and Musical Times of David Amram*. Westport, Conn.: Greenwood Press.

Baker, Dorothy. 1961. *Young Man With a Horn*. 1938. Cambridge, Mass.: Houghton Mifflin Co.

Baker, Houston. 1984. *Blues, Ideology, and Afro-American Literature: A Vernacular Theory*. Chicago: The University of Chicago Press.

Baldwin, James. 1990. Sonny's blues. In *Hot and Cool: Jazz Short Stories*, edited by Marcela Breton. New York: Plume.

Balliett, Whitney. 1956. The measure of "Bird." *Saturday Review of Literature*, 17 March, 33–34.

Banes, Sally. 1993. *Greenwich Village 1963: Avant-Garde Performance and the Effervescent Body*. Durham, N.C.: Duke University Press.

Baraka, Amiri. 1963. *Blues People: Negro Music in White America*. New York: Morrow Quill Paperbacks.

———. 1964. *Dutchman and The Slave*. New York: William Morrow and Co.

———. 1984. *The Autobiography of LeRoi Jones/Amiri Baraka*. New York: Freundlich Books, 1984.

———. 1987. Interview with Amiri Baraka. In *The Beat Vision: A Primary Sourcebook*, edited by Arthur and Kit Knight. New York: Paragon House.

———. 1990. The screamers. In *Hot and Cool: Jazz Short Stories*, edited by Marcela Breton. New York: Plume.

———. 1994. *Conversations with Amiri Baraka*, edited by Charlie Reilly. Jackson: University Press of Mississippi.

Baraka, Amiri, and Amina Baraka. 1987. *The Music: Reflections on Jazz and Blues*. New York: William Morrow and Company.

Baraka, Amiri, and Norman Podhoretz. 1958. Correspondence: The Beat generation. *Partisan Review* (spring): 472–79.

Bebop. 1948. *Life*, 11 October, 138–42.

Bell, Bernard. 1987. *The Afro-American Novel and Its Tradition*. Amherst: The University of Massachusetts Press.

The Benny Goodman Story. 1955. Directed by Valentine Davies. Universal International.

Benston, Kimberly. 1976. *Baraka: The Renegade and the Mask*. New Haven, Conn.: Yale University Press.

Berliner, Paul F. 1994. *Thinking in Jazz: The Infinite Art of Improvisation*. Chicago: The University of Chicago Press.

Boddy, William. 1990. *Fifties Television: The Industry and Its Critics*. Urbana: University of Illinois Press.

Boyer, Richard O. 1948. Bop. *The New Yorker*, 3 July, 26–32.

Breines, Wini. 1992. *Young, White, and Miserable: Growing Up Female in the Fifties*. Boston: Beacon Press.

Brown, Frank London. 1968. McDougal. In *Black Voices*, edited by Abraham Chapman. New York: New American Library.

Carney, Ray. 1984. *American Dreaming: The Films of John Cassavetes and the American Experience*. Berkeley: University of California Press.

———. 1994. *The Films of John Cassavetes: Pragmatism, Modernism, and the Movies*. Cambridge: Cambridge University Press.

———. 1995. No exit: John Cassavetes' *Shadows*. In *Beat Culture and the New America 1950–1965*, edited by Lisa Phillips. Paris and New York: Flammarion, 1995.

Charters, Ann. 1987. *Kerouac: A Biography*. 1974. New York: St. Martin's Press.

Charters, Samuel, and Leonard Kunstadt. 1981. *Jazz: A History of the New York Scene*. 1962. Reprint. New York: Da Capo Press.

Collier, James Lincoln. 1978. *The Making of Jazz: A Comprehensive History*. New York: Delta.

———. 1983. *Louis Armstrong: An American Genius*. New York: Oxford University Press.

Cripps, Thomas. 1993. *Making Movies Black: The Hollywood Message Movie from World War II to the Civil Rights Era*. New York: Oxford University Press.

Cruse, Harold. 1984. *The Crisis of the Negro Intellectual: A Historical Analysis of the Failure of Black Leadership*. 1967. New York: Quill.

Damon, Maria. 1988. "Unmeaning jargon"/uncanonized beatitude: Bob Kaufman, poet. *South Atlantic Quarterly* (fall): 701–41.

Dardess, George. 1975. The logic of spontaneity: A reconsideration of Kerouac's "spontaneous prose method." *Boundary* 2: 729–43.

Davis, Miles, with Quincy Troupe. 1989. *Miles: The Autobiography*. New York: Simon and Schuster.

Dent, Tom. 1993. Lower East Side coda. *African American Review* 27: 597–98.

Dyer, Richard. 1993. *The Matter of Images: Essays of Representations*. London: Routledge.

Ellison, Ralph. 1964. *Shadow and Act*. New York: Random House.

The Five Pennies. 1959. Directed by Melville Shavelson. Paramount.

Floyd, Samuel A. Jr. 1995. *The Power of Black Music: Interpreting its History from Africa to the United States*. New York: Oxford University Press.

Frankenberg, Ruth. 1993. *White Women, Race Matters: The Social Construction of Whiteness*. Minneapolis: University of Minnesota Press.

Franklin, John Hope, and Alfred A. Moss Jr. 1988. *From Slavery to Freedom: A History of Negro Americans*. 6th ed. New York: Alfred A. Knopf.

Frederickson, George M. 1987. *The Black Image in the White Mind: The Debate on Afro-American Destiny, 1817–1914.* 1971. Middletown, Conn.: Wesleyan University Press.

Gabbard, Krin. 1996. *Jammin' at the Margins: Jazz and the American Cinema.* Chicago: The University of Chicago Press.

Garon, Paul. 1975. *Blues and the Poetic Spirit.* New York: Da Capo Press.

Gates, Henry Louis. 1988. *The Signifying Monkey: A Theory of African-American Literary Criticism.* New York: Oxford University Press.

George, Nelson. 1988. *The Death of Rhythm and Blues.* New York: Plume.

Giddins, Gary. 1987. *Celebrating Bird: The Triumph of Charlie Parker.* New York: Beech Tree Books.

Gilbert, James. 1981. *Another Chance: Postwar America, 1945–1968.* Philadelphia: Temple University Press.

Gillespie, Dizzy, with Al Fraser. 1979. *To Be or Not to Bop: Memoirs.* New York: Da Capo Press.

Gilroy, Paul. 1993. *The Black Atlantic: Modernity and Double Consciousness.* Cambridge: Harvard University Press.

Ginsberg, Allen. 1967. Interview. In *Writers at Work: The Paris Review Interviews.* Third series. Introduced by Alfred Kazin. New York: Viking Press.

Gitler, Ira. 1985. *Swing to Bop: An Oral History of the Transition in Jazz in the 1940s.* New York: Oxford University Press.

Gitlin, Todd. 1987. *The Sixties: Years of Hope, Days of Rage.* Toronto: Bantam Books.

The Glenn Miller Story. 1954. Directed by Anthony Mann. Universal International.

Grennard, Elliott. 1947. Sparrow's last jump. *Harper's Magazine,* May, 419–26.

Hall, Stuart. 1992. What is this 'black' in black popular culture? In *Black Popular Culture,* a project by Michele Wallace, edited by Gina Dent. Seattle, Wash.: Bay Press.

Haney Lopez, Ian F. 1996. *White by Law: The Legal Construction of Race.* New York: New York University Press.

Harris, William J. 1985. *The Poetry and Poetics of Amiri Baraka: The Jazz Aesthetic.* Columbia: University of Missouri Press.

Hartman, Charles O. 1991. *Jazz Text: Voice and Improvisation in Poetry, Jazz, and Song.* Princeton, N.J.: Princeton University Press.

Hebdige, Dick. 1987. *Subculture: The Meaning of Style.* 1979. London and New York: Routledge.

Henderson, Stephen. 1973. *Understanding the New Black Poetry: Black Speech and Black Music as Poetic References.* New York: Willliam Morrow & Company.

Hentoff, Nat. 1975. *The Jazz Life.* 1961. New York: Da Capo Press.

———. 1976. *Jazz Is.* New York: Random House.

Hernton, Calvin. 1993. Umbra: A personal recounting. *African American Review* 27: 579–83.

Hodeir, Andre. 1979. *Jazz: Its Evolution and Essence.* 1956. New York: Grove Press.

Holmes, John Clellon. 1967. *Nothing More to Declare.* New York: E. P. Dutton and Co.

———. 1988a. *Go.* 1952. New York: Thunder's Mouth Press.

———. 1988b. *The Horn.* 1958. New York: Thunder's Mouth Press.

Hughes, Langston. 1926. The Negro artist and the racial mountain. *The Nation,* 16 June, 662–63.

Huggins, Nathan Irvin. 1971. *Harlem Renaissance*. London: Oxford University Press.

Ignatiev, Noel, and John Garvey, eds. 1996. *Race Traitor*. New York: Routledge.

Ismalli-Abu-Bakr, Rashidah. 1993. Slightly autobiographical: The 1960s on the Lower East Side. *African American Review* 27: 585–89.

Jacoby, Russell. 1987. *The Last Intellectuals: American Culture in the Age of Academe*. New York: Basic Books.

Jezer, Marty. 1982. *The Dark Ages: Life in the United States 1945–1960*. Boston: South End Press.

Johnson, Joyce. 1983. *Minor Characters*. Boston: Houghton Mifflin Company.

Jones, Gayl. 1991. *Liberating Voices: Oral Tradition in African American Literature*. Cambridge: Harvard University Press.

Jones, Hettie. 1990. *How I Became Hettie Jones*. New York: Penguin.

Kalaidjian, Walter. 1993. *American Culture Between the Wars: Revisionary Modernism and Postmodern Critique*. New York: Columbia University Press.

Kart, Larry. 1983. Jack Kerouac's 'Jazz America' or who was Roger Beloit? *Review of Contemporary Fiction* (summer): 25–27.

Kelley, William Melvin. 1965. *A Drop of Patience*. Garden City, N.J.: Doubleday and Co..

Kerouac, Jack. 1957. *On the Road*. New York: Signet.

———. 1961a. Belief and technique for modern prose. In *A Casebook on the Beat*, edited by Thomas Parkinson. New York: Thomas Y. Crowell Co.

———. 1961b. The essentials of spontaneous prose. In *A Casebook on the Beat*, edited by Thomas Parkinson. New York: Thomas Y. Crowell Co.

———. 1961c. The origins of the Beat generation. In *A Casebook on the Beat*, edited by Thomas Parkinson. New York: Thomas Y. Crowell Co.

———. 1968. The art of fiction XLI. Interview by Ted Berrigan et al. *Paris Review* (summer): 61–103.

———. 1971. *The Subterraneans*. 1958. New York: Grove Press.

———. 1990a. *The Jack Kerouac Collection*. Rhino World Beat. R-70939.

———. 1990b. *Mexico City Blues (242 Choruses)*. 1959. New York: Grove Weidenfeld.

———. 1995. *Jack Kerouac: Selected Letters, 1940–1956*, edited by Ann Charters. New York: Penguin.

Knight, Arthur, and Kit Knight, eds. 1987. *The Beat Vision: A Primary Sourcebook*. New York: Paragon House.

Lears, Jackson. 1989. A matter of taste: Corporate cultural hegemony in a mass-consumption society. In *Recasting America: Culture and Politics in the Age of Cold War*, edited by Lary May. Chicago: The University of Chicago Press.

Leeming, David. 1994. *James Baldwin: A Biography*. New York: Henry Holt and Company.

Leonard, Neil. 1987. *Jazz: Myth and Religion*. New York: Oxford University Press.

Levine, Lawrence. 1977. *Black Culture and Consciousness: Afro-American Folk Thought from Slavery to Freedom*. New York: Oxford University Press.

Lhamon, W. T. Jr. 1990. *Deliberate Speed: The Origins of a Cultural Style in the American 1950s*. Washington, D.C.: Smithsonian Institution Press.

Lipsitz, George. 1990. Listening to learn and learning to listen: Popular culture, cultural theory, and American studies. *American Quarterly* (December): 615–36.

———. 1995a. The possessive investment in whiteness: Racialized social democracy and the "white" problem in American studies. *American Quarterly* (September): 369–87.

———. 1995b. "Swing low, sweet Cadillac": White supremacy, antiblack racism, and the new historicism. *American Literary History* (winter): 700–725.

Lipton, Lawrence. 1959. *The Holy Barbarians.* New York: Julian Messner.

Lott, Eric. 1988. Double V, double-time: Bebop's politics of style. *Callaloo* (summer): 597–605.

———. 1993. *Love and Theft: Blackface Minstrelsy and the American Working Class.* New York: Oxford University Press.

Mailer, Norman. 1981. *Advertisements for Myself.* 1959. New York: Perigee Books.

Mariani, Paul. 1981. *William Carlos Williams: A New World Naked.* New York: McGraw-Hill Book Co.

Maultsby, Portia. 1990. Africanisms in African-American music. In *Africanisms in American Culture,* edited by Joseph E. Holloway. Bloomington: Indiana University Press.

Maynard, John Arthur. 1991. *Venice West: The Beat Generation in Southern California.* New Brunswick, N.J.: Rutgers University Press.

McKean, Gilbert. 1947. Memo: On bebop. *Saturday Review of Literature,* 30 August, 18–19.

Mezzrow, Mezz, and Bernard Wolfe. 1990. *Really the Blues.* 1946. New York: Citadel Press.

Miles, Barry. 1989. *Ginsberg: A Biography.* New York: HarperCollins.

Miller, James. 1987. *Democracy Is in the Streets: From Port Huron to the Siege of Chicago.* New York: Simon and Schuster.

Miller, Terry. 1990. *Greenwich Village and How It Got That Way.* New York: Crown Publishers.

Morgan, Edward. 1991. *The 60s Experience: Hard Lessons about Modern America.* Philadelphia: Temple University Press.

Muller, Gilbert H. 1984. *John A. Williams.* Boston: Twayne Publishers.

Munro, C. Lynn. 1978. Culture and quest in the fiction of John A. Williams. *CLA Journal* 23 (December): 71–100.

Murray, Albert. 1976. *Stomping the Blues.* New York: Da Capo Press.

———. 1983. *The Omni-Americans: Black Experience and American Culture.* 1970. New York: Vintage Books.

———. 1996. *The Blue Devils of Nada: A Contemporary American Approach to Aesthetic Statement.* New York: Pantheon Books.

Nelson, Dana D. 1992. *The Word in Black and White: Reading "Race" in American Literature, 1638–1967.* New York: Oxford University Press.

Nicosia, Gerald. 1983. *Memory Babe: A Critical Biography of Jack Kerouac.* New York: Penguin Books.

O'Brien, John, ed. 1973. *Interviews with Black Writers.* New York: Liveright.

Omi, Michael, and Howard Winant. 1986. *Racial Formation in the United States: From the 1960s to the 1980s.* New York: Routledge & Kegan Paul.

Otis, Johnny. 1993. *Upside Your Head! Rhythm and Blues on Central Avenue.* Hanover and London: Wesleyan University Press.

Pascoe, Peggy. 1996. Miscegenation law, court cases, and ideologies of "race" in twentieth-century America. *The Journal of American History* (June): 44–69.

A passage for trumpet. 1960. Directed by Don Medford. *The Twilight Zone*. CBS Television.

Petry, Ann. 1990. Solo on drums. In *Hot and Cool: Jazz Short Stories*, edited by Marcela Breton. New York: Plume.

Phillips, Lisa. 1995. *Beat Culture and the New America: 1950–1965*. Paris and New York: Flammarion.

Poggioli, Renato. 1968. *The Theory of the Avant-Garde*. Translated by Gerald Fitzgerald. Cambridge: The Belknap Press of Harvard University Press.

Polenberg, Richard. 1980. *One Nation Divisible: Class, Race, and Ethnicity in the United States since 1938*. New York: Penguin.

Polsky, Ned. 1967. *Hustlers, Beats, and Others*. Chicago: Aldine Publishing Co.

Pratt, Mary Louise. 1991. Arts of the contact zone. In *Profession 91*. New York: MLA.

Quadrano, Jill. 1994. *The Color of Welfare: How Racism Undermined the War on Poverty*. New York: Oxford University Press.

Reisner, Robert, ed. 1977. *Bird: The Legend of Charlie Parker*. 1962. New York: Da Capo Press.

Rivers, Larry, with Arnold Weinstein. 1992. *What Did I Do? The Unauthorized Autobiography*. New York: HarperCollins.

Ro, Sigmund. 1984. *Rage and Celebration: Essays on Contemporary Afro-American Writing*. Atlantic Highlands, N.J.: Humanities Press.

Roediger, David R. 1991. *The Wages of Whiteness: Race and the Making of the American Working Class*. London: Verso.

———. 1994. *Towards the Abolition of Whiteness*. London: Verso.

———. 1995. *Guineas, wiggers*, and the dramas of racialized culture. *American Literary History* (winter): 654–68.

Rogin, Michael. 1996. *Blackface, White Noise: Jewish Immigrants in the Hollywood Melting Pot*. Berkeley: University of California Press.

Ross, Andrew. 1989. *No Respect: Intellectuals and Popular Culture*. New York: Routledge.

Russell, Ross. 1961. *The Sound*. New York: E. P. Dutton and Co.

———. 1971. *Jazz Style in Kansas City and the Southwest*. Berkeley: University of California Press.

———. 1996. *Bird Lives: The High Life and Hard Times of Charlie (Yardbird) Parker*. 1973. New York: Da Capo Press.

Said, Edward W. 1978. *Orientalism*. New York: Vintage Books.

———. 1993. *Culture and Imperialism*. New York: Vintage Books.

Santoro, Gene. 1996. All that jazz. *The Nation*, 8 & 15 January, 34–36.

Schaub, Thomas Hill. 1991. *American Fiction in the Cold War*. Madison: The University of Wisconsin Press.

Shapiro, Nat, and Nat Hentoff. 1966. *Hear Me Talkin' to Ya: The Story of Jazz as Told by the Men Who Made It*. 1955. New York: Dover Publications.

Shadows. 1959. Directed by John Cassavetes. Castle Hill.

Sidran, Ben. 1971. *Black Talk*. New York: Holt, Rinehart and Winston.

Simmons, Herbert. 1965. *Man Walking on Eggshells*. Boston: Houghton Mifflin Co..

Sitkoff, Harvard. 1978. *A New Deal for Blacks: The Emergence of Civil Rights as a National Issue: The Depression Decade*. Oxford: Oxford University Press.

Sorrentino, Gilbert. 1972. Remembrance of bop in New York, 1945–1950. In *Things in the Driver's Seat: Readings in Popular Culture*, edited by Henry Russell Huebel. Chicago: Rand McNally.

Southern, Eileen. 1983. *The Music of Black Americans: A History*. 2d ed. New York: W. W. Norton and Co.

Spellman, A. B. 1985. *Four Lives in the Bebop Business*. 1966. New York: Limelight Editions.

St. Louis Blues. 1958. Directed by Allen Reisner. Paramount.

Stearns, Marshall W. 1958. *The Story of Jazz*. London: Oxford University Press.

Steinberg, Stephen. 1995. *Turning Back: The Retreat from Racial Justice in American Thought and Policy*. Boston: Beacon Press.

Stephenson, Gregory. 1990. *The Daybreak Boys: Essays on the Literature of the Beat Generation*. Carbondale: Southern Illinois University Press.

Stowe, David W. 1994. *Swing Changes: Big Band Jazz in New Deal America*. Cambridge: Harvard University Press.

Stuckey, Sterling. 1987. *Slave Culture: Nationalist Theory and the Foundations of Black America*. New York: Oxford University Press.

Such, David G. 1993. *Avant Garde Jazz Musicians: Performing "Out There"*. Iowa City: University of Iowa Press.

Sukenick, Ronald. 1987. *Down and In: Life in the Underground*. New York: Beech Tree Books/William Morrow.

Szwed, John. 1980. Josef Skvorecky and the tradition of jazz literature. *World Literature Today* (autumn): 586–90.

Tallman, Warren. 1961. Kerouac's sound. In *A Casebook on the Beat*, edited by Thomas Parkinson. New York: Thomas Y. Crowell Co.

Taylor, Henry Louis Jr. 1995. The hidden face of racism. *American Quarterly* (September): 395–408.

Thomas, Lorenzo. 1992. "Communicating by horns": Jazz and redemption in the poetry of the Beats and the black arts movement. *African American Review* 26: 291–98.

———. 1993. Alea's children: The avant-garde on the Lower East Side, 1960–1970. *African American Review* 27: 573–78.

Too Late Blues. 1962. Directed by John Cassavetes. Paramount.

Tytell, John. 1986. *Naked Angels: The Lives and Literature of the Beat Generation*. 1976. New York: Grove Press.

Wakefield, Dan. 1992. *New York in the 50s*. Boston: Houghton Mifflin/Seymour Lawrence.

Weinreich, Regina. 1990. *The Spontaneous Poetics of Jack Kerouac: A Study of the Fiction*. 1987. New York: Paragon House.

West, Cornel. 1984. The paradox of the African American rebellion. In *The 60s Without Apology*, edited by Sohnya Sayres, Anders Stephanson, Stanley Aronowitz, and Frederic Jameson. Minneapolis: University of Minnesota Press.

Where mixed couples live. 1955. *Ebony*, May, 61–65.

Williams, John. 1964. *Night Song*. 1961. London: The Jazz Book Club.

———. 1970. The literary ghetto. In *The Black Novelist*, edited by Robert Hemenway. Columbus, Ohio: Charles E. Merrill Publishing Co.

————. 1973. *Flashbacks: A Twenty-Year Diary of Article Writing*. Garden City, N.Y.: Anchor Press/Doubleday.

Williams, Raymond. 1977. *Marxism and Literature*. Oxford: Oxford University Press.

————. 1983. *Keywords: A Vocabulary of Culture and Society*. Rev. ed. New York: Oxford University Press.

————. 1995. *The Sociology of Culture*. 1981. Chicago: The University of Chicago Press.

Williams, William Carlos. 1967. *I Wanted to Write a Poem: The Autobiography of the Works of a Poet*. 1958. Boston: Beacon Press.

Wright, Sarah E. 1993. The Lower East Side: A rebirth of world vision. *African American Review* 27: 593–96.

Yates, Richard. 1990. A really good jazz piano. In *Hot and Cool: Jazz Short Stories*, edited by Marcela Breton. New York: Plume.

Young, Al, Larry Kart, and Michael S. Harper. 1987. Jazz and letters: A colloquy. *Tri-Quarterly* (winter): 118–58.

Young Man With a Horn. 1950. Directed by Michael Curtiz. Warner Bros.

Index

Weinreich, Regina, 136, 138, 139

West, Cornel, 14, 15

White by Law (Haney Lopez), 142

"White Negro, The" (Mailer), 18, 20, 31, 34, 54, 56–57

Whiteness, xii, xiii–xv, xvi, xviii–xix, 6, 8, 19, 20, 22, 146, 147 n 3

Williams, John A., xii, 33, 35, 74, 75, 121, 122, 127–28, 131, 151 nn 2, 7

Williams, Raymond, x–xi, 119

Williams, William Carlos, 120

Winant, Howard, 148 n 1

Wolfe, Bernard, 54

Woodstock, 22

World War II, xx, 13

Wright, Sarah E., 29, 30

Wyse, Seymour, 38

Yates, Richard, 93–96

Young, Al, xix

Young, Lester, 61, 64, 77

Young, Trummy, 63, 64

Young Man With a Horn (Baker), 49–51, 55

Young Man With a Horn (film), 49, 51–52

Youth culture, 18, 20, 39–40